EDUCATION AT THE CROSSROADS

EDUCATION AT THE CROSSROADS

EDITED BY:

APOORVANAND & OMITA GOYAL

India International Centre

PAPER MISSILE

NIYOGI BOOKS

Published by
NIYOGI BOOKS
Block D, Building No. 77,
Okhla Industrial Area, Phase-I,
New Delhi-110 020, INDIA
Tel: 91-11-26816301, 26818960
Email: niyogibooks@gmail.com
Website: www.niyogibooksindia.com

Editors: Apoorvanand and Omita Goyal
Design: Shashi Bhushan Prasad
Cover Illustration: Qamar Dagar
(Karmanye waadhikaarastemaphaleshukadaachanaa)

ISBN: 978-93-86906-34-2
Publication: 2018

Printed at: Niyogi Offset Pvt. Ltd., New Delhi, India

CONTENTS

FOREWORD

Education is an area that lends itself to extensive analysis and, often, intense controversy. This volume brings together a large number of contributions by many well-known scholars in the areas of their expertise from around the country.

Instead of attempting a synoptic view of the whole problem, I will confine myself to a single set of issues involving what may be called 'value-based education.' Educational technology is changing rapidly; the traditional classroom is in danger of disappearing, and even the arts of reading and writing that were so crucial in our lifetimes are getting displaced by increasingly sophisticated gadgets. The whole area of educational technology aside, however, it is crucial to pay attention to the content of our education. Education is not merely an exercise in transmitting information. It must also involve the transmission of certain values that we consider essential to the very welfare of human civilisation. In the face of the overwhelming threat of violence and fanaticism, it is, in my view, important to lay stress upon value-based education.

Today, humanity stands at a crucial and potentially decisive crossroad in its long and tortuous history on Planet Earth. On the one hand, the 20th century witnessed an astounding development in almost every sphere of human activity, with science and technology transforming life on this planet in a couple of generations. Breaking the space barrier, landing on the moon, probing the planets and the stars beyond, are all symbols of the astounding creativity of the human mind. Instant communication has now become routine, and the Internet and other aspects of Information Technology have spread around the globe. For tens of millions of human beings there has been a substantial rise in living standards; some have reached levels of affluence unimaginable in the recent past. The world has literally shrunk before our eyes, and whether we are probing the majestic rhythms of the galaxies or the subatomic dance of the neutrinos, human ingenuity has broken all barriers. We now have enough resources, if used with wisdom and compassion, to ensure for every human being the material, educational and vocational inputs necessary for a decent human existence.

On the other hand, the 20th century has been perhaps the most lethal and destructive in the recorded history of humanity. The First and Second World Wars, and dozens of regional conflicts, some of which are still raging, have killed millions of human beings—men, women and children alike—and dislocated many millions more. The ideological systems of Nazism, Marxism–Leninism, and Maoism resulted in immense human suffering, death and disaster. The advent of nuclear power has introduced a new and deeply disturbing dimension into possible future conflicts. Fundamentalism, fanaticism and terrorism are on the rise in many parts of the world, and while the number of nations endorsing a democratic system has considerably increased, many authoritarian regimes still prevail, and grave threats to global peace and stability remain. Unilateralism has become a new doctrine, casting a cloud over attempts by the United Nations to build a more democratic global society.

In this ambiguous situation, educating children and youth for intercultural and inter-religious understanding assumes tremendous significance. The UNESCO Commission for Education in the 21st century published a report in 1996 entitled *Learning: The Treasure Within.* 1 I commend this document to educationists around the world as it covers—in a comparatively short compass—a broad gamut of educational problems and challenges. In it are identified 'Four Pillars of Learning'—'Learning to Know', 'Learning to Do', 'Learning to Live Together', and 'Learning to Be'. Here, I will focus on the third of these, 'Learning to Live Together'.

There is an ancient Sanskrit hymn which exhorts: 'Let us work together, let us enjoy together, let us achieve together, may there be no hatred between us'. Highly consistent with this framework, 'Learning to Live Together' implies that value education should include at least six interrelated dimensions. The first of these relates to *family values*. By these, I do not mean a reversion to conservative or retrogressive social structures, but the necessity for harmony within the family, which, after all, is the first classroom and laboratory for every child. If there is constant conflict within the family, the effect upon children cannot but be negative. Family values, such as respect and regard for elders by children, and children by elders, helpfulness, cooperative functioning and mutual affection help lay the foundation for how we learn to live together over the whole of our lives. Although our educational systems do not integrate the family lives of individual children into the classroom, there can be no doubt that the first elements of education are inculcated within the family, which also requires strong parent–teacher associations within our schools.

The second set of values, which I call *societal values*, include courtesy, consideration to strangers and elders, punctuality, cleanliness and cooperation. After the family, it is in school that these values need to be inculcated. Although competition is important, we must cultivate the art of cooperative functioning within our educational institutions. Among many other avenues, sports and involving students in community service projects can be excellent training for intercultural understanding. For example, in developing nations like India, the concept of Socially Useful Productive Work (SUPW), in which students make periodic visits to slums or villages in the vicinity and assist in projects designed to improve standards of living in areas such as health and education, seems full of promise. This training facilitates social consciousness among students, and is designed to foster a society that is distinguished by cooperation and service to others.2

The third set of values involves *environmental sustainability*. It is now well known that the 20th century witnessed a massive exploitation and degradation of the biosphere. Millions of acres of forests have disappeared, tens of thousands of species have vanished, the ozone layer is steadily attenuating, glaciers are melting, and sea levels rising. If these trends continue, even the medium-range prospects for the very survival of the human race will be in question. It is therefore necessary that students develop an awareness of the importance of preserving and protecting the natural environment. Importantly, all religions address the value of preservation and protection of nature. The historic conference at Assisi in Italy in 1986 resulted in the Interreligious Declarations on Man and Nature. Although written from the point of view of different religions, these declarations are remarkable in that they all emphasise the spiritual significance of nurturing Mother Earth. A World Wildlife Fund-India publication containing these declarations is invaluable as an educational tool.3

The fourth set of values involves *interreligious understanding*. Historically, religion has a decidedly mixed track record. On the one hand, much that is great and noble in human civilisation—art and architecture, painting and sculpture, scriptures and literature, moral codes and social organisations—have their genesis in the great religions of the world. At the same time, countless millions of human beings have over the ages been massacred and burnt, tortured and persecuted, in the name of religion. Even as I write, fierce conflicts are raging around the world between and within religions, causing havoc and massive suffering. The astounding rise of the Islamic State of Iraq and al-Sham (ISIS) has introduced a new dimension of violence and terror.

Complicating matters, in many countries, school textbooks have misleading and biased information about religions that are not in the mainstream, thus imprinting negative archetypes on children from a young age. In order to counteract these distortions, the Interfaith Movement emerged over the last century, seeking to bring people of different religious persuasions together in a harmonious and creative dialogue. Between the First Parliament of the World's Religions in Chicago in 1893, and the Sixth in Salt Lake City last year, there have been hundreds of interfaith meetings around the globe, along with the development of several major interfaith organisations, including the Temple of Understanding.4 The key to interreligious understanding lies in the acceptance that there are multiple paths to the divine. In declaring that 'The truth is one, the wise call it by many names', the Rig Veda recognises a growing global sensibility that there can be no monopoly of divine wisdom or spiritual methodology. In other words, if the divine exists, surely it cannot be monopolised by any one creed or religion. Whereas it may be acceptable for us to claim that our own religion is the most effective way to achieve a spiritual goal, it is manifestly not acceptable to persecute and terrorise people who belong to different religious traditions or on the basis of gender, caste or sexual preference. Who are we, denizens of a tiny speck of dust that we call Planet Earth, to declare that in the infinite billions of galaxies that surround us, the illimitable spirit of the divine can appear only in one form or at one place or at one time?

For these and other reasons, the time has come when the great religions of the world must forgo their mutual antagonism and work together for the abolition of poverty and deprivation, hunger and malnutrition, disease and poverty that still engulf more than half the population of our planet. At a corresponding level, interfaith education must become part of educational curricula and programmes around the world. I am aware that such a call is inherently sensitive, but if a basic introduction to the great religions of the world could be available to students as a matter of course, it would help them broaden their outlook and prevent extremism, while furthering interfaith and intercultural understanding.

The quest for greater interreligious understanding inevitably leads to the question of *spiritual values*, the fifth domain which may facilitate our capacity for learning to live with one another. There is a distinction between religion and spirituality, although these spheres are usually closely intertwined. Religion necessarily involves a great deal of outer conformity, whereas spirituality attempts to access the divine power that resides within the deeper recesses of our consciousness, and cuts across theological and denominational divides. In this regard, the 'Noor-I-Ilahi' of Sufism, the 'Bodhi-chitta' of Buddhism, the 'Light that lighteth every man that cometh into the world' of the Bible, and the seers of the Upanishads who exclaim in ecstasy, 'I have seen that great being shining like a thousand suns beyond the darkness', are all manifestations of deep spiritual awareness. All religions emphasise this 'inner light', this 'treasure within' to which so many aspire through an array of methodologies such as prayer, meditation, yoga, Zen, Tao and Zikr. Rather than focusing on differences, therefore, our education would do well to reflect on the fundamental spiritual values that we share across religions, including the most basic contention regarding our essential essence as human beings.

Sixth and finally, we must embrace the shared values of an emerging *global society*, displaying the courage to think and act globally, and abandon rigid, traditional paradigms. In so doing, we must mobilise our inner and outer resources in order to construct a new world based on mutually assured welfare, rather than destruction. As global citizens committed to human survival, we must use the most recent array of innovative and interactive pedagogic methodologies to structure a worldwide programme of education for children and adults alike. Such an approach should open our eyes to the reality of this global age and our hearts to the cries of the oppressed and the suffering. There is no time to lose. Even as the global society inexorably emerges, regressive forces of fundamentalism and fanaticism, exploitation and intimidation are also growing. As we conceptualise and create a global society grounded in shared values of coexistence, we must not underestimate these destructive forces, while simultaneously seeking to understand and address the fears of such individuals and groups within the broader international community.

In conclusion, I feel that with our rich and multifaceted religious and cultural heritage, India is in a significant position to promote and indeed spearhead the whole concept of value- based education.*

KARAN SINGH

◆

NOTES

1. http://www.see-ducoop.net/education_in/pdf/15_62.pdf
2. http://education.nic.in/cd50years/q/38/3V/383V0301.htm
3. http://www.nvo.unep.org/eaf/eafadec.pdf
4. http://www.templeofunderstanding.org

◆◆

PREFACE

According to the Ministry of Human Resource Development,

> the essence of human resource development is education, which plays a significant and remedial role in balancing the socio-economic framework of the country… the youth of this great nation awaits a new paradigm of education that fosters knowledge with analytical skills, logical reasoning and the ability to imagine beyond the given.

The current events on university campuses fly in the face of these very pronouncements.

A little over 36 years ago, I was catapulted from the sheltered and homogeneous environs of a convent school to Delhi University's North Campus. It was an eye-opener. I shared space with students from across the country, some of whom were more comfortable speaking Hindi. One of the first questions I was asked by my classmates was, 'what is your caste?' It brought home the reality that is India. Today, it is difficult to comprehend the efforts to stifle rational, questioning voices. My best memories of those five years are the after-class gatherings of students, talking animatedly about the state of the nation at large, voices getting louder as opinions clashed. We were often joined by our professors, who sharpened our thinking and made us question even more. Is that a thing of the past? I sincerely hope not.

But we should remind ourselves that the state of education in India today goes deeper and further back. Some of the concerns are brought out in this collection of papers. Quite deliberately, we decided not to concentrate on the specifics of primary, secondary and tertiary education, nor is there a lot by way of statistics of literacy, dropout, enrolment rates, etc. These are certainly important, and have been touched upon by the contributors, but data for these is available in other sources. Here, the contributors ask a fundamental question: What is education? While there is no one answer, the papers provide a clear understanding of the current state of education which, we all agree, stands at the crossroads. There is limited space here to give a short summary of all the articles. Instead, I highlight some salient issues that have been dealt with individually and across papers.

So, what is education? First and foremost, it is a fundamental right for the empowerment of every citizen, and the holistic development of the human personality. It is not only about literacy and grades and rankings, nor merely about knowledge creation. A common theme that runs through the collection is the recognition that education has to teach us to think and question. If this is the imperative, education must take cognisance of disparities in incomes and social status, the heterogeneity of culture, religion, language and lived reality.

At the primary level, the Right to Education has in some small measure helped reduce inequality in access to education. But we need to reaffirm our faith in public schooling and invest more funds for basic amenities and good teachers. In higher education, there has been breakneck expansion, particularly with the growing number of private providers. What is not clear, however, is whether this expansion has in any way improved the quality of education. This is not to say that privatisation of education is in itself a bad thing: the concern is the real danger of education becoming a commodity with a market value. What is needed is better regulation and a clear government policy.

There is much, much more that this volume offers, but there are also some areas we could not include for want of space. However, we believe it is a significant contribution to the current debate on education in India.

◆

OMITA GOYAL

INTRODUCTION
Indian Education in Turmoil

APOORVANAND

Education seldom makes news in India. Very few occasions attract media attention: there is the annual ritual of national lament when India fails to appear in the list of the top two or four hundred universities globally. The discussion on school education is also largely restricted to controversies about the content of textbooks. Then, too, it is only history textbooks and controversies around them which hog the limelight.

At the time of writing, the Indian media is full of reports about campuses. They seem to suggest that campuses have turned into battlegrounds and a nationalist anxiety has gripped the Ministry of Human Resource Development, and university leaders are vying with each other to prove their credentials. This battle of nationalism is being presented as a war between the elite and the subaltern. It is claimed that these elite institutions are eating into scarce national resources, using their privilege to shelter anti-national elements and foster their ideology. Interestingly, the nationalist argument is now being spelt out in a language of equity. It is laced with the data of per capita expenditure on students, teacher–pupil ratio and the like, to prove that the common taxpayer's money is being used by students and faculty of privileged institutions like Jawaharlal University (JNU) and Hyderabad Central University (HCU), without making any significant contribution to the national economy.

It was amusing, but also worrisome, to see the government and the ruling party contrasting the image of a soldier buried under tons of ice at Siachen with students and teachers comfortably ensconced in those campuses. A language implying betrayal and ungratefulness is being used to question the very existence of such universities. Army personnel being invited to campus to seek their advice on how to run a university deepens this perception. It is a fusion of utilitarianism and nationalism to redefine the very purpose of education.

All this could have been a blessing in disguise: it should have ideally led to a fresh discussion of the aims of education and the role of educational institutions in the new national and international scenario. Economies ridden with crises, large-scale forced displacement due to unending wars, failed nation states, violence and mistrust that defines human relationships in the globalised world, and ecological predicaments facing humanity have placed new challenges before education. Education is expected to first identify and articulate these challenges coherently, and then suggest ways to deal with them. It is a huge task if we consider the fact that education, in a way, is itself a product of the very forces responsible for the planet's problems. If it takes only a subservient role and legitimises the status quo, the university or school systems run the risk of failing in the original mandate of providing solutions through critical study and thinking.

In the Indian context in particular, the present crisis of education has awakened sleeping ghosts. The suicide of Rohith Vemula in HCU has brought the question of caste-based discrimination in educational institutions into sharp focus. We are repeatedly told that caste is no longer a marker of inequality and we need to move beyond it in formulating policies to ensure equitable quality in higher education. And yet, the letter written by Vemula before his tragic death brings to the fore the painful reality of discrimination in educational spaces, and the insensitivity of policymakers and university leaders towards it.

The tragedy at HCU is reminiscent of an incident at the All India Institute of Medical Sciences (AIIMS) 10 years ago. We were there to seek facts about a reported incident of caste-based discrimination. When we reached the complainant's room, we were shocked to see the choicest abuses scribbled as graffiti across his walls. There was cunning behind them; they did not mention caste specifically so as to evade the provisions of the SC/ST atrocities act. Later, the then director of the Institute mobilised the full force of his faculty to assure us that caste was alien to the Institute, which was concerned only with producing excellence. We could sense the embarrassment which this incident had caused to the members of the Institute and could understand their denial. The investigation could not proceed further as the complainant disappeared. One faculty member explained that the threat of punishment for violating the privacy of the 'family', i.e., the Institute, could, in such cases, ruin the career of the complainant, forcing him to withdraw.

Clearly, we can see that far from being engines of transformation in our social relations, educational institutions are mostly unequal spaces in themselves. The story is similar if we look at schools, where children from the scheduled castes and tribes still do not feel at home. Stories of villages boycotting schools with a Dalit cook, for instance, are not exceptions. If we do not hear of such instances more often, it is because the authorities address communitarian sensitivities right in the beginning.

Apart from the scheduled castes and tribes, the absence of minorities, especially Muslims, from higher education has not even entered the discourse on exclusion. The 'Muslim issue' remains confined to a discussion on madarsas and institutions like Aligarh Muslim University (AMU). The intervention of the state is in the guise of modernising and secularising Muslims. The minority status of institutions (AMU, for instance) is seen as a special concession given to Muslims and is used to create resentment against them. Instead, the larger and more crucial question of their exclusion from educational spaces needs to be brought to the forefront.

The question of the autonomy of universities has not been discussed sufficiently. We know that this word has become irrelevant in the context of state universities, where vice chancellors work at the mercy of their political masters. The Acts, which govern the functioning of central universities, provide safeguards for vice chancellors against the whims and fancies of the political power of the day. Despite this, many have been seen to voluntarily act as agents of the government. If the Acts ensure autonomy, how was it lost? Does autonomy mean autonomy of the vice chancellor alone, or is it a sum total of the autonomy of all the constituent units of the university?

The universities gave in to the demands of the government to first implement the semester system across India, irrespective of the nature of the university. Next, they implemented the Choice Based Credit System (CBCS), which also means that the universities would have to follow a common curriculum prepared by the University Grants Commission (UGC). All this was done in the name of ensuring efficiency and uniformity without an adequate consultative process. The opposition by teachers was portrayed as being supportive of the status quo and driven by the interest in protecting their privileges. That teachers should also have a right to decide the content and form of teaching is treated as a principle fit only for universities of the first world.

It has often been said that institutions should first prove that they deserve autonomy, and that autonomy always comes along with accountability. Is autonomy then to be treated as a reward for excellence, or is it a necessary condition for it? Professor Upendra Baxi once remarked that we should use the word responsibility in place of accountability. Responsibility should be read here as *response-ability*. The manner in which the organs of the university are made response-able should lead us to the question of governance and structure of the university. How is it that the IIMs or the IITs have managed to be autonomous and excellent institutions at the same time? Somehow, they have been able to ward off attempts by successive governments to tamper with their functioning. Do central and state universities have something to learn from them?

The issue of governance, too, needs to be foregrounded. Not just central universities, but state and private universities should also be brought into the discourse. We need to examine the processes and structures that govern a university. Why is it that the head of the institution is not accountable to the university community? The relationship between universities and the apex regulatory body—in this case the UGC—does not make for a pleasant story. At the same time, the weakening of the autonomy of the UGC by successive governments has made it so fragile that it now resembles a subsidiary of the Ministry.

Does this insensitivity towards autonomy have something to do with the erosion of the agency of teachers? If we look beyond the central universities, there are universities and colleges across India that have functioned without teachers for decades. Turning teachers into informal, contract labour is a phenomenon which started with schools and was ignored by the teaching community in universities. Unfortunately, it is now a reality. Despite these open positions, universities and colleges conduct examinations regularly. The most important, rather the only function of the institution, is to provide certificates to students. Everybody is happy as long as examinations are held peacefully and results are out on time. It should be noted that students no longer agitate to extend the dates of examination, which was a fairly regular demand three decades back. What does it signify? The total dissociation of classrooms from examinations has become a fact for state-run universities in India.

The collapse of state-run universities is a tragic story, which is waiting for a narrator, to be told with all its poignancy. In the ruins of the public university system, experiments like the Nalanda University and South Asian University are like blossoms in a desert, but their claim and clamour for autonomy in all aspects seems to suggest that autonomy flows from eminence. It is not a right for commoners, who are to be found in the hinterland or backwaters of education.

Professor Baxi had once suggested that we need to do away with the term 'higher education'. What is high about it? Higher education in India has arrogantly placed itself on a pedestal much above the one on which our schools rest. And, today, they mirror the morass and morbidity our schools have experienced for decades.

Advocates of the autonomy principle often argue that universities cannot be treated like schools. There seems to be general agreement amongst our university dons, irrespective of their ideological colour, that schools are mostly places where knowledge is transferred to children. Teachers have a responsibility and duty to do the job of faithfully transferring the 'right' kind of knowledge. In this discourse, a schoolteacher is not given the autonomy that university teachers claim as their right. Neither are the children treated as free minds. Their susceptibility, vulnerability and impressionability is invoked to save them from 'unwarranted' and 'unhealthy' information. All attention is focused on textbooks which are repositories of authorised, official knowledge. All that is required is proper training for teachers to be able to transact this in their classrooms.

These questions were raised in the Report of the Yashpal Committee (2009) that advised on the 'renovation and rejuvenation of higher education'. Unfortunately, the Report was put in cold storage by the then government. The issue of institutional autonomy, independence of the apex regulatory body in the field of higher education, bridging the gap between the state and central educational institutions, ending the fragmentation in every aspect of higher education, including policy making, were flagged for urgent attention. The urgency remains.

The National Curriculum Framework for School Education (NCF), 2005, tried to take the debate to a different plane. It advocated the centrality of teachers and students in the scheme of school education. Textbooks were to be treated as one of the actors in this drama to help teachers and students explore the expanse of knowledge with freedom. The idea of the school classroom as a site for the creation of knowledge has been heard with suspicion and derided even by those who want freedom for teachers and students in universities.

The NCF tried to move away from prescribing what to teach, to questioning the need to teach it, and how it should be taught. By privileging the learner and teacher, and emphasising the processes, the NCF sought to free the discourse of school education from restrictive ideological frames of nationalism and secularism. If the democratising potential of education has to be realised, it cannot but treat teachers and students as independent thinking agents.

The NCF was making a very sophisticated argument, which was lost on both the right and the left. The left found it wanting in its duty of secularisation of education. It forgot that, essentially, secularism had to be a principle that emerges from democratic processes. Failing that, secularism will always remain an alien notion and always have an equal competitor in nationalism. In this battle, unfortunately, given the balance of forces in the Indian context, right-wing nationalism is bound to win.

The fundamental challenge facing education today, therefore, is to conceive and design all its elements in such a way as to realise its democratic potential. In a highly unequal world such as ours, which has to deal with a societal mind in which inequality and discrimination are deeply ingrained, it would mean equal and equitable distribution of resources at all levels. Bypassing this question does not help.

The experience of newly created universities has shown that nearly all of them resemble their state counterparts. It is not surprising that they lack vigour and freshness and look fatigued, lacking the desire to undertake bold experiments in their selection processes or curricular exercise. Experimentation cannot be the preserve of a privileged few like Ashoka or Shiv Nadar University; it is the right of all universities. This is not to say that private initiatives need not be taken in the field of education. In fact, we would need many more private interventions to bring energy and innovation to this field, but yet treat education as a public good and part of the commons.

Instead, very often, the rich and privileged first cut themselves off from the masses, establish their own educational zones, and then defend them from being contaminated with the ordinary. In my opinion, one example is the case of Sanskriti School, Delhi, which was established by the elite civil services. They approached the Supreme Court to exclude themselves from conditions placed by the Right to Education Act. This battle, as Professor Krishna Kumar points out, shows how far the elite can go to fortress their privileges. Similarly, the Right to Education Act was sought to be diluted by the powerful lobby of private schools which took the matter to the Supreme Court. The destruction of the common school system had to be followed by the crumbling of the public university system. The severe curtailment in budgetary provision for the public university system would further weaken its already fragile structure. This tottering figure is being adorned with nationalist armour. Which war will this caricature of a warrior fight, let alone win?

We need, therefore, to move beyond the momentary excitement that we see in the media, and look at more long-term structural issues of education that also have a great impact on the everyday functioning of educational institutions. We need to inculcate a policy-oriented mindset which does not treat education in an episodic and disjointed manner. Similarly, we need to resume the discussion that NCF and the Yashpal Committee Report had started. This volume is an effort in this direction.

◆

WHY EDUCATE?

ROMILA THAPAR

When we speak of education we tend to confine ourselves to discussing categories of institutions, their numbers, and the figures of those that qualify. This is fine up to a point, but there is obviously far more to what we want from education. A question that we seldom stop to explore fully concerns its purpose and function. The easy answer is that education provides us with information on various subjects, it equips us to better understand the world we live in, and is necessary to many jobs. The next question is whether education does this in India. The answer is, generally, that it does so only to a limited extent. There are an exceptional few for whom education goes beyond that limited point, and this exception does not constitute the critical mass that ensures the proper function of education in a democratic society.

Since 1947, governments have spoken of the importance of education, yet, in the same breath, have allocated minimal funds to its furtherance. This paucity is explained as the budget having had to be adjusted to other national requirements. When budget cuts are required, then the finances for education are easily reduced without any public outcry. There have been many Education Commissions suggesting ways of improving both the quality of education and the number of educational institutions. But it cannot be said that educational activities have registered a striking improvement; in fact, in some areas, there has been a decline. Can this, perhaps, be due to a political discomfort with having to cope with literate, educated citizens who will of course make demands on, and more critically assess, governments? This can be avoided by leaving people ill-educated or uneducated.

Winter 2015–Spring 2016, Volume 42, Numbers 3 & 4

What, then, would one want from a system of education should one, as a citizen, have a chance to make demands? As a first step, education means acquiring information and the information comes from the knowledge that is conveyed through the process of education. Two important questions arise. Is the knowledge up-to-date, irrespective of the field to which it refers? Endlessly passing on information that is out-of-date is not education. At best it will assist basic literacy, but literacy alone, however valuable it is in itself, is not the end purpose of education. It is a means to education. Second, how can there be an improvement on what is being taught. One tested method of improving the quality of knowledge is by teaching students to think critically, or by what is known as critical inquiry. This does not come through opening up the country to schools and universities run by private agencies, both national and foreign. It comes from understanding the purpose of education.

Critical inquiry is not acquired in passing. It has to be taught, inculcated and made relevant. This, of course, is the one procedure that we generally do not teach. Some discover it by accident, others may meet a rare teacher who can teach them how to proceed, or they might accidentally have access to a good library from where they can read in a way that encourages such inquiry. Instead of its being the foundation of an educational system, its acquisition has become what a student may arrive at despite it.

The initial step in any inquiry is to collect data pertaining to a subject, and such data increases as more and more information is discovered, unearthed and revealed. As subjects begin to get connected through research, there are new aspects that are discovered. Inter-disciplinary research, for instance, reveals new connections and requires fresh questions.

For example, even in a relatively remote subject new perspectives and techniques become necessary. A century ago, historians researching the Vedic period of ancient Indian history would have consulted only the Sanskrit texts of the Vedic corpus for information. A few decades later this changed and there was new information from an entirely new source—the excavation of settlements associated with those times—and this required some corelation of textual and archaeological evidence. Fifty years ago came the results from linguistics, indicating the use of more than one language in the texts. The relationship between the speakers of these languages became an obvious question. In examining the choice of settlements, the ecology of the region demanded attention. Information on changing river courses or deforestation became relevant. In the last few years there has been the intervention of genetics, and although the results of DNA analyses have neither been definitive nor sufficient, it is a study that may possibly provide interesting information. A single scholar may not have expertise in such diverse disciplines. But there should be an awareness that evidence from just one discipline may no longer suffice for an in-depth study. An earlier, relatively uncomplicated history has now become a complex subject. Yet the textbooks, from which this subject is taught, are unaware of this complexity. Instead, the subject is cut down to simple statements that discourage students from asking questions.

After the information has been collected, there is the essential question of checking its reliability that alone allows it to be treated as evidence. How does one distinguish fact from fantasy, or between reliable evidence and an imaginary belief? This is particularly important in both natural and social sciences, since knowledge in these subjects cannot advance without reliable evidence. In scientific experiments, some evidence can be tested and, if it is faulty, the experiment can fail. The fantasies current these days about scientific achievements in ancient India, when tested through experiments, calculations and information on the technology used, have failed. Genuine achievements have stood the test; spurious ones have not. So whereas we know that there were substantial contributions from Indian scholars to the world's knowledge of astronomy, mathematics and medicine, claims to aeroplanes, motor-cars and stem-cell research three thousand years ago are untenable. For much of social science, testing a hypothesis through experiments is not always possible; nevertheless, there are other dependable methods of checking the reliability of evidence.

With reliable data one can proceed to making causal connections. These require that they be based on logic and rational argument. It is only if this process is followed can we then claim that the new knowledge being proposed is an advance on what exists. This, then, is the process that should underlie much of education. To make education suitable to the needs of society, its contents must be relevant and tested. Does this happen? Or is there a preference for keeping the status quo and not assessing what is being taught? Or else, does it merely impose the diktat of those who govern and teach what they want taught? Since those who govern change with every general election, this does rather make a joke of education, as has happened with the NCERT History Textbooks.

Education does not function in isolation. It is part of the larger vision of society. Therefore, questions relating to human rights and social justice are relevant to its implementation. Education has to be made available to even the most under-privileged citizen and has also to be, as far as possible, relevant to their needs. This is why schooling—both primary and secondary—is crucial and is the right to which every citizen is entitled. This also requires that the content of education should emphasise the inclusion of all members of society in creating the category of citizen. A democracy, for instance, cannot have primacy of citizenship given to those of one religion alone.

This brings me to the crucial question of who decides what constitutes knowledge, and how it is to be taught. Since education is not just a matter of being literate and getting grades, even an awareness of the answer to this question is central to the process of education. Learning how to think and to interrogate knowledge is a primary function of education. Admittedly, not every student is expected to respond equally to this, but if there is awareness of at least some of the broader questions that relate to knowledge, then the idea of education will have come a long way. This requires that courses and syllabi, and the contents of these, should be in the hands of specialised professionals and not be dictated by politicians and casual bureaucrats, as they frequently are.

Those who have been the decision-makers in defining what constitutes education have obviously changed fundamentally over the centuries. In the absence of secular education, the institutions involved in educating people came from those propagating religions of various kinds, and the socio-religious function of their institution has defined the nature and content of their education.

Institutions where education was imparted were associated with religious sects, especially those that received patronage from royalty and the rich. This consisted of monetary donations and wealth, as well as large grants of land that enabled them to finance themselves and provide them with the required social status. These institutions were not isolated from social concerns. Their categories of knowledge included not only that which pertained to religious beliefs but also to social codes.

These were the *ashramas*/hermitages in the forest, superseded by the wealthy *mathas* and *gurukulas*. The Buddhists had their *viharas*/monasteries, where much of the study of Buddhist and other texts was carried out. The complex of monasteries at Nalanda was such a place. With the expulsion of Buddhism in most parts of the country, these came to a close. Then came the *madrassas* and later the schools run by *gurudwara* committees. Christian missions established their individual schools. Serfoji II, ruling from Tanjore in the late 18th century, attempted to introduce the views of the Enlightenment, emphasising the rational in its curriculum. But these institutions did not survive colonialism.

Colonialism introduced some schools and colleges with a rather more non-religious curriculum, but the earlier ones were not replaced and grew in numbers. Colonial syllabi underwent a different kind of filtration. For example, Kalidasa's play *Abhijnana-shakuntalam* was taught in Sanskrit classes, but it was an expurgated version where passages thought to be too erotic were deleted; or books on liberty and the right to free speech were omitted from the syllabus. There was a difference in these schools with respect to the content of education, and how information and knowledge are to be investigated.

The religion-based schools continued after independence and to these were added the new religio-political schools—the Shishu Mandirs and others run by the organisations of the Sangh Parivar—reflecting the ideology of their umbrella organisation. It would be worth counting the number of properly secular schools as compared to all the religion-oriented schools. A secular society would discourage education with a religious bias.

A religio-political ideology determines the authority that controls the information taught in the curriculum, and what areas of knowledge are to be explored, if at all. This form of teaching more often follows a kind of question–answer format, with set questions and set answers, deviating from that which is not encouraged. Schools run by the state would carry the imprint of the state and its ideology. The latter is often determined by who is governing it, although it should ideally be independent and determined by the requirements of the discipline.

The question, therefore, remains as to who decides on these fundamentals of education. Much depends on what we visualise as the purpose of education. If we limit it to just being literate and getting good grades, then it can be reduced to memorising a set of formulae. This has been on the increase over the years and explains in part why there are complaints now from those teaching at graduate and postgraduate levels about the poor training of the students coming to them. The question is whether they should be failed and asked to repeat the degree, or if the levels of education should be lowered still further so that students can scrape through and proceed to a further degree, where they will meet the same problem, but intensified. Poorly trained students neither have the required information, nor the training in how to think. Yet this is a requirement that is pertinent to all forms of education. If properly internalised, it becomes the foundation for tackling a range of professional and other problems of life.

Have we seriously addressed the question of what constitutes education and enquired as to what needs to change to ensure its relevance? Discussions on the New Education Policy, to be implemented shortly, have not even begun in any systematic manner, and yet the decisions are imminent. To list themes and hope for useful discussion is unlikely to give results unless information and experience are analysed in depth, and systematically discussed. Themes relating to broad questions of public and private education, and of the contribution of the state, will bring forth reactions differing according to the socio-economic background and aspirations. One size does not fit all.

As usual, a policy will be imposed given the absence of time and extensive discussion. One can predict the nature of the policy, given that it has to apply to more than half-a-million young Indians. They will not be taught to think independently or to question; they will be taught to accept, without a murmur or a question, what they are told by those in authority.

Would this be yet another example of inefficiency in handling a project that was, in any case, too extensive to be systematised in such a short time? Or is it deliberate? The predictable confusion will be solved by continuing with the simple dog-eared system that exists, but there will be a major change, viz., the content of what is taught will be dictated to by the ideological needs of the 'cultural organisations' in which the party in power is rooted.

The reworking of educational policy may produce better results if two immediate actions are taken. One is that the orientation to the purposes of education has to start from the first level of schooling and proceed systematically from primary to secondary school. For the last few years we have heard dramatic announcements about the tertiary level. This makes for good propaganda but little else. If the quality of education at these two levels of schooling can be significantly improved, some improvement will be possible further up as well. Improvement does not mean reducing everything to the Lowest Common Denominator, but upgrading levels.

An upgrade is not as fierce and frightening as it sounds because surprisingly good results can emerge if the process of education and its contents are properly systematised. What it does mean is that the content of textbooks has to be improved by having textbooks written and vetted by specialists in the subjects, and not merely by casual writers wanting to make quick and easy money, or in keeping with the heavy imprint of self-declared 'cultural and religious organisations'.

If good teachers are to be attracted to teaching, there have to be some inducements. If taken seriously, teachers have to be better trained and given facilities to upgrade. This can be done with a reasonable budget focusing on frequent local workshops, better equipped schools, and with the help of radio and TV through setting up separate education channels. Ensuring that the technology required for education is available will mark a change for the better as indeed is the sensible use of the wider technology as an aid to extensive education. Maps and charts, and even minimum laboratory facilities for the sciences, would make a difference.

For all our apparent respect for *rishis* and *munis*, we are a society that generally has little or no respect for teachers, academics and intellectuals. We are currently experiencing the worst forms of anti-intellectualism than we have known since independence. The freedom to present explanations other than the propagated one is curtailed by the claims of a few that their sentiments are hurt by certain opinions. The silence of the majority is bought by assassinating rationalists. Ethics that pertain to human qualities of understanding the world we live in, and are essential to education, are difficult to find these days, although they did exist a half-century ago.

It does little good to education if those controlling it insist on only one explanation for any matter being discussed, and where there is no scope for assessing the viability of the evidence and considering other plausible explanations. Even if one explanation is chosen, it has to be arrived at by analysing the various explanations for viability and demonstrating why the others are not viable.

Can the assessment of knowledge, or its explanation, be unbiased? This issue is as pertinent to the natural sciences as the social sciences, although it was once thought that the former is based on rational thinking and thus protected from bias. This argument no longer holds. That research often begins with a hypothesis means that the researcher may not be liberated from predetermined ideas; but the fact that it is treated as a hypothesis also means that the theory on which it is based can be modified, or even changed, should the investigations suggest otherwise. The openness of the exploration of knowledge can only succeed if the training and education is not forced to conform to one explanation, or to one that is not based on critical inquiry.

If students are to be accommodated in a global system there has to be an emphasis on teaching them to think and to question what exists, and to relate it to the aspirations that they demand from a system of education. A crucial question that we need to ask today is whether the education proposed will assist in creating a secular democracy, together with its components of human rights and social justice. Will education help bring about the society for which we are waiting?

◆

THE UNIVERSITY AND ITS OUTSIDE*

UDAYA KUMAR

Recent events in JNU and the strong, widespread responses they provoked indicate two things. First, what is at stake in the JNU crisis goes beyond the destiny of a particular university, or even questions of higher education, foreboding wider repression of freedoms in society. Second, in the current contestation over the scope of democracy, the public university as an institution and intellectual space is placed in a position of vital significance. Similarities between the situations that arose in Hyderabad Central University, Jadavpur University and JNU have been instructive. In all these instances, the state and a section of the population sought to reconfigure the university space and enforce new limits to what can take place there. Has the Indian university become the visible site where the imminent futures of freedom and democracy are being thought and fought over?

SPECIAL RELATIONSHIP

The university as an institution has a special relationship to society at large: it is commonly recognised that its larger societal functions can be fulfilled only under certain conditions of autonomy. At the same time, shifts in the relationship between the university and its outside can have a vital impact on its space and the energies mobilised there: they may enhance the university's autonomous responsiveness to society or hamper its institutional integrity.

The past four or five years, dating from the last years of the UPA II government, saw an intensification of government interference in the functioning of university administrations. Fresh dimensions have been added to this under the new regime: now government intervention has become more blatant and direct; it is often prompted and accompanied by aggressive political campaigning against the freedoms enjoyed by universities, sometimes leading to violent onslaughts from politically organised vigilante groups. Student protests have been increasingly confronted by belligerent mobs and a police force that seems to abdicate all autonomy of functioning. The events that unfolded in the Patiala court compound on 15 and 17 February offer the starkest example of this, but are by no means unique. Occupy UGC protests and students' march near the RSS office in Jhandewalan in the wake of Rohith Vemula's suicide were handled with brute force, with newspapers and television channels reporting the participation of plainclothes men in the latter crackdown.

CATCHWORD OF 'ANTI-NATIONAL'

The catchword 'anti-national' has been prominent in these aggressive campaigns as a tool for mobilisation and self-justification. Although the phrase has been in active use in right-wing political discourse for some time, it has acquired a new salience in the attack on universities. It was heard repeatedly during the developments in Hyderabad Central University that led to Vemula's suspension and later his suicide. It has acquired a new, deafening loudness in the past weeks in the context of JNU. Whether it be capital punishment, or judgements pronounced by courts, or human rights violations by armed forces, or the suppression of political dissent by the state, the expression of views critical of them within university campuses are portrayed as 'anti-national' actions. Devoid of conceptual specificity, the phrase 'anti-national' does not allow patient scrutiny: it does not permit critical unpacking, invalidation, or self-delimitation. Without any foundation in the constitution or legal structures, the phrase works as aggressive name-calling which singles out persons and views to publicly incite and direct punitive action.

Branding adversaries as 'anti-nationals' allows political formations to mobilise an irate public whose self-authorisation as spokespersons for the nation resides solely in the divisive force of accusation and in the violent demand for punishment. Courts have in the past cautioned that opinions against the government or belief in an alternative vision of society cannot in itself be termed as illegal, in the absence of evidence of actions aimed at destroying the state. Such vital distinctions are erased by the punitive rhetoric of offended nationalism. The alarming frequency with which cases are registered and people arrested for expression of views on social media or campus publications indicates that the harassment of prosecution is being used as a form of punishment, regardless of the legal tenability of the charges. The convergence of state machinery, political discourse and mob aggression has produced an atmosphere of siege in many university campuses.

LINK TO OTHER CHANGES

These recent developments, however, cannot be viewed in isolation. Under the UPA-II regime, major changes in higher education were initiated and imposed on universities without consultation or public discussion. This was dramatically demonstrated in the case of Delhi University, where a series of hastily formulated curricular reforms were forced without serious academic deliberation by making a mockery of institutional mechanisms. Ironically, the very argument about university autonomy was used then in order to pre-empt critical scrutiny by courts or Parliament. Autocratic methods of bullying the academic community into submission have been used in other Indian universities as well. Such moves have often been viewed by critics against the backdrop of a projected transformation of Indian higher education through increased privatisation and globalisation. Their immediate consequence, however, has been a dramatic erosion in institutional procedures and academic standards caused by the hasty cobbling together of syllabi and teaching programmes, questionable appointments, and a cynical disregard for collective deliberation.

The recent escalation of government intervention has made the university alarmingly vulnerable to an outside beyond its control. Over the past year, newspapers reported several standoffs between the government and the administration of central universities and IITs. Many vice-chancellors and administrative heads now face the same sense of disenfranchisement that faculty members in universities experienced for the past few years. Press reports on the high-handedness displayed by the government in its interactions with university vice-chancellors and other institutional functionaries seem to confirm the change in the relations between the state and the university. The earlier pretence of non-expertise on the part of the Ministry has given way to the discrediting of expertise and autonomy with an ugly insistence on showing who is boss, taking the form—if the press is to be believed—of asking 'who pays your salary?'

RECONFIGURING THE RELATIONSHIP

This question may be read as a sign of current attempts to reconfigure the relationship between the university and its outside in a language of hostility and control. This is present not only in governmental intervention in the university's functioning; we also find it in the recent prominence of the figure of the 'taxpayer' in public discussions on education. Although tax regimes are devised for the fulfilment of larger societal objectives and do not confer any special rights to those who pay personal taxes as opposed to sections of the population that are exempted from taxation, the 'taxpayer' is projected as a figure of special entitlement in contrast to the 'public' or 'society'. The rhetoric around the taxpayer subverts inclusive conceptions of public interest by producing a distinction between 'taxpayers' and 'spongers', and arrogates a differential right to dictate the terms on which public funds should be spent. Education is seen less as a vital resource valued and maintained in collective interest than as a site of economic investment where the funders, i.e., the taxpayers, have a right to set societal agendas and objectives. This differentiation of the public—dividing it on the basis of graded rights in deciding public matters—is interestingly accompanied by a trend in the opposite direction. That which is excluded appears not as an inclusive, deliberating public before which contesting views on public interest and public spending—ranging from military expenditure to health and education—can be raised. It assumes the form of aggressive trolls or politically organised mobs that regard inclusive public discussion as an enemy.

EXPANSION OF THE UNIVERSITY

We should not think that shifts in the relationship between the university and its outside have always been towards hostile confrontation. The most significant change in higher education in independent India has perhaps been the expansion over the last decade of reservation to backward classes, and this has led to major changes in the texture of central universities. This, combined with the award of scholarships for MPhil and PhD students who did not have funding through UGC's competitive JRF (Junior Research Fellowship) examination (a measure whose withdrawal provoked the Occupy UGC protests) made it possible for the first time for students of weaker social backgrounds to pursue university education to advanced levels on a large scale. This has significantly altered the predominantly upper-caste, middle-class character of the student body, redefining the relations between the intellectual activities in the university and the world outside. This unprecedented enhancement of diversity in economic, social and linguistic backgrounds has posed important challenges for mass higher education in India in terms of facilities, infrastructure, provisions for close academic support and mentorship, and—importantly—attitudes, much of which remains insufficiently addressed till now. However, the presence of a large student population from socially underprivileged sections has increasingly inflected and transformed idioms of political thinking and practice on campuses. Many institutional habits, which remained invisible, naturalised and unchallenged over decades have been questioned in recent years for their discriminatory character, and a new, more inclusive academic culture is being demanded. The public university seems placed at the moment at the crossroads of these two forces: the state and a punitive public trying to curtail its autonomy as a space, and the democratisation of the student body altering the character, concerns and relationship of the university to society at large.

The last government and the present one have emphasised the need for a massive expansion of higher education to larger numbers of students. However, this is not conceived as an expansion of what we have known as the university space. Mass higher education is increasingly conceived as a technological endeavour realisable through online courses or mass contact classes, which does not need to create the time and space for debates and discussions typical of university campuses. Projected descriptions of the public university dispense with 'critical thinking,' an idea that has been central to the university's self-image as knowledge-creator for a long time. The vital contribution of the university to the world was understood as not merely as supplying skills needed by society, but also critical and innovative thinking, which enabled social transformation in accordance with the times. Criticism works by an inherent tension with dominant norms and structures, through a refusal to accept the authority of ideas as given and by opening them up for scrutiny. The acquisition and dissemination of knowledge within the university takes place within the horizon of this larger aspiration to innovate and critically transform existing fields of knowledge and life.

UNIVERSITY AS A SKILL FACTORY

In the new conception being put forward by the government, the university is considered as a skill factory, which, through mass production, will address the needs of the country's economy. Critical thought is regarded as an outmoded ambition, an irritant that impedes the smooth accomplishment of this aim. In the protected space of the university, the implicit valorisation of critical thinking has served to link the classroom to its outside: political debates and intellectual conversations on campus connect in creative ways with the classroom, and serve as much as sources of education as formal academic instruction. Universities can foster critical thinking only if they permit students to engage and experiment with diverse points of view in an atmosphere free of fear and the threat of violence. New policies seem to envisage a different kind of public university, where the disciplined acquisition of skills is the only role assigned to students. They are not imagined as possessing any non-curricular intellectual subjectivity. Thought and expression outside the classroom are considered as part of the domain of discipline. The suggestion seems to be that governments will decide on what sorts of non-curricular activities are permissible.

This approach does not recognise the university student as an adult, as an autonomous individual. He/she has voting rights and can thus participate in the most important political choice exercised by citizens, but does not have the right to thought and expression and the freedom to experiment with ideas in the free and protected space of the university. Such activities are becoming matters for surveillance and discipline. The increasing obsession on the part of the UGC and university authorities with surveillance measures, such as CCTV cameras and police presence on campuses, illustrates this. This is particularly pronounced in relation to women students. This new idea of the university denies adulthood to students, and considers them as in a state of tutelage and intellectual heteronomy. The university is being thought of as an extension of the school, where external guidance and necessary force are seen as essential to the maturation of the child into the adult.

These moves place not only the university student in a state of tutelage, but the university itself as an institution is reconceived as properly belonging to such a state. The university is divested of the rights to decide for itself, to govern itself, and set its norms and objectives. It is treated as a child who cannot be trusted to decide what is best for it. Who decides, then, for the university? Who has the right to say what is right for higher education? In the current situation, the government seems to be usurping that position from the university, aided by political formations and self-authorising sections of the public. RSS publications have compiled detailed information on events that take place in campuses like JNU and have outlined plans of 'course correction'. In both Hyderabad and New Delhi, right-wing legislators, armed with such information, asked the government to intervene in the university space and set limits to permissible activities. Nationalism is used as a tool to legitimise efforts to determine from outside what the university ought to allow by way of independent thinking. The government, in a recent meeting, decided to install large national flags on appropriately high flagpoles in central universities to help induce a spirit of nationalism. It has been suggested that military tanks on display on university campuses will have the necessary totemic force. Instead of critical practices that draw their energies from multiple voices and debate, an intellectual ethos of silent veneration or choric acclamation is being proposed. This model thinks of universities not as laboratories of thought but as factories, where activities are performed in unison. Instead of a cohabitation of differences in friendship and respectful, heated disagreement, you have a paranoid fantasy that gets rid of all real diversity.

WHICH FUTURE?

Which of these images will fit our public universities in the years to come? Will they emerge with a stronger sense of autonomy and intellectual vibrancy by drawing on the democratisation of their space and the new energies of critical thought this has brought in? Or will they turn into extended schools which impart skills and impose discipline? At stake in current battles is the fate both of the university and of our democracy.

◆

NOTE

*This essay was first published in *Economic and Political Weekly*, Vol. LI, no. 11, 12 March 2016, pp. 29–31.

◆◆

CHALLENGES OF HIGHER EDUCATION POLICY

Accountability vs. Capabilities

SUDHANSHU BHUSHAN

INTRODUCTION

Higher education is at the crossroads in the 21st century, and is facing new challenges from the roles and expectations of all its stakeholders—students, teachers, administrators and, last but not least, society and state. The question is: can policy help to fulfil the expectations and new roles of different stakeholders? In this article, I argue that the greatest challenge is to define the transformative role of a teacher and the teaching–learning process, and create conditions for achieving the same. The article takes an analytical perspective of 'capabilities' discussed by Amartya Sen (2009) and Martha C. Nussbaum (2013). Ingrid Robeyns (2011) notes that 'Nussbaum describes the capabilities approach as a new theoretical paradigm in the development and policy world, which poses the questions: "What are people actually able to do and to be?"' Put differently, the capabilities approach questions which genuine opportunities are open to people. It shifts the focus of policy and development analysis from resources to capabilities. The capabilities approach allows teachers the freedom to effectively engage with students, but this freedom is coupled with responsibility. It is argued that unless the capabilities of teachers are developed, it would be difficult to raise the standards of higher education and fulfil the expectations of stakeholders.

The competing approach to policy prevalent today is the one guided by formal—bureaucratic and technological—rationality. From this point of view, rules and regulations guide decision making

Winter 2015–Spring 2016, Volume 42, Numbers 3 & 4

from an external source. Formal rationality also imposes the use of technology in order to improve efficiency in higher education, and aids in its progress. Stephen Kalberg notes that,

> from a technical point of view, the most 'rational' type of domination is found in the bureaucracy simply because it aims to do nothing more than calculate the most precise and efficient means for the resolution of problems by ordering them under universal and abstract regulation (1980: 1158).

For example, the current discourse in higher education policy is guided by formal rationality that advocates the idea of the credit system, the Academic Performance Indicator (API), the National Eligibility Test (NET), model-course prescription, accreditation, rankings impact factors, research-evaluation exercises, prescribed hours of teaching, research and extension, students' feedback, etc., which are said to be universal, calculable, and efficiency and productivity driven. These factors become instruments of domination and control aimed at directing action. Max Weber notes that formal rationalisation has led to purposive rational action in terms of a means-end type of social action (ibid.).

The paper argues that the present policy dialogue compels the need to move away from the rationalisation constructed by leading decision makers. Policy, guided by rationalisation, has led to too much regulation aimed at uniformity and standardisation. It completely bypasses the heterogeneous field reality of higher education. The variation in student-body size and composition is one such challenge that no one standard practice can deal with. On the other hand, it may be argued that the capabilities approach allows an understanding of the transformative role of a teacher who can, with a greater degree of empowerment, deal with varying situations within the context in which she works.

The challenge that a large higher education system such as ours faces is to develop a bridge of trust and cooperation between the state and the community of teachers. This foundation of mutual trust is missing today. As a result, the state uses various forms of control and directs decision making. From this perspective, policy uses various norms for accountability and becomes the tool for efficiency-driven measures, while the productivity rationale dominates thinking. However, it is opposed by the community of teachers which wants decisions to be guided by discussion amongst itself. Freedom, wherever it is curtailed, becomes the cause of dissent and conflict. The policy that ignores this space for a teacher gives rise to opposition, covert or overt. Therefore, I believe that bridges of trust are necessary for policy. In the various deliberations on policy of which I have been a part, I find that there is a lack of trust. The community of teachers believes that freedom would be curtailed as many decisions taken through policy would ignore the field reality of colleges and universities and, therefore, stand little chance of success.

This dilemma of freedom to teachers may be resolved by using the capability approach. It also helps build the competency that is necessary for a teacher. Further, freedom can be used only with a democratic decision-making process, as a result of which impartiality can be maintained. The capability approach also differs in a significant way from the state-directed accountability perspective. It is not the rule-oriented perspective of justice guiding policy. It is very much a *nyaya*-based perspective that guides policy and it means that, in actual situations, the 'well-being' of a student is examined. As soon as a student enters the portal of higher education she is assessed, and the deficit addressed to further her advance in the pursuit of skill and knowledge. It is important to understand advancement within the capability approach in terms of actual achievement, and not in terms of what is desirable.

The point to be noted is that if policy aims to build trust, not control over the community of teachers, then it should be open to deliberation and allow decision making by them. The capabilities approach allows the basic and advanced capabilities of a teacher to use freedom with responsibility. Unless teachers are thus empowered, higher education cannot progress to fulfil the expectations of students and the community. It will remain an ivory tower; it will not connect itself with the community.

FORMAL RATIONALITY

Formal rationality in the present industrial society may be said to exist in terms of the domination of 'bureaucratic rationality' and 'technological rationality' in the legal, economic and scientific spheres of life.

Unlike purposive rational action under bureaucratic and technological rationality, substantive value rationality, on the other hand, directs action in terms of the value postulate of the past, present and potential. Value postulate implies friendship, trust, collegiality, equality, and so on. Of the multitude values held by individuals, some values become dominant and guide action.

The interactions of the two previously mentioned forms of rationality—formal and substantive—noted by Weber point to the policy dilemma in modern higher education. From the point of view of formal rationality, rules and regulations guide decision making from external sources. It also imposes technology designed to improve the efficiency of higher education. The progress in higher education is said to take place with the imposition of formal rationality. This creates a disturbance for teachers, students and other stakeholders, who are guided by substantive value rationality. Teachers are guided by a world view in which scholars with a passion for knowledge are of universal value. However, there may be social and cultural differentiation amongst teachers, which encourages them to think differently, creating interests in various subjects. Although the choice of discipline and specialised areas of work might vary, the differentiation that characterises higher education is also its unifying element, which is the search for knowledge through questioning. The domination of formal rules and technology causes interruptions and destroys world views held by teachers. This standardisation of higher education through formal rationality erases the highly differentiated characteristics of higher education.

Formal rationality, as noted earlier, leads to both the 'loss of meaning' and 'loss of freedom'. In higher education, the former takes place in the mind of the teacher. Here, the teacher fails to comprehend that education should be treated as a value proposition—the main aim of which is to inculcate a critical understanding in the endeavour towards achieving a better society. Formal rationality, through rules and techniques, however, constantly directs a teacher to treat higher education as an instrument to achieve certain ends. These ends are predefined in terms of material progress achievable through the capitalist order of society. There is no scope to critically understand the institutional and organisational structure that directs them to follow rules. Therefore, the loss of meaning is to be understood in terms of the disenchantment created by external formal rationalisation that directs a teacher to work for the reproduction, efficiency and productivity of the system.

To a teacher, the loss of freedom is manifest in the power of the bureaucracy and technology that enforces submission. The teacher, being a paid employee[1] and bound by the rules of the organisation in which he works, feels impelled to preserve the substantive value that has thus far guided his action—the preservation of the liberal values of argumentation, the critical understanding of facts, and habits of questioning. The loss of freedom amounts to the submission of the teacher's attempts at a variety of methods to a standard format, the negation of which might lead to the infringement of rules. Bureaucratisation, too, imposes a social control over almost every aspect of the intellectual life of a teacher. Moreover, the loss of freedom associated with formal rationality makes him feel powerless. Thus, the impression created is that rules are universal, concrete and objective, with a boundary which cannot be overstepped, and this alienates the teacher from his own life world of diverse values.

Weber was personally dissatisfied with the bureaucratic domination in German universities in the first quarter of the previous century. His candid expressions of the dominance of the bureaucracy and the fear amongst academics of its power, and, consequently, the demoralisation of the academic community, is no less relevant today in Indian higher education as it was in Weber's day.

STUDENTS' EXPECTATIONS

The students of colleges and universities belong to diverse social groups representing rural, urban, middle-, high-, and low-income groups from every part of the country. This diversity spans mixed religious groups with affiliations to their respective cultures that can be quite rigid. The gender mix in different disciplines of study usually varies. Higher education needs to be receptive to both slow and fast learners, the physically and mentally disabled, and transgenders, to whom social stigma is attached.

It is quite clear that students from diverse groups and communities come from their local environments to institutions of higher education with personal biases and expectations. The immediate objective of higher education is to free their minds from narrow interests and personal biases through liberal education that cultivates the mind through systematic reasoning. Reason allows them to escape from partisan interests, preparing them for the world of work in which they earn their livelihood in a manner that should not be in conflict with others with similar goals.

Students come to institutions of higher education to make their transition to the world of work. In certain cases, the opportunity cost of higher education might be quite high, and for some students a quick transition may be required. For such students, skill building through vocational education and training is desirable. Hence, an efficient vocational pathway might be appropriate for large numbers entering higher education.

Policy in higher education is challenged by the need to meet the diverse expectations and requirements of students as follows:

(i) All barriers to entry should be minimised, implying that higher education should be affordable. Besides, social or cultural barriers must be removed.
(ii) Students need to be introduced to the world of objective reason that is free from biases.
(iii) Language may be an important bottleneck for students so far trained in vernacular languages.
(iv) They must have the option of selecting subjects of their choice.
(v) Curricular design should be flexible enough to allow slow learners to learn at their own pace. It implies that the teaching–learning process should be supported by teachers.

As far as the first requirement is concerned, the role of the state is to ensure that all such barriers to entry are reduced to the minimum. Higher education should be affordable. The government should take complete responsibility for establishing colleges and universities, and the fees charged in these institutions should not be burdensome or prohibitive. Proper infrastructure must be ensured, with teachers posted in the colleges.

THE FAILURES OF RATIONALISED POLICY

It is important to note that policy guided by formal rationality aims at following an efficient path towards the achievement of a certain goal. For example, in the direct recruitment of teachers, and the Career Advancement Scheme (CAS) for promotion, the use of the Academic Performance Indicator (API) is mandated by the University Grants Commission (UGC) through regulation. Under API, minimum scores must be earned under different categories to make up a prescribed total required for entry or promotion. The broader aim is to maintain the standards of higher education through certain quality controls of the qualifications of a teacher. It is common knowledge that it is difficult to keep a record of every single activity to credit a point under API. Second, under the varied conditions that a teacher works, it may not be possible to earn the point under different categories. Third, various ways are adopted to earn a point. One of the most common methods is the use of ISSN and ISBN by the publication to which the contribution is made. Points may be earned by publication in journals, which could, however, be substandard. These methods, besides being a distraction, also lead to dubious ways of publishing which, in turn, lead to further regulation of the quality of journals. Several universities went a step further and clarified a large number of issues that related to the earning of points under API. As the failure of one regulation (policy of API) in turn leads to another regulation (policy on the quality of publication), it results in a chain reaction in which regulation after regulation is pursued, following repeated failures.

The API was suggested after the introduction of the 6th Pay Commission appointed by the UGC. However, even before its introduction, and well after, NET continues to be a means to control the entry of candidates of a certain quality into the teaching profession. While NET, API and regulations on publication operated simultaneously to maintain standards, there was already in existence further regulation governing the quality of PhDs, requiring the mandatory six-month course. When all regulations fail, the evaluation of the quality of institutions is attempted through ranking and accreditation and, further, institutions are mandated to follow the credit system as examples of various strategies. Bureaucratic and technological rationality, with a view to efficiently controlling quality, is never questioned in policy circles. Attempts are then made to further design policy that will control quality with even more precision. All discourses on policy concerning quality are attempts to move towards more accurate measures, which are frustrated time and again.

Policy is a tool used to dominate and disempower the teacher through the loss of freedom and loss of meaning. The fact that students are a diverse community with different needs is never examined. This diversity can never be treated through homogeneous means of control through regulations. There are students who may face language barriers, which teachers need to address. Some students may be first-generation learners and the deficit of cultural capital from which such students suffer is the first important challenge for a teacher. Students, in the light of disciplinary and interdisciplinary knowledge, need to be trained in objective reasoning and, further, they must be freed from the biases that imprison their minds. Teachers need freedom with responsibility to address these different requirements. However, the measures that are taken to maintain standards, which bind teachers to bureaucratic rationality, are impediments.

The way out of the complex rational structure within which a teacher functions is to impose minimum regulation. At the same time, the capabilities of teachers need to be addressed. My plea, therefore, is that the regulatory perspective needs to be substituted with the capabilities perspective in new policy discourse.

THE CAPABILITIES PERSPECTIVE OF POLICY

Capability without accountability is meaningless. Consider the following statement:

> Freedom to choose give[s] us the opportunity to decide what we should do, but with that opportunity comes the responsibility for what we do—to the extent that they are chosen actions. *Since a capability is the power to do something, the accountability that emanates from that ability—that power—is a part of the capability perspective* [italics mine]...(Sen, 2009: 19).

This may appear to be a duty-centred, deontological perspective. Amartya Sen, for a variety of reasons, distances himself from it and prefers the perspective of social realisations for which capabilities are of central importance. An important reason to move away from the deontological form of duty-based accountability relates to the opposition to transcendental institutionalism, which Rawls proposed to present as a rule-based system (ibid.). Essentially, it assumes the organisational propriety and behavioural correctness for rules to be observed and duties to be performed. And, if this happens, society, through the right institutions and right conduct, moves towards perfect justice. What Sen proposes is a much more inclusive perspective of nyaya, which is linked with realisation, the lives of the people and the process through which the realisation takes place, not just the institutions or rules we happen to have. Sen no longer believes in the dichotomy that traditionally exists between consequentialists and deontologists. He clears the ground for the consequential perspective that takes into account comprehensive outcomes, inclusive of the role of the agency and the processes. Hence, while neither duty nor rules are removed from the scenario, the realisation of the goal for improving the lives of the people is proposed. The whole concept of accountability with a view to meeting the goal is supplemented with the 'freedom to choose'—thus developing capabilities. The capabilities approach, according to Sen, focuses on human lives and not just resources. Only then does accountability become meaningful. In the context of higher education, the whole notion of accountability, following from Sen, has to be understood in terms of a realisation-based perspective and the development of the capabilities of a teacher.

The freedom of teachers is important for the achievement of students' interests by giving them more opportunities to pursue the realisation of these interests. This aspect of freedom relates to the choice (or opportunity) that helps to realise the goal. Another aspect of freedom that relates to the process is that a teacher should not feel constrained by others or be forced to follow the prescribed process. Both the opportunity and the process aspects of this freedom are important constituents of capability.

Consider the case of a college teacher who has to implement a teaching strategy to address the problems of slow learners in his class. The UGC regulation, 2010, Clause 17, code of professional ethics, sub clause II (iii) states that teachers should 'recognise the differences in aptitude and capabilities among students and strive to meet their individual needs'. The teacher wants to have the opportunity to go to the university library, which is a few miles away from the college. He, therefore, wants to spend the first half of the day in his college and the second half in the library, for at least two weeks. In situation A, the principal of his college permits him to do so—the opportunity to use the library as well as the process (choice) is facilitated by the former. In situation B, the principal does not permit him to use the library in view of the circular from the university requiring him to be present in the college throughout the day. In the latter situation, the opportunity aspect of the freedom to remain in the college during the first half of the day is fulfilled, but not the freedom to use the university library during the second half. As he is forced to remain in the college, the process aspect of freedom is also lost. It is quite clear that in spite of his accountability towards the slow learners in his class, he is unable to deliver. Therefore, unless capability, in terms of the freedom or opportunity to choose, is ensured, accountability has no meaning as the objective is not realised for want of capability. What is important is the manner in which a teacher achieves the objective of addressing the needs of slow learners by making full use of the opportunity to consider the alternative of going to the library. A teacher's capability must be understood in terms of the process of the choice involved within the actual ability to do so.

An examination of the capabilities of teachers in higher education requires a focus on information. The informational focus should be assessed in terms of the overall freedom and the restraints that are imposed on that freedom. The implication of Sen's argument does not lead us to a specific design based on which an educational institution should be organised. However, the informational material about the constraints on the freedom of a teacher will be useful in the assessment of how far the loss of capabilities is responsible for the non-realisation of the objectives of higher education. It is questionable, however, as to how far these capabilities should be enhanced, thereby enabling teachers to achieve their objectives with complete responsibility.

It must be pointed out that rules and regulations for the maintenance of standards in higher education by the UGC assumes, given the organisational propriety, behavioural compliance in terms of the duty of teachers. It is then assumed that the maintenance of standards will occur in a transcendental manner. However, given the objectives of higher education, the realisation perspective examines the degree of capability of teachers, and the opportunity or the freedom to achieve the outcome in a comprehensive sense. In other words, 'capabilities are important because of the way in which they may lead to functionings' (Nussbaum, 2011: 25). While the former is necessary for the latter, without the latter the former would be pointless. Without capabilities, of course, accountability has no meaning. As teachers are all different, the development of capabilities would imply a plurality of the ways in which they use that freedom for certain functioning.

An essential area of research pertains to the assessment of the constraints on the freedom of a teacher, in terms of those aspects of freedom which are basic to a teacher, in order to have the minimum 'basic capability'. The concept of basic capability was advanced by Nussbaum. 'Basic capabilities are the innate faculties of the person that can make later development and training possible' (ibid.: 24). Sen notes that a basic capability is 'the ability to satisfy certain elementary and crucially important functions up to certain levels' (1992: 45, n. 19). In the context of a teacher, it may be said that a basic capability is measured in terms of the knowledge of the subject—the opportunity to discuss the subject. It is quite possible that all teachers may not have the same basic capability. The goal of public policy should be to develop basic capabilities upto a threshold level so that teachers are able to satisfy certain elementary and crucially important functions of teaching. This might require the basic capability of a teacher to be ensured before entering the profession. If a teacher does not possess this basic capability, he fails to ensure accountability in terms of the delivery of the subject knowledge. Basic capabilities are, however, not simply confined to the merit of the teacher.

Every teacher has some capacity for self-reflection, without which the delivery of the subject is highly monotonous and mechanical. The practice of teaching, and theories about learning, are specialised branches of knowledge, and the teacher must have a basic understanding of the processes of teaching and learning. Teaching is not simply a monologue. It requires an active learner who has to be motivated to ask questions based on his understanding of the subject. The delivery requires a systematic process of imparting subject knowledge from the simple to the complex. The enormous preparation for each class requires some basic capability. If there is a large inequality in the basic capabilities of teachers, special interventions would be required through policy and planning to equip them suitably.

The later development of a teacher in terms of teaching skills, innovations, the analytical abilities of questioning, writing, and shaping the life of a student to develop capabilities for different functions, requires advanced capabilities on the part of the teacher. However, if a teacher does not have some basic capability, such as the knowledge of the subject, it is highly unlikely that advanced capabilities can be developed in terms of the opportunity to make choices.

ADVANCED CAPABILITIES

I shall not attempt to draw up an exhaustive list of advanced capabilities, which can be built from basic capabilities. However, the development of advanced capabilities needs some discussion in order to comprehend the idea of education and training.

(i) Commitment to liberal democratic values: No distinctions of rank in the functional division of labour and facilities is to be made except for special reasons; participation on an equal footing in the decision-making process.

(ii) Development of the capacity for imagination: The teacher should have the proper environment, skill and training to develop a capacity for imagination. The development of questioning and critiquing are aspects of advanced mental faculty that are necessary.

(iii) Nurturing talent: The individual talent of teachers needs to be nurtured for them to develop special abilities (specialisation).

(iv) Development of work ethic: Regular and sustained work without which a teacher can easily slip into apathy and negligence.

(v) Effective engagement of students in the teaching–learning process: e.g., tutorials, seminars, workshops, IT-enabled learning.

(vi) Peer-group cooperation: The development of cooperation in all matters of academic life.

Nussbaum notes that internal capabilities are not simply basic capabilities. They are 'trained or developed traits and abilities in interaction with the social, economic, familial and political environment' (2011: 21). They are states of persons that are sufficient conditions for the exercise of the corresponding function. Internal capabilities build on pre-existing basic capabilities by processes such as education and training. Many internal capabilities require a more structured educational environment. In other words, the advanced capabilities of a person are internal capabilities. It is important to note that internal capabilities can function only when supported by the environment in which a person works. Nussbaum terms internal capabilities and environment as combined capabilities.

COMBINED CAPABILITIES

Combined capabilities are defined as internal capabilities in conjuction with the external conditions that make the exercise of a function a live option. The aim of public policy should be the promotion of combined capabilities. This requires two kinds of efforts: (i) the promotion of internal capabilities (say, by education or training); and (ii) making available external institutional and material conditions.

ENVIRONMENTAL FACTORS

The following environmental factors may be considered necessary for combined capabilities to work.

(i) A room to work for every teacher: Without a room, gossip and aimless discussions lead to wasted time and prevents students from meeting with teachers to clarify doubts, share personal problems, etc. An individual room is also security against the intrusions that prevent sustained academic work.

(ii) Diverse and heterogeneous groups: The faculty should be from different regions, social and cultural groups, and of both genders, which facilitates the truly democratic ethos of the work environment. The representation of students from different groups, regions, gender and nationalities enables a lively social environment.

(iii) The dignity of the academic profession: While human dignity is of utmost value in political liberalism

(Nussbaum, 2011), the dignity of the academic profession enhances the reputation of a teacher and institutions of academic excellence—persons of great academic dignity command respect and it keeps intellectual activity at a high pitch.

(iv) Physical and material conditions: Some basic requirements are adequate classrooms, clean washrooms, sports facilities, laboratories and a well-stocked library.

NEGATIVE CAPABILITIES

It would not be inappropriate to mention that negative capabilities that immediately restrict freedom must be minimised. Bureaucratic and centralised decision making discourages the participation and freedom of the teacher to make choices in the academic interests of students. Populism is another stumbling block that invites vested interests and supports negative capabilities.

It must be noted that capabilities are important for every teacher. However, 'Every teacher has to shape his own evolution, gaining from his own environment, from his colleagues and from the intellectual provocation received from intelligent students' (Dutta, 1990: 14). It is also incorrect that the capabilities earlier mentioned need to be ensured in totality. It may be argued that there are resource constraints. Furthermore, it may also be argued that autonomy to the teachers may be dangerous for want of its judicious use. However, the change in higher education can be progressively ensured by raising the capability of teachers from a lower to a higher level. At one point, capital punishment was the order of the classroom. However, this was removed from teaching practices once it was shown that the incentive system worked better in motivating learners, and it allowed teaching to be more enjoyable. It shows that the education system has moved towards greater justice with the higher capability of teachers.

CONCLUSION

It was earlier noted that the current policy discourse is weighed in favour of rational decision making, dominated by bureaucratic and technological rationalities. These rationalities have attempted to define and measure with precision the accountabilities in order to ensure the efficiency and productivity of the system. This approach leads to a complex system of rules and regulations. It is assumed that under proper institutions and behaviours, policy will be realised in a transcendental manner. However, the failures of rationalised policy making and, further, the cover-up of these failures by means of another policy, have only accumulated over the past years, and have led to the demoralisation of the teachers. I have suggested in this article that the capability approach to policy is a far more useful approach as it empowers the teacher to use freedom with responsibility and effectively fulfil the diverse needs of students from differing backgrounds. It is necessary that a bridge of trust be developed between the teaching community and the state.

◆

NOTE

1. Often such an economic bargain has resulted in academic employees of the government showing loyalty and conforming to the power of state authority without realising that their independence is critical to the creative construction of the society, which the state has to administer for their well-being.

REFERENCES

Dutta, Bhabhatosh. 1990. 'The Adventure of Teaching', in Amrik Singh (ed.), *On Being a Teacher*. Delhi: Konark Publishers Pvt. Ltd.

Kalberg, Stephen. 1980. 'Max Weber's Types of Rationality: Cornerstones for the Analysis of Rationalization Processes in History', *The American Journal of Sociology*, Vol. 85, no. 5, March, pp. 1145–79.

Nussbaum, Martha. 2011. *Creating Capabilities: The Human Development Approach*. Cambridge, Massachusetts and London, England: The Belknap Press, Harvard University Press.

Robeyns, Ingrid. 2011. Review of Martha C. Nussbaum, 2011, *Creating Capabilities: The Human Development Approach*, Harvard University Press, available on http://ndpr.nd.edu/news/26146-creating-capabilities-the-human-development-approach-2/

Sen, Amartya. 1992. *Inequality Re-examined*. Oxford: Clarendon Press.

———. 2009. *The Idea of Justice*. US: Allen Lane and Harvard University Press.

◆◆

EDUCATION INDIA PRIVATE LIMITED[1]

JYOTSNA JHA

Education in India is experiencing an unprecedented crisis at all levels in the form of increased and unregulated commercialisation. This is not an allusion to privatisation in its obvious form of private, fee-charging schooling, which, while acknowledged as the first step, is only one amongst the many taken towards commercialisation. I am referring to the commercialisation where education is viewed merely as a product, determined and guided by the market, and the market alone. This trait is worrisome for any country, more so for one that claims to be 'the world's largest democracy' and aspires to the title of a 'developed' nation by 2020.

Democracy and development go hand-in-hand if we abide by Amartya Sen's notion that 'development consists of the removal of various types of unfreedoms that leave people with little choice and little opportunity of exercising their reasoned agency' (1999: xii). Public policy in a democratic polity has a responsibility to work continuously towards reducing the 'unfreedoms', or various forms of disadvantage, restrictions and oppressions that an individual or a community or a group faces. Education is a Right and, at least in its 'ideal' form, has both intrinsic and instrumental values: it serves to widen world views and knowledge, thus enabling people to assert their rights, question the injustices around them, and to build a cohesive and continuously evolving society that is truly democratic in spirit and not just in name; it widens opportunities and enhances the capacities required to use those opportunities in a manner that also helps in enhancing their livelihood, as well as other forms of securities; and, in reducing the inequalities that exist due to caste, class, religion, language and location. Sen and other proponents of the capability theory clearly establish that greater public engagement with, and investment in, the areas of education and health is critical for removing deep-rooted inequalities and improving the well-being of all, especially those who are more vulnerable. If education, in its form and delivery, is guided almost entirely by commercial concerns, it cannot fulfil this role and, therefore, the commercialisation of education is dangerous for a country desirous of attaining both economic growth and reduced inequality while, at the same time, sustaining and deepening its democracy.

Broadly, this paper makes two arguments: (i) the penetration of commercialisation into the Indian education system in various forms and shades, with the fee charged in private schools or colleges only one end of the spectrum; and (ii) the argument regarding this aspect as beneficial for improving the quality of education and, therefore, enhancing the nation's development, is misleading. I use some of my own as well as research by others and, in addition, a few individual experiences in support of these arguments.

PRIVATISATION ON THE RISE

The phenomenal increase in the numbers of fee-charging private schools and colleges is the first sign of commercialisation. In the last two decades, the rates of increase in the numbers as well as enrolment of private unaided schools and colleges has been much higher than that for either public or private aided institutions. As against the private aided, where the teachers' salaries largely come from public sources and fees are regulated closely, the private unaided are fee-charging institutions with little or no regulation. This is despite the access to public resource support in many cases, in some form or the other, such as public land at subsidised rates.

An analysis of the National Sample Survey Organisation (NSSO) data for two time periods—1995–96 and 2014–15—using the 52nd and 71st Rounds, clearly reveals that the enrolment share for both urban and rural areas has remained either static, or declined in both public and aided institutions, and has increased almost universally in private unaided institutions. Himachal Pradesh, where government educational institutions are widely reported to function better in comparison to other northern and eastern states, has reported one of the sharpest increases in the enrolment share of private unaided institutions at all levels in these two decades:

from 1.7 to 36.4 per cent at the primary; from 4.8 to 23.4 per cent at the upper primary; from 5.5 to 17.8 per cent at the secondary and higher secondary; and from zero to 47.0 per cent at the undergraduate and above. In general, the rate of increase is sharpest for the highest level, undergraduate and above, in most states. At the all-India level, the enrolment share at the tertiary level in private unaided institutions has increased about five times in both rural and urban areas in this period, covering one-fourth of rural and one-third of urban enrolment.

COMMERCIALISATION IN THE SCHOOL SECTOR: SHADES AND FORMS

The tuition fee is not the only element of 'commerce' in the private school. It is just one and, perhaps, the most consistent element. Despite the RTE (Right to Education) banning capitation charges, most (all?) private schools continue to charge it in the name of either admission or development fees. The amount, even for low-fee schools, is substantial, ranging from ₹10,000 to ₹50,000, which, apparently, goes up to several lakhs for middle- and high-end schools. One study in Bangalore suggested that almost all parents who admitted their children to private schools under the RTE provisions for the weaker sections also paid ₹10,000 to ₹15,000 as admission fee.[2] But it does not end here; this, in most cases, is just the beginning.

A number of directions and demands, all guided by market interests, follow next; these include particular brands of uniforms and shoes and, at times, learning resources and sports equipment. Apparently, with Continuous and Comprehensive Evaluation (CCE) becoming mandatory in the post-RTE phase, some schools are also marketing 'projects'—all information pertaining to one discovery-based project can be 'discovered' in one packet, at a cost! It has been an old practice for schoolteachers to ask students to attend private tuition on additional payment; newer options have been added in the form of tuition chains, both real and virtual. A number of edu-corporates have entered the school market with both technology- and non-technology-based learning tools and techniques, which a large number of private schools are 'buying' and offering to students for an additional price. These are adopted and sold by the school as being important for 'speaking English', 'better scores in tests' and 'computer literacy'; no one asks why the school itself is not responsible for imparting these skills. The market principle runs supreme in which the consumers of one school are forced to become the consumers of all these add-on brands. It can be likened to a consumer who, once having bought a particular brand of car, is left with little choice but to buy its spare parts, irrespective of price. Education is increasingly becoming like other industries in which production is increasingly deterritorialised, and parts are procured in bits and assembled by a global firm at high cost. In the case of the edu-industry, the consumer is definitely not king. The consumers are voiceless children, and their parents an insecure lot who want to buy everything possible to make their children's future secure.

That such practices are inherently exclusive, and therefore divisive, is self-explanatory. If parents cannot afford to pay for a particular service, the child is physically separated from those who can; this can deepen the child's experiences of exclusion. The case of Bala Vidya Mandir, a private school in Chennai, which tried to introduce a differential fee structure—one basic, and one advanced with access to the canteen, sports and robotics—is well-documented in media reports.[3] Added to this montage of commercial brands are school managers who seem to have entered not only private schools but public ones as well. In order to understand this, let us move from the shades and come to the forms of privatisation.

Until about two decades ago, the private schooling scenario in India was dominated by two kinds of schools: (i) denomination-based schools, commonly known as convents; and (ii) private trust-run schools, both largely patronised by the middle and the upper-middle classes. An important departure at the two ends of this spectrum came in the form of (i) the entry (and also partial exit) of the so-called budget schools at the elementary school level; and (ii) the entry of high-fee, high-end 'international' schools offering IB (International Baccalaureate) curriculum, along with the choice of Indian as well as external Board certifications, e.g., the British General Certificate of Education (GCE), giving O (Ordinary) and A (Advance) level certificates. Interestingly, these models all offer a deviation, not just by way of fee-range and clientele-base, but in terms of their approach to the curriculum and teaching–learning practices as well. While the high-end ones emphasised a deep inquiry-based approach aimed at developing thinking, analytical and reflective skills amongst students using highly qualified, well-paid teachers, the lower-end budget schools have been looking for approaches that encourage the use of technology-based or/and structured teaching–learning, tool-based 'learning' solutions with the help of low-paid, less-trained teachers. The rich shifted from traditional private schools and patronised the high-end alternatives as a deviation from the rigid, rote learning-based schooling system, whereas the budget private schools, run largely by 'education managers', were advocated vociferously as an 'affordable and effective' alternative to the 'dysfunctional, low-quality state schools' for the poor.[4]

In recent years, there has been persistent and motivated advocacy in favour of policy support and public investment in various forms for low-cost or affordable private schools in the name of offering 'school choice' to the poor (e.g., providing vouchers to parents that could be encashed at any school of their choice, rather than the public school). These efforts are aimed to create public opinion and receive policy support for low-budget, but clearly for-profit schools, in the name of equity and quality. Given that these are the two major concerns of the Indian school education system, it is not difficult. The advocacy has been crafted largely by powerful networks of Indian IT companies and transnational organisations with roots in the UK and USA that are committed to promoting market-based interventions in all sectors, including education. The sophisticated nature of this advocacy includes intellectual exercises in which research and widespread efforts towards media attention are part of the strategy. The objective is not limited merely to gain legitimacy for the edu-business in India, but to use the success here to promote the same in other countries and continents (Nambissan and Ball, 2010: 324–43).

The private has also penetrated the public, and it is increasingly common for various state governments to hand over public schools to private 'school managers' for an 'improvement in quality' and 'accountability'. Many of these school managers, with roots and connections to the wider advocacy networks mentioned earlier, are making profits by using public money under the guise of helping state schools improve quality. Public–private partnership is the new name for contracting out public works, or transferring public money to private parties at a subsidised rate or as a subsidy, often without commensurate accountability. It is important to point out that although it has now become much more rampant and visible with the participation of international players, the practice started in some form or other about two decades ago. One example comes from Uttar Pradesh where, in 1997, the state government had adopted a policy of giving ₹10 lakh to any new, unaided private girls' school in blocks in which there was no secondary school for girls, in order to boost female enrolment. This amount was later enhanced to ₹20 lakh for any girls-only secondary school being started in a *nyaya* panchayat, a unit covering about 20 primary schools. A number of new schools used this scheme to access the subsidy to build physical infrastructure, but female enrolment did not pick up as these were fee-charging schools, and parents were perhaps not ready to pay for girls' education in those areas. The state government later permitted these schools to admit boys through an Office Order; however, they continued to be called *balika vidyalayas* in official records. Most of these schools were set up by local politicians and other 'influential' people, who first used the schemes to access public money, and later their influence to get an order passed that would make their enterprise more profitable and, in the process, subverted the policy objective of promoting girls' secondary education in backward areas. This also revealed that the policy initiative of promoting girls' secondary education in rural areas through the provisioning of fee-charging private unaided schools was misplaced right from the beginning (Jha and Subrahmanian, 2006).

A more recent example comes in the form of the Model School scheme, launched by the Government of India, in November 2008, which had articulated clearly that of the 6,000 schools sanctioned, 2,500 would be built under PPP. The infrastructure for the model school was provided by private entities legally competent to run an educational institution. The government was to contribute recurring costs on a per capita basis for the students it sponsored. Besides, an additional 25 per cent support was to be provided in respect of sponsored students towards capital cost.[5] The scheme is under suspension at the moment.[6] It is clear that although the presence of for-profit educational institutions is not legal in India, profit is finding a place and legitimacy through various avenues, policy itself being one of them.

PRIVATISATION IN THE TERTIARY SECTOR: FROM THE UNIVERSAL TO THE LOCAL

The rate of privatisation at the tertiary level has been higher than that at the school level because, unlike the elementary school sector, public investment in the expansion efforts has been very low. A high proportion of the expansion in services has taken place through the opening of new colleges and universities in the private sector. A number of features deserve attention but, here, I will concentrate on one: the growth of mono-discipline universities, especially in the areas of engineering, medicine and management. These colleges, which are often stand-alone universities, have mushroomed in the private sector because of their potential for high revenue generation. Public universities are following suit as these are also considered lucrative areas for revenue generation; and in response to pressures to earn their own revenue from the respective governments, the trend to build stand-alone medical, engineering or management universities is being increasingly witnessed in public sectors. This is contradictory to what a university should be: the word university derives its root from 'universe', referring to the presence of a wide range of subjects and disciplines, including the possibility of pursuing a specialised or a single-discipline-based study in a multidisciplinary environment—something that is considered essential to foster knowledge. The students of these applied courses in stand-alone universities remain deprived of any exposure to fundamental subjects, and that limits their opportunities to enhance their understanding and ability to connect their own subjects to wider social and natural phenomena. This focus on applied skills, without exposure to fundamental theories and interlinkages, often prevents new and innovative thinking. This, in turn, reduces the potential for the larger societal externalities that higher education usually has and, therefore, brings down the quasi public-good nature of education.

This focus on applied courses alone is undesirable also because it privileges these disciplines at the cost of others, even in universities which do not necessarily offer only applied courses; often, these include the humanities and social sciences and, at times, basic sciences as well. What is forgotten is that the basic sciences, social sciences and humanities are key to creativity, innovation and knowledge creation, and a country aspiring to, or even claiming to promote, a knowledge society and knowledge economy would ignore these subjects at its own peril. Commerce and utilitarianism become the driving factor—often, the buildings for these disciplines are better maintained. It is common to find a shining building fitted with computer labs, surrounded by decrepit buildings housing the humanities, pure sciences and social sciences departments in state universities—an indicator of what is valued, and what is not. Moreover, this divides the teaching and student communities: those who pay higher fees and generate higher revenues perceive themselves as being 'more useful' than those in the other category—again, it is commerce that determines 'utility'.

It is important to mention skill-based education in the context of commercialisation. In general, skill-based education has not received the desired attention from either public- or private-sector providers. An important, and disagreeable, feature of the skill-education policy in India is that it has been promoted for 'failures': those who are unable to continue with academically focused higher education are required to choose skill-based education. The students are labelled even before making this choice, and this becomes even more objectionable in a society where caste–class–skill linkages are strong and discriminatory. The only exception to this has been IT- and computer-based skill-education, which private companies have utilised fully by promoting high-fee courses that have penetrated the public sector as well. This high demand and the readiness to pay for these courses emanates from the perception of these courses as 'intellectual activity', leading to white-collar jobs as compared to most other skill-based courses that are viewed as 'manual' activities. To quote from what was written long ago but is relevant even today:

> The society which scorns excellence in plumbing as a humble activity and tolerates shoddiness in philosophy because it is an exalted activity will have neither good plumbing nor good philosophy: nether its pipes nor its theories will hold water (Gardner, 1961: 86).

The fate of our society in which philosophy, shoddy as it may be, is not valued—let alone plumbing—must give us cause for concern. The better delivery of 'English-medium education' at the school level, of 'useful courses' at higher levels, and an improvement in quality at all levels, are the main selling points for privatisation in education. Therefore, it is essential to examine the extent of the validity of prevalent perceptions regarding higher-quality education in private institutions. While nobody can disagree that state schools, colleges and universities are struggling with major issues of inclusion and learning, it remains highly debatable if privatisation is the solution.

WHETHER QUALITY OR WITHERING QUALITY?

The debate surrounding quality at the primary level has been dominated by the issue of learning outcomes. Periodic surveys, although quite rudimentary in approach and, therefore, not necessarily robust, have brought the issue of poor learning levels in India to the fore. In general, a variety of surveys undertaken by various organisations in several states have shown that age and grade-specific learning outcomes are poor, both in state and non-state schools throughout the country, and there is no conclusive evidence in favour of private schools. The available evidence on the impact of vouchers on the learning levels of those choosing private schools has been inconclusive as well.[7] Although bringing quality to the fore as an issue central to education is a positive trend, reducing it to merely learning outcomes is cause for concern. This is especially so when it is continuously, and insidiously, used to critique the public system of education, which is now overwhelmingly represented by the poorer and weaker sections of society.

This is not to say that quality is not an issue, but to assert that it is an issue both in private and public institutions; however, private schools fare better in manipulating 'quality'. A few examples are enough to illustrate this trend. It is common practice for a large number of 'reputed' schools to encourage, or compel, those students in terminal grades who are not expected to perform well in the regular boards to register with the Open School boards, most often the National Institute of Open Schooling (NIOS).[8] This is to avoid any dent in the pass percentage and to ensure 'high' average performances. Such practices are common at the tertiary level as well. A 'prestigious' private college in a hill station in Tamil Nadu claims 'high standards' as no one securing less than 50 per cent marks is passed—in reality, no teacher is allowed to give less than 50 per cent marks to any student. Another private 'autonomous' college in Bangalore that conducts its own examinations, clearly directs teachers to keep the level of tests low to ensure high performance.[9] In other words, the relationship between education providers and consumers is completely determined by commerce where consumers, having paid the price, are ensured of the product, i.e., certification with a certain minimum level of marks, in this case.

Not a single Indian institution, not even any of our 'best', finds a place in the top-200 list published by the Times Higher Education Supplement and other similar international rankings. Even if we were to consider these rankings as stemming from cultural biases, any other indications through a variety of sources are not very complimentary. This is largely true for both public and private universities, with a few exceptions. A recent article in *The Economist* quotes Aspiring Minds, a company that surveys student capabilities, to claim that,

> If university exams were run properly, 70% of students would fail. Of 700,000 engineering graduates in India each year, only 3% are employable without many months of post-recruitment training. Only 15% of computer-engineering graduates could complete a basic task set in one assessment and language and other 'soft' skills are often poor.[10]

The same article also articulates a well-known fact about private higher education institutions:

> The worst private outfits serve, in effect, as money-launderers. Even honest ones emphasise marketing over teaching: glitzy ads lure students with swimming pools, marble foyers, or guarantees of jobs. Colleges often devote over a fifth of their revenue to acquiring new students, which is more than they pay faculty. Students care little for study, as few are ever allowed to fail exams.

Quality, quite obviously, withers in such situations.

Schools, colleges and universities across the world as well as in India have been the harbingers of social movements, determining political agendas and providing intellectual leadership; this cannot be considered even distant reality if education is reduced to a mere commodity. It is not simply a coincidence that in order to understand whether India's higher education is effective in nurturing democratic citizenship amongst urban youth, CMCA, in a recent survey of more than 10,000 high-school and college students in 11 state capitals, including five metros, concluded that:

> ...youth are growing up without adequate critical knowledge and skills, and the desirable attitudes and values necessary to evolve as humane and democratic citizens who can meaningfully participate in governance and politics while staying committed to democracy, equality, human rights and social justice.[11]

Clearly, there is a need to pay greater attention to quality, including its definition, in both public and private institutions.

NEEDED: PUBLIC INVESTMENT FOR A PUBLIC GOOD

Education has been recognised largely as a public or a quasi public good, as it produces a 'wide variety and huge magnitude of externalities'. Commerce-driven education can enhance private gains and contribute to the country's economic growth in the short term, but in the long term it is bound to face severe limitations as it does not allow the reduction of inequalities, kills intellectual engagements that can help society evolve, and adversely impacts social cohesion. The highly unequal access to education, besides being unacceptable as an undesirable feature of a democratic society, continues to fuel further inequalities in income. Such a situation is even more precarious in a society that is highly heterogeneous in terms of language, culture and religion, and in which the general political environment is that of increased intolerance towards dissent.

There is no other policy option available other than making the required public investment in education at all levels, while also paying attention to reforming it to promote both quality and social justice. While the universalisation of elementary education might, for obvious reasons, be accorded higher priority vis-à-vis secondary and higher education, it does not automatically imply that funds for the former are necessarily at the cost of the latter. The access to secondary and higher education is a major equaliser in terms of facilitating occupational mobility and also in the simple sense of being equal to others. Given India's demographic, with the population tilted proportionately towards the young, higher education is deeply linked with people's aspirations and desires. The level of higher education is often a marker of social status and its role in a highly stratified society cannot be underestimated. The commercialisation of education can only exacerbate the challenge, taking it to a level from where recovery would be even more difficult, or, perhaps, irreversible.

◆

NOTES

1. This article has benefited from inputs and comments received from my colleagues, R. Maithreyi and Shreekanth Mahinderan.
2. See Centre for Budget and Policy Studies (CBPS). 2013. 'A Study on Quality of Acceptance of Children admitted in Private Unaided Schools in Bangalore under section 12(1)(c) of the RTE Act, Bangalore.' http://www.cbps.in/wp-content/themes/cbps/pdf/CBPS_FinalReport_30June2014%20(1).pdf
3. Various newspaper reports consulted include: http://www.newindianexpress.com/cities/chennai/More-Fees-for-Better-Facilities-Bala-Vidya-Mandirs-Circular-Causes-Uproar/2015/06/01/article2842970.ece, http://www.thehindu.com/news/cities/chennai/fee-row-school-replaces-principal/article7280261.ece, http://www.thehindu.com/news/cities/chennai/school-circular-on-differential-fee-upsets-parents/article7266133.ece, http://www.deccanchronicle.com/150603/nation-current-affairs/article/probe-ordered-bala-vidya-mandir-school-fee-structure
4. See Nambissan (2012) for a review of papers and articles supporting low-cost budget schools.
5. See Luthra and Mahajan (2013). http://www.ripublication.com/gjmbs.htm (accessed September 2014).
6. http://mhrd.gov.in/model_school_ppp (accessed September 2015).
7. See Karopady (2014) and Day, *et al.* (2014). https.://www.gov.uk/government/uploads/system/uploads/attachment_data/file/307032/Private-schools-2014.pdf (accessed October 2014).
8. Based on the findings emerging from an ongoing study led by the author entitled 'Open and Distance Learning as a Cost-effective Option for Secondary Level Schooling in India: Potential and Prerequisites', CBPS, Bangalore.
9. Personal interviews with teachers from these institutions.
10. http://www.economist.com/news/21631948-big-quantity-short-quality-indias-university-challenge
11. Children's Movement for Civic Awareness. 2015. Results shared in a workshop held on 7 October 2015 in Bangalore.

REFERENCES

Day, Ashley L., C. Mcloughlin, M. Aslam, J. Engel, J. Wales, S. Rawal, R. Batley, G. Kingdon, S. Nicolai and P. Rose. 2014. *The Role and Impact of Private Schools in Developing Countries: A Rigorous Review of the Evidence.* Department for International Development.

Gardner, John W. 1961. 'Excellence. Can We be Equal and Excellent Too?' New York: Harper.

Jha, Jyotsna and Ramya Subrahmanian. 2006. 'Secondary Education in the Indian State of Uttar Pradesh: An Exploration of Gender Dimensions of State Policy and Practice', in Shahra Razavi and Shireen Hassim (eds.), *Gender and Social Policy in a Global Context.* London: UNRISD/Palgrave.

Karopady, D. D. 2014. 'Does School Choice Help Rural Children from Disadvantaged Sections?' *Longitudinal Research in Andhra Pradesh*, Vol. XLIX, no. 51, 20 December.

Luthra, Manisha and Shikha Mahajan. 2013. 'Role of Public Private Partnership in School Education in India', *Global Journal of Management and Business Studies*, Vol. 3, no. 7, pp. 801–10.

Nambissan, Geetha B. and Stephen J. Ball. 2010. 'Advocacy Networks, Choice and Private Schooling of the Poor in India', *Global Networks,* Vol. 10, no. 3, pp. 324–43.

Nambissan, Geetha B. 2012. 'Private Schools for the Poor: Business as Usual', *Economic & Political Weekly,* Vol. xlvii, no. 41, 13 October.

Sen, Amartya. 1999. *Development as Freedom.* Oxford: Oxford University Press.

◆◆

MOOCs
Virtual, but not Virtuous

APOORVANAND

Massive Open Online Courses (MOOCs) are part of the agenda of the present government in Delhi. In 2015, Smriti Irani, Minister, Human Resources and Development, called upon the youth of India to sign up for MOOCs and take the examinations for which a certificate would be issued. The students were assured that the central government had been working on its creation, and the facility would be offered by the finest universities in India and made available absolutely free of cost.

MOOCs were mentioned in the first presidential speech in Parliament last year, soon after the new government assumed power in Delhi. The central cabinet had approved an agreement between the Ministry of Human Resource Development and the US Department of State for cooperation in the field of higher education for Study Webs of Active-Learning for Young Aspiring Minds (SWAYAM), a programme for online education.

The SWAYAM platform server was to be based in India, and US universities would be invited to offer postgraduate academic programmes with certification. Officials said that this would be offered using open edX. The Indian partners of edX are the Indian Institute of Technology (IIT), Bombay; the Indian Institute of Management (IIM), Bangalore; and the Birla Institute of Technology and Science (BITS), Pilani.[1]

The academic community of India is largely unaware of this move. The government did not consider it necessary to consult universities and academics before taking such a momentous decision, which, if implemented, would have a deep and long-term impact on the system of higher education in India. The institutions

Winter 2015–Spring 2016, Volume 42, Numbers 3 & 4

collaborating in this initiative did so without consultations with their faculty members.

The Government of India is pursuing this path at a time when the enthusiasm for it is ebbing. According to a survey conducted by the Babson Survey Research Group in 2014, only 16 per cent of academic leaders surveyed thought that MOOCs were sustainable. Of 2,800 academic leaders consulted, 51 per cent were of a contrary view. This is considerably low if we look at the numbers in 2012, when MOOCs had begun thriving. Only 28 per cent of academic leaders then believed that MOOCs were the future of higher education; 26 per cent felt otherwise. The basic concern of these administrators had more to do with the economics as they did not see much potential to generate an income. Any return would be indirect in nature and hard to quantify, although MOOCs could serve the purpose of increasing the visibility of their institutions and help recruit students from far and wide.

MOOCs began with the promise of subverting the existing brick and mortar university structure. The *New York Times* declared 2012 the first year of the MOOCs era. That year, two Stanford professors founded Coursera—an online platform for free lessons—and MIT released its edX online teaching programme together with Harvard University. In the same year, most major developed countries introduced their own MOOCs, such as 'Future Learn' in the UK, 'FUN' in France, 'iUniversity' in Germany, 'JMOOC' in Japan, and 'Open2Study' in Australia. The EU, too, had its own platform called 'OpenupEd'.

Within one year, hundreds of lessons were contributed to Coursera by more than 100 top international universities, such as Princeton and Stanford, and the number of registered students from various countries worldwide exceeded seven million. Clearly, MOOCs were now the most discussed subject on the international education scene.

In China, Shanghai Jiaotong University (SJTU) and Tsinghua University have taken the lead by launching online classes, with other higher education institutions also presenting bold ideas and initiatives in this direction. Some high schools have created 'Khan Academy' micro-courses to free students from remedial classes and excessive piles of books.[2]

◆◆◆

Recently, I read *Choori Bazar Mein Ladki* (A Girl in a Bangle Market) by my colleague, Krishna Kumar, a distinguished teacher of Education in Delhi University. The book was the result of an educational journey that he undertook along with his MEd Class to Firozabad, a small town in Uttar Pradesh well known for its glass industry. Women students of the class experienced the dreadful working conditions of the small factories that produce various products of daily use.

They came face to face with the hard reality of child labour employed in large numbers in these small-scale factories. They also visited one of the non-formal educational centres set up for these children, where they are expected to be educated under a government programme. The children assembled there after a long, arduous day. Kumar noticed a little girl trying to read from her textbook; it was the story of a child seeking *dua* from Allah. 'If you chance to meet Allah, what would you tell Him?' he asked the child. With tears streaming down her small cheeks, she replied, 'I would ask him, why did He give birth to me in this poverty?' Silently, with her head bowed, she wept, her tears falling on the hard, cold floor of that non-formal school.

The next morning, the class assembled at the Taj Mahal in Agra to share and interpret their experiences at Firozabad. The challenge before them was to turn their personal experiences into educational ones. 'My self-identity as a teacher was shaken...,' said Kumar. In desperation, he turned to his students, and they struggled collectively to make sense of their trip. Kumar has dedicated a chapter, *Taj par Kaksha* (Class at the Taj), to this struggle.

Kumar confesses that before this journey it had not occurred to him that there were some experiences that he, as a man, would never be able to understand with the same intensity as his women students. His educational journey to Firozabad forced him to examine his self-awareness, the so-called neutrality of social spaces. He said,

> At the root of education is the concept of learning. It has been the axis of my life as a teacher to keep exploring it. However, even after having taught thousands of girls, I had remained oblivious of [to] the process of learning they undergo to become Indian women.

This painful discovery—that the most crucial learning had been taking place independent of the syllabus and curriculum—led him to reorganise his self-awareness, and so the book was born.

This is what makes teaching, learning and knowledge creation indivisible. Kumar understands that an experience in itself is not knowledge. However, if experiences that shake you to your core are allowed to pass through a thought process, the knowledge generated in due course will have a certain radiance about it.

What is left unsaid in the book is that the exercise of teaching and learning is a very local affair and the teacher cannot succeed without an active student body. It underlines the fundamental unity between 'the knower and what is known', as explained by Bernstein (1996) in his paper 'Thoughts on the Trivium and Quadrivium: The Divorce of Knowledge from the Knower'.

Who creates knowledge and who is the knower? Is it only the student who knows or, as we can see from the preceding example, the teacher is also the knower? Can the two be separated?

Bernstein published his paper in 2000 at a time when MOOCs were nowhere on the horizon. But he gives us a very critical term—'official knowledge'. He says, '...we have, for the first time, a dehumanizing principle, for the organization and orientation of official knowledge'. Bernstein was prophesying that commercial interests would soon take over the business of certifying which branch of knowledge would be worthwhile.

I have been wondering whether it is at all possible for Krishna Kumar to prepare a MOOC, which will communicate the same pain, the agony and joy of going through this educational journey.

What was largely an American phenomenon barely three years ago very soon caught the fancy of policymakers, education planners and leaders worldwide. MOOCs began to be viewed as viable alternatives to the brick and mortar university system, which are, according to them, increasingly becoming costlier and unviable. Governments claim that it is difficult to provide funds to match the ever-increasing demand for tertiary or higher education. The existing university structures are unable to accommodate the new aspirants. European countries are not far behind. In 2014, a summit of European MOOCs was held, which has now become an annual feature. All governments in Europe are taking steps to create their own models of MOOCs. In the Middle East, the Queen Rania Foundation is collaborating with edX to create MOOCs in Arabic.

As expected, India did not lag behind and joined the race in 2012–13. The first major indication came from Sam Pitroda, advisor on innovations to the then prime minister. Speaking at the convocation ceremony of the University of Delhi, he claimed that we did not need too many teachers. The very idea of higher education was being transformed and the time was not far when it would turn from being teacher-centric to student-centric. We would need only four or five good, world-class teachers for a discipline, and technology would enable students in any part of the world to access their courses.

Anant Agrawal, founder of edX, one of the major companies offering MOOCs, believes that they are the future of higher education. The days of professors with yellow notes are over. Teachers cannot take their students for granted any longer as the latter would be able to access a good course, which is constantly evolving through MOOCs.

The underlying assumption in these claims is that the experience of good teaching can now be availed of with the help of MOOCs. It is also assumed that students have a right to the 'best'. If the best is available at one of the Ivy League universities, why should a student from Patna be deprived and settle for a much lower teaching talent?

The promise of MOOCs is found to be so great that Zhen Huang, Vice President of SJIU, Chinese Dean of SJTU–Paris Tech Elite Institute of Technology, warns,

> MOOCs break time and space confinements and radically change the way people acquire knowledge. University walls come down and national boundaries become unimportant. If our teachers continue the traditional cramming method of teaching, students will vote with their 'eyes and ears'. They very well may sit in a Chinese classroom, only to be looking at a laptop with a MOOC made by a US university. Education reform is imperative.

The belief behind such assertions is that the best knowledge is being produced in the universities of the US and it is only democratic that students who are not privileged enough to enrol there get a chance to access this knowledge. Hence, MOOCs become a means to realise this democratic dream.

Who knows what is good for the students? Decisions on behalf of students and teachers are taken either by governments or leaders of universities. In 2013, the President of the San Jose State University introduced MOOC-based courses in various departments. The Department of Philosophy was asked to integrate a course on Justice prepared by the renowned professor, Michael Sandel, into its curriculum. Professors of the department refused. They decided to write an open letter to Professor Sandel to explain their decision.

> In spite of our admiration for your ability to lecture in such an engaging way to such a large audience, we believe that having a scholar teach and engage with his or her own students is far superior to having those students watch a video of another scholar engaging his or her students.
>
> ...There is no pedagogical problem in our department that JusticeX solves, nor do we have a shortage of faculty capable of teaching our equivalent course.
>
> ...the thought of the exact same social justice course being taught in various philosophy departments across the country is downright scary—something out of a dystopian novel. Departments across the country possess unique specializations and character, and should stay that way. Universities tend not to hire their own graduates for a reason. They seek different influences. Diversity in schools of thought and plurality of points of view are at the heart of liberal education.

Advocates of MOOCs claim that they contain not only lectures but also reflections of students. Questioning this claim, the letter raised an issue which has not been debated fully in this context,

> ...what kind of message are we sending our students if we tell them that they should best learn what justice is by listening to the reflections of the largely white student population from a privileged institution like Harvard? Our very diverse students gain far more

> when their own experience is central to the course and when they are learning from our own very diverse faculty, who bring their varied perspectives to the content of courses that bear on social justice.

Professor Sandel did not think it fit to engage with these substantive issues. In his reply, he merely said that he respected the right of the faculty to design their own courses. The letter had, however, made another significant point which Professor Sandel chose to evade. The ethical issue of 'famous' or 'star' professors collaborating with companies like edX remains unaddressed. Why do they want to reach millions using the MOOC platform? Would the population thus reached be called their student mass even if they would never get a chance to interact with the 'teachers' and they themselves would never know who these anonymous students are? Pankaj Chandra once suggested that the best way to start a discussion on MOOCs could be by asking: Whose alma mater would a MOOC be?

The idea of education or learning has traditionally been associated with students and teachers interacting with each other in close proximity. It is not just the discipline they engage with—they engage with each other. Gayatri Chakravorty Spivak says that for teaching to happen in a meaningful manner, the teacher has to know her student.

Professor Castillo of Cornell University teaches theatre. Discussing the pressure she feels from the MOOC ideology, she says that it is based on certain tech myths.

> Following upon the recent work of Judith Burnet and her colleagues, let us remind ourselves of a few of the dangerous tech myths in education, before we ponder a bit more closely why they are important to us as gender conscious/feminist scholars and teachers. Burnet et al. (2009) ask, schematically, what kinds of myths we implicitly use to define what our technologized society is like. Here are some of their suggestions. Modern society is:
>
> (i) Connected and global—there is no one and nowhere 'outside'.
> (ii) Time and space have changed, and we can talk to anyone, anywhere, at anytime in the twinkling of an eye, that is, we can transcend our bodies.

(iii) The new age is more democratic, open and accessible to all, with more opportunities to exercise choice and participate in decision making.
(iv) We can address the division of the world between developed and wealthy and the developing world by taking the technology of the developed world and diffusing it to everyone everywhere.[3]

Is media transparency and technology an unequivocal good? Raising this issue, Castillo suggests that

> in its ideologically charged erasure of ethnicized and sexed bodies, the current trends in higher education are returning us precisely to the 1960s mindset decried by McLuhan—an illusion of control over highly fragmented systems comes down to privileging precisely and exclusively the things those systems do well. The scaling effects of MOOCs tend to push ever more to the background precisely those unexplored gendered, raced dynamics.[4]

It has often been said that there could be problems with Humanities courses being conducted through MOOCs; sciences and technology courses lend themselves more easily to this medium.

There is another, sinister, implication as well to do with social class, access and the politics of location. I return here to one of the myths cited by Burnet and her collaborators, the myth that 'we can address the division of the world between developed and wealthy and the developing world by taking the technology of the developed world and diffusing it to everyone everywhere'. Much of the praise for online education is focused precisely on this aspect: that anyone, anywhere, can access the best and most advanced education in the world, taking courses from leading professors at Harvard, MIT, Stanford, Berkeley, among others.

It would be difficult for many, especially for those who live in first world countries, to comprehend that people might be ready to face physical attacks of all kinds to be able to belong to a space called school or college or university. As I write these lines, I think of the Dalit families of a small village in Haryana, barely 100 km from Delhi, who spent months at Jantar Mantar, a central site of protest in New Delhi, in the winter of 2014. They had to flee their village, as four school-going girls from their community were abducted and raped by 'higher caste' people of their own village.

Feminist scholar Mary E. John speaks of the increasing incidents of sexual assault Dalit girls face and suspects that they are connected with these girls crossing traditional boundaries by insisting on going to school and college. The 'upper castes' are outraged at the invasion of these educational spaces, which were once naturally theirs, by traditional 'idiots'. What is it that they seek, and why does it make the traditional elites feel threatened? Education and knowledge, of course, and also a desire to enter shared spaces and claim knowledge centres as their own.

It has been a long and tortuous battle for these castes, as testimonies from the 19th century onwards demonstrate; it still continues. Despite the burning of their homes, beatings, humiliation, rapes and murders, and discrimination at educational centres, Dalits and the so-called 'lower caste' people have not ceased their fight to storm the citadels of knowledge which had been impenetrable for thousands of years.

What do MOOCs offer these Dalit girls? Or girls like Malala Yusufzai of Pakistan, or those of Afganistan, who are threatened, shot and killed by religious extremists like Boko Haram in Nigeria? One view postulates that MOOCs can act as a liberating force for these girls. It can protect them from bullets, yet help them attain knowledge within the safe confines of their homes, on their computers or laptops. In short, they would adopt anonymity to attain knowledge, which would, in turn, help them free themselves.

Let us first examine the promises of MOOCs. 'Massive' is only one aspect of it. Here is a possibility of reaching millions of students through this platform. A teacher's labour in preparation for a course is optimised by access to an unimaginable number of students. They will, in turn, benefit by the opportunity to learn from an educator whom they could ordinarily never have afforded, given their social and economic constraints.

As one of the providers for MOOCs, Coursera claims 8.2 million registered users and 678 courses from 110 colleges, universities and other institutions. These users, who would be called students in traditional universities, are spread all over the globe. The courses are offered by some of the best on the faculty of universities in the US. These numbers are staggering and it is easy to persuade the education planners of a 'Third World' country like India that instead of investing in long-term liabilities called teachers and universities, buying licenses to use MOOC-based courses prepared by these companies is a less expensive way to satisfy the urge of the ever-increasing student population.

Studies done to assess the reach and significance of MOOCs tell a different story. A large study by a joint Harvard–MIT research team, after examining 68 certificate-granting courses, 1.7 million participants, 10 million participant hours, and 1.1 billion participant logged events, found that nearly 39 per cent of the users were teachers. Almost half the registered users were not interested in, and were unsure about, certification. A significant number of participants were mid-career professionals.

A study covering India was conducted by the University of Pennsylvania in 2013 which looked at the participation pattern of all students who had ever enrolled in one of the MOOCs offered in collaboration with Coursera, the largest provider of MOOCs. At the time of the survey, the University of Pennsylvania had offered 32 courses to over 800,000 students.

Gayle Christensen and Brandon Alcorn, reporting the findings of the survey, write,

> Results from the survey, which included responses from about two thousand students, suggest that Indians taking MOOCs are generally young, male, and well educated, with about two-thirds under the age of thirty, and more than three-fourths male and with a college degree. While some of those with college degrees are students pursuing postgraduate studies, the majority are employed full time (the remainder are either self-employed or working part-time). This user base is unsurprising and similar to early adopters of cell phone, new media, and other technologies.[5]

Both surveys indicate that MOOCs as yet are not being seen as substitutes for regular courses offered by traditional, brick and mortar universities and colleges. A vital concern is that of certification. Since courses offered as MOOCs do not offer credentialisation, they are used as add-ons or as supplementary material. This has led MOOC-providers to lobby with policymakers in the developing world to force universities to imbed these courses in their regular syllabi.

I argue that for the vast majorities of this world (if not worlds), knowledge or education is about making a claim for their share of cultural capital. Space is a very critical aspect. Education has to be a physical reality for them. They want to feel it on, and through, their skins, and sit in those places from which they were kept away for centuries.

Education is a communitarian affair for such societies. It has other implications for classrooms as well, the composition of which has changed dramatically. It is now very challenging for teachers to find a new common language, and who find themselves stripped of the security with which they had worked all along.

Education is an individual affair, but it is also crucially about creating collectivities. It cannot be done by making learning an activity pursued in isolation from messy daily realities. It has also been repeatedly said that more than lectures, it is the learning environment which infects people with novel ideas. Students from diverse disciplines meeting each other at a public talk or a coffee shop gain something which falls outside the structured space of syllabus or curriculum. It cannot be assessed or evaluated, but it changes the worldview of young boys and girls which, in turn, changes the world.

Education, for new societies or societies in formation, has to be about the creation of new communities and new proximities. Physical campuses are an excellent opportunity for this and the reason that American universities score over others globally. Not only are they cosmopolitan in character, but also attract the best minds in their faculty and a very diverse international student population. In my opinion, the biggest challenge all knowledge systems face today is the creation of dialogic societies. This can only take place by the creation of more and more shared spaces. It is not about saving costs, but about creating international sensibilities.

In the campuses of the University of Delhi or Jawaharlal Nehru University, youth from Mizoram, Manipur, Jammu and Kashmir, and Bihar mingle with one another. Their ears tune themselves to the sounds of languages they would ordinarily never hear in their native geographical or cultural areas. This should not be treated as incidental to university education. On the contrary, I believe that it is one of the defining features of a university to create possibilities for strangers to come together in classrooms and in other activities on the campus, and help them to understand and appreciate this uniqueness.

Brick and mortar universities privilege physicality. Education is an embodied experience for the students and teaching community. I would go as far as to say that being in a university also means trying to cope with the town or city of which it is a part.

The question of the success of MOOCs is closely associated with the uneven nature of the universe of knowledge. With the passage of time, the knowledge divide between the North and South grows wider and deeper. Some MOOC enthusiasts claim that only 10 great universities would, or should, function in this century. All that would be required is to produce smart knowledge technicians, who would then create platforms to make knowledge produced by them accessible to the masses. In this manner, MOOCs would act as equalisers—as an act of redistributive justice. After all, knowledge aspirants living in the Third World also have a right to access the knowledge that Ivy League university students enjoy.

The equalising claim of MOOCs divides the world in two neat categories: learner and knowledge provider. The companies involved in this business validate the knowledge that people should aspire for. Since much has been said on the subject of professors who attain the status of rock stars, which we know are manufactured in the mediatised world, the unequal knowledge world would force universities lower on the ladder to accept their choice. The courseware produced by MOOC companies would form part of the syllabus of these universities. It takes away from the teacher the right to structure and design his/her own course.

There is a lot of interest in the Indian corporate sector around MOOCs. A simple Google search would direct you to the official page of the Federation of the Indian Chamber of Commerce (FICCI), where an exciting discussion is taking place on its efficacy. Indian universities have absolutely no idea about the future that is being planned for them. There is genuine fear that the unequal power that corporates wield in the planning process of state schemes would ensure a privileged position to their ideas and, gradually, MOOCs would be forced down the throat of reluctant, and resisting, faculty.

MOOCs do offer a lot to free-floating learners who are not looking for credentials to enter the job market, and can also be treated as excellent supplementary material by teachers or students. In fact, one of the leaders of a MOOC company asks people to view them as textbooks as well. Critics have pointed out that there is a significant difference between courseware and a course.

That being said, we must ask: Whose knowledge is this, and who creates it? The epistemological premise of MOOCs assumes that knowledge is something you can produce independent of the diverse contexts in which we live. Educational theories suggest that knowledge is not brought into the classrooms from outside, but is constructed right there. It is not only the student who learns—it is also the teacher. Expertise is equally of importance, and universities are also a place to create and nurture it. All societies need it; they need to produce their own philosophers, psychologists and literary theorists.

A key issue that currently engages us is whether money will be invested in hiring teachers. In a country like India, teaching is increasingly contractual. Teachers are hardly viewed and respected as knowledge creators. They have long been seen as a community of evaluators. Scholars have questioned if the judgement of teachers was only important for endorsing the peer assessment process introduced by MOOCs. With MOOCs claiming to provide high-quality education at a very low cost, would planners start motivating university leaders to opt for MOOC-based courses?

The corporate world foresees a stage in which education would be untethered from physical campuses. The mobile phone revolution would help MOOCs reach a number unimaginable by current standards. However, other challenges remain. Many feel that MOOC-based courses are of a very high quality and that the majority of undergraduate aspirants are simply not prepared for them. What, then, is the solution? Should the courses be diluted to suit student capabilities? Would that, then, not perpetuate the knowledge divide between elites and subalterns? The idea that students can cherry-pick from freely available courses is seductive. But can 18- and 19-year-olds really decide in an informed manner? Are they sufficiently aware of the implications of the choice they are making? My final question is: Would those who can afford to attend top-end universities stop going there in favour of the virtual learning space called MOOCs? We know the answer.

◆

NOTES

1. http://www.business-standard.com/article/management/online-education-gains-traction-114100200299_1.html
2. http://www.paristechreview.com/2014/08/26/MOOCs-education-china/
3. From a lecture by Debra Castillo in her presentation 'Performing Gender in the Classroom and on the Stage', at a seminar organised by the Department of Germanic and Romance Studies, University of Delhi. 13 January 2015.
4. Ibid.
5. 'Can MOOCs Help Expand Access to Higher Education in India?', Gayle Christensen and Brandon Alcorn. 30 December 2013. https://casi.sas.upenn.edu/iit/christensenalcorn

REFERENCES

Bernstein, Basil B. 1996. *Pedagogy, Symbolic Control, and Identity: Theory, Research, Critique.* London; Washington, D.C.: Taylor & Francis.

Burnet, Judith, Peter Senker and Kathy Walker (eds.). 2009. 'Introduction.' *The Myths of Technology: Innovation and Inequality*. New York: Peter Lang.

Kumar, Krishna. 2013. *Choori Bazar Mein Ladki.* New Delhi: Rajkamal.

◆◆

THE GIFT OF KNOWLEDGE

Philanthropy and Higher Education*

PUSHPA SUNDAR

Private philanthropy has played a significant role in educating India. Traditionally, Indians have had a high reverence for education, especially higher education. In American historian Stanley Wolpert's evocative words, education is 'the swiftest elevator to the pinnacles of modern Indian power and opportunity' (1999). It is this veneration for education which has attracted philanthropy. Education has ever been a favoured field for Indian philanthropy—it was so in ancient times, and it is so now.

A BRIEF HISTORY

Epigraphical records indicate that the support for education was a favoured form of charity, even in ancient times, and took the form of free feeding houses for poor students, the construction of college buildings and endowment of chairs, or the grant of land to meet the recurring expenses of educational institutions.

After the establishment of British rule in India, education along Western lines served as a ladder to official favour as well as the means to optimise new opportunities offered by industrialisation and contact with Western civilisation. The Indian intelligentsia and the new rich, from personal inclination and aided by government policy, directed their philanthropy to establishing Western educational institutions.

In Bombay, leading merchants Jaggananth Shankarshet, Framji Kavasji Banaji and Jamsetji Jijibhai gave considerable amounts to fund Elphinstone professorships and Grant Medical College; Kavasji Jehangir Readymoney's generous donations to Bombay University and hospitals totalled ₹14 crore. The J. J. School of Art owes its

Winter 2015–Spring 2016, Volume 42, Numbers 3 & 4

existence to the endowment by Jamsetji Jijibhai. Numerous other philanthropically-minded merchants, and others, came forward in Bombay and elsewhere to fund colleges (Sundar, 2000: 72–73).

Education, especially for girls, was one of the favoured causes supported everywhere. Millowner Bechardas Ambaidas of Ahmedabad, who endowed the Mahalakshmi Female Training College, was one such donor.

In Madras, one of the earliest great philanthropists was Pacchaiyappa who, inspired by his English friend Norton, established an educational trust which set up the first private college in Madras—Pacchaiyappa's College. In Bengal, Motilal Sheel endowed the Free College.

A catalogue of philanthropy for education before Independence would be incomplete without mention of one of India's greatest philanthropists, Jamsetji Tata, who launched the J. N. Tata Endowment Scheme in 1892, well before the first major foundation in America. With a capital of ₹25 crore, it gave scholarships to deserving students for higher studies abroad. But, since he did not believe in encouraging dependence through free charity, the scholarships were loans at a nominal rate of interest, to be paid back in easy instalments. By this means, the fund was also conserved for future generations.

Tata's biggest contribution, however, was the establishment of the Indian Institute of Science for which, in 1898, he set aside 14 of his buildings and four landed properties in Bombay, to create an endowment for an institute of science at Bangalore. The aim was to give India the technological personnel that would enable her to step into the industrial age. As the government did not accept the offer immediately, the Institute was completed only in 1911, seven years after Tata's death. It is noteworthy that in order to attract more funds to the Institute, Tata insisted that his own name not be attached to it, a rare phenomenon in today's philanthropy.

In the rest of India, too, the wealthy were giving large donations for education, fired by the nationalist ideals of a free and progressive India. Inspired by Mahatma Gandhi's struggle for freedom, many of the new rich funded the new Nationalist education, contributing generously to causes such as the setting up of Benaras Hindu University by Pandit Madan Mohan Malviya.

In Delhi, Sri Krishna Dass Gurwale, one of the promoters of Delhi Cloth Mills, established Hindu College in 1899. It was set up for those Hindu students as would not be sent by orthodox parents to St. Stephen's Mission College, the only other institution of higher learning at the time.

The years immediately following Independence also resulted in the establishment of several well-known educational institutions such as the Shri Ram College of Commerce and Lady Shri Ram College for Women; medical institutions such as Sulochana Devi Singhania School, Bombay; J. K. Institute of Applied Physics and Technology, Allahabad; and, J. K. Institute of Sociology and Human Relations, among others. Almost every city in India has at least one or two colleges endowed by a private donor. Philanthropy thus played an important role in building the higher educational infrastructure in pre- and immediate post-Independence India.[1]

In this brief summary, four points stand out. One, the motives for starting such institutions were perhaps more purely altruistic than in later times. It was clear to the pioneers of the first wave of wealth creation that for sustained development, massive social investment in education, especially vocational and technical education, was necessary. And just as they had initiated a number of new industrial projects, irrespective of tariff protection or without the expectation of government aid, they began to make good the gaps in the social field themselves. The result was a proliferation of colleges, universities, technical and research institutes, which were later taken over or supported by the government.

Two, many of the pioneers were self-made men with little education, with the exception of the Tatas and later technocrat entrepreneurs. Despite that, or perhaps because of it, they placed a great deal of importance on education as the golden key which would unlock the doors to prosperity and progress, and therefore gave freely to move India from a backward, agricultural and tradition-bound society to a strong, modern one (ibid.).

Three, most of the educational initiatives were confined to urban areas, particularly to major towns.

Four, the government played a very positive role in moving the wealthy towards philanthropy by offering tax concessions, and titles and awards.

After Independence, with a socialistic pattern of society as the avowed goal of state policy, the state became the predominant actor in development. Higher education became a government preserve. Since a deficit in technology was identified as the reason for India's backwardness, priority was given in higher education to the creation of the prestigious institutes of technology (IITs) which, although predominantly funded by government, also received research funding from private business.

The most significant *private philanthropic* contribution of the 1960s and '70s was the setting up of the Birla Institute of Technology and Science (BITS), Pilani, by G. D. Birla's eponymous Education Trust in 1964. It was later converted into a deemed university.

The three premier Indian Institutes of Management (IIMs) at Ahmedabad, Calcutta and Bangalore followed between 1961 and 1973. In the creation of IIM, Ahmedabad (1961), rich business leaders of the city such as Vikram Sarabhai and Kasturbhai Lalbhai made valuable contributions in terms of money, time and expertise. The IIM, Calcutta, too, benefited from the contributions of the West Bengal government, as well as foreign donors such as the Ford Foundation and Indian industrialists. However, after the '70s, genuine philanthropic contributions became rarer as the government raised tax rates to high levels in deference to the socialistic ideal, and to finance plans for development. There was a disinclination to invest in big-ticket institutions without government aid.

Philanthropy, if any, largely became an outlet for the huge amount of black money generated by high tax rates and the license-permit raj. It encouraged the establishment of numerous charitable trusts as tax-saving devices. This was the beginning of the privatisation of higher education in the name of philanthropy, much of which owed little to genuine philanthropic instinct.

EDUCATION AND PHILANTHROPY TODAY

The higher education system today has become a large and complex one because of public investments, foreign aid and private contributions. Still, many challenges remain. One of these is a well-documented supply–demand gap. India's growth rate of enrolment in higher education is only 12–15 per cent compared with 26 per cent in China, and 36 per cent in Brazil. There is an enormous unmet demand, a large proportion of which is being met by private, often for-profit, 'unaided' colleges and universities in which standards are often questionable.

By and large, the quality of teaching and learning in both public and private institutions is low. The system churns out ill-prepared and unemployable graduates because of a chronic shortage of faculty, the poor quality of teaching, outdated and rigid curricula and pedagogy, the lack of accountability and quality assurance, and the separation of research and teaching. Consequently, the state of academic research is abysmal. India spends less on research and development than other fast-growing economies.

Other challenges include uneven growth and a lack of access for lower castes and backward regions, as well as the absence of autonomy for prestigious institutions, with much intervention and interference by the HRD ministry. Because of these constraints the quality of Indian education is terrible, by and large, with the result that only 10 per cent of general graduates, and 25 per cent of both engineers and MBAs are estimated to be employable.

A major reason for this state of affairs is the lack of funds. Although public expenditure at all levels of education has increased tremendously since independence from ₹64.46 crore or 0.64 per cent of the GDP in 1951, to 3.2 per cent of the GDP in 2010–11, and then to 4.29 per cent in 2012–13,[2] this is clearly insufficient to ensure both the expansion of seats and an improvement in the quality of education. This is even more so as the total public spending on higher education alone, in 2013–14, was only ₹26,750 crore, a mere 1.33 per cent of India's GDP for that year.

What is needed is more private investment to supplement public expenditure. In fact, the unaided private sector's share has increased significantly since 2001, in terms of the number of institutions and enrolment. As of 2012, the share of unaided private institutions accounted for 64 per cent of the total number of educational institutions, and 59 per cent of enrolment—an increase of 48 per cent and 79 per cent, respectively, from just a decade ago.[3] Today, about 60 per cent of higher education is provided by the private sector. Private investment has been particularly steep in professional education, especially in the medical, technological and management sector.

Unfortunately, much of this increase in private investment is powered solely by the interest in the profits to be harvested, not in the improvement of standards, whereas what is needed is disinterested investment, which is represented by philanthropy. Even in what is termed philanthropy there is a cynical use of the institution of charitable trusts for the sake of profit and personal gain.

NEW TRENDS IN PHILANTHROPY

PRIVATISATION, NOT PHILANTHROPY

Increased private investment in education is composed of two parts: the greater one represents a privatisation of education in the name of philanthropy, with a smaller one representing genuine philanthropy.

Most universities and colleges are set up as not-for-profit, tax-exempt ventures under Section 25 of the Companies Act, of which only a small number are philanthropic in intent or practice. This is because the larger number operate as for-profit entities, charging high capitation and tuition fees without giving corresponding value-added services. Their income is derived from fees rather than endowments and investments, and they make large profits without having to pay taxes on them. This is especially true of professional colleges. The evil of capitation fees continues to grow like a hydra-headed monster that feeds on political patronage and unsatisfied demand, because of which virtually any institution has a market.

Tax exemptions have attracted huge amounts of black money into the higher education sector. Registering as a non-profit charitable trust also allows for easier land acquisition without inviting public interest litigation (PIL).

The result is that although there are some private institutions of a high standard, on the whole there is a rapid increase in the number of private, often for-profit, 'unaided', academically-mediocre schools and colleges, in which standards are often questionable. These colleges and institutes are little more than teaching shops, the mushrooming of which has been aided by the tax incentives offered by the government. Because of this, the contribution of the private sector to superior education has, by and large, lagged considerably behind that of the public sector.

A majority of these 'teaching shops', in which there is no pedagogical innovation or excellence, have thrived only due to the connivance and active involvement of politicians and officials. The special investigative team (SIT), recently appointed by the government to check black money, has in its reports mentioned several studies that highlight the higher and technical education sectors, as well as the health sector, as major sources of black money. These studies mention that entities engaged in education through trusts accept large, unaccounted amounts as donations which, in a number of cases, are used for personal benefit and tax evasion.[4]

ESTABLISHMENT OF NEW UNIVERSITIES

There is some good news as well. Although smaller in size than private investment in education for profit, genuine philanthropy also exists alongside the crass commercialisation of education, and is growing. Three distinct trends are visible: first, the establishment of several large, well-funded universities in preference to donations to existing public institutions; second, alumni funding of existing institutions of excellence; and, third, the internationalisation of Indian philanthropy with several big-ticket contributions by Indian philanthropists to universities abroad, and to outreach initiatives of foreign universities in India.

Several new universities have been, and are being, set up by the new philanthropists who have made vast amounts of money as a result of India's rapid growth. These are either eponymous, or named for the donor's company, or in memory of a family member. Since 2000, several new private universities have been set up by business tycoons. As is the case with non-philanthropic private investment in education, many newly endowed philanthropic institutions offer professional education rather than one in the liberal arts—as was the case in an earlier era—because of the great demand for such qualifications, from both students and employers.

Some new universities, mentioned at random, are:

(i) The Nirma Institute of Technology, established in 1995 by Karsanbhai Patel, the founder of the ₹2,500 crore Nirma group, which was followed by the Nirma Institute of Management, and, finally, the Nirma University in 2003;

(ii) The Dhirubhai Ambani Institute of Communication & Technology in Gandhinagar, Gujarat, established in 2001 by Mukesh Ambani, in memory of his father;

(iii) The NIIT University of computer technology, founded by Rajendra Pawar and Vijay Thadani;

(iv) The O. P. Jindal Global University, founded in 2009 by Naveen Jindal, chairman of Jindal Steel & Power, in memory of his father;
(v) The Ashoka University in Sonepat, near Delhi, as a collective effort by 46 philanthropists, led by Ashish Dhawan and Sanjeev Bikhchandani;
(vi) The Shiv Nadar University, set up by Shiv Nadar of HCL;
(vii) The Azim Premji University, by the promoter of Wipro; and,
(viii) The Adani Institute of Infrastructure Management, created by Gautam Adani, chairman of the USD 5 billion Adani Group.

A few more such institutions are in the process of being set up.

There are several reasons why philanthropists have taken to setting up new universities on a very large scale, rather than donating to existing institutions. One is, of course, the oft-cited need to give back to society. Nevertheless, the fact that most universities are set up as not-for-profit ventures under Section 25, which gives the donor tax concessions, also helps.

The mandatory contribution of 2 per cent of profit before tax for corporate social responsibility (CSR) programmes under the Companies Act, 2013, is also pushing companies in this direction. For many companies, the amounts governed by CSR are so large that only a big project can absorb such sums. Among other reasons are that many leading business houses already run schools and colleges; they have gained enough expertise to make a university the logical next step; and, finally, quite simply, the huge demand. The gross enrolment ratio (GER), or the ratio of young people who are signing up for courses to the total number of people of that age, is increasing rapidly. By 2030, the number of students in colleges is estimated to go up to 7 crore.[5]

The reason for the distinct preference for endowing professional and technical institutions, rather than institutions for the social sciences and humanities, is obvious. The greatest demand from students is for technical and management education of all kinds, since it commands the highest salaries. Second, there is a huge demand for such skills from employers, too, who are faced with a shortage of the required technical and managerial skills. Endowing technical and management institutions, in which they can set the agenda, provides them with a captive supply of the numbers and type of skills they need, and is also more profitable.

Although donations to existing Indian institutions by Indian philanthropists pale in comparison with the amounts spent in setting up their own universities and colleges, in addition to big-ticket donations given to institutions abroad, they are not non-existent either. Most of these donations come from alumni of Indian public institutions, and are beginning to grow, although they are most noticeable in the case of the IITs and IIMs, which have been able to tap into a large base of professional alumni amongst the Indian diaspora.

One of the biggest donations to an Indian alma mater by an NRI was made by Frank Islam, an Indian–American entrepreneur. Islam donated USD 2 million to Aligarh Muslim University to build the Frank and Debbie Islam School of Management, with an emphasis on entrepreneurship.

Besides this bequest to a public university, most alumni donations are made to the IITs, now 15 in all, and the IIMs. These donations to their alma mater institutions represent a payback from those who have received the finest education at highly subsidised rates. Notable donations by alumni and non-alumni have been made by Nandan Nilekani, N. R. Narayana Murthy, Kris Gopalakrishnan, Bhupat and Jyoti Mehta, and Kishore Chivukula. These donations go mainly towards research in professional institutes and research institutions, rather than to public institutions of the liberal arts or science. It is heartening that many of these donations support non-traditional scientific research and development, which augurs well for breakthroughs in different fields.

INTERNATIONALISATION OF INDIAN PHILANTHROPY

Thus far, India has been a net receiver of international philanthropy, with much of it going to higher education. It is a telling comment on India's growth story that rich Indians are now reversing the flow of philanthropic funds by giving to educational institutions abroad. These big-ticket donations by leading Indian philanthropists to institutions of higher learning abroad have brought Indian philanthropy to global attention.

Among those who have donated to foreign universities are: (i) Naveen Jindal, to the University of Texas, Dallas; (ii) Shiv Nadar, for the creation of the Shiv Nadar Professor of Engineering Chair at Carnegie Mellon University; (iii) Ratan Tata, of USD 50 million to Cornell, in 2008, for agricultural and nutrition programmes, and USD 50 million, in 2010, to Harvard Business School, to fund a new academic and residential building; and, (iv) Anand Mahindra's bequest of USD 10 million to the Humanities Centre at Harvard.

Such donations to foreign institutions have naturally caused much heartburn in Indian institutions. Questions have been raised about the need for Indian philanthropists to donate to institutions as well-funded as Harvard University, particularly when there is a crying need to improve standards in Indian universities and Indian think tanks, which are hamstrung for resources.

That major philanthropists have chosen to donate to foreign institutions rather than Indian ones is unfortunate, but understandable. Given the state of higher education institutions in India, donors of large sums believe that they would be unable to absorb funds of the kind that were offered to Harvard, and others. Besides, many of these donors have also given substantially to other causes, and other organisations in India. While international philanthropy undoubtedly deprives Indian institutions, it offers personal benefits to donors in terms of recognition abroad, and also serves as an acknowledgement of their gratitude for the excellent education received from their alma maters, which has enabled them to succeed in their careers.

There is also the simple fact that the top echelons of Indian capital are becoming increasingly global, jockeying for access and influence. Large donations to highly visible institutions serve to boost the brand image of their companies and add to their market value.

If the highly sophisticated fundraising campaigns of premier institutions such as Harvard, Cambridge and the University of Chicago, some of which offer honorary doctorates to large donors as an incentive, are juxtaposed to the total absence of any fundraising efforts by Indian public institutions for higher education, then it is not difficult to understand the big donations.

Finally, the internationalisation of many endeavours is inevitable in today's networked world, and also has the benefit of the cross-fertilisation of ideas and innovations.

CONSTRAINTS ON GIVING

So far, the government has allowed private players to expand higher educational facilities only because of its own fiscal deficits; its own need to meet the increased reservation requirements by expanding supply; and, because education offers a convenient source of patronage (Kapur and Mehta, 2004: 26). But it needs to encourage philanthropy for its own sake. However, several constraints prevent philanthropy from growing. One of these is the government's refusal to offer autonomy to public or publicly-aided educational institutions. Donors of scale, whether NRIs or Indians, hesitate to commit large resources unless they also have a say in its use, and an institutionalised mechanism present to have their voice heard. However, such mechanisms tend to be non-existent in the governance structures of most higher education institutions, with governmental interference in institutional autonomy rampant. One reason why the Indian Institute of Science (IISc) has attracted such a large donation from Kris Gopalakrishnan is that it has set up the new Brain Research Centre with his donation as an autonomous society, which gives it full freedom to operate free from government rules and regulations, while also drawing on the intellectual and physical facilities of the institute's campus.

Second, while the corporate sector and India's elite can be criticised for not paying sufficient attention to India's public universities, where many of them studied, universities must also be willing to shoulder blame. Other than a few exceptions, such as the IITs and the Indian Institute of Science, Bangalore, higher education institutions have not attempted to tap the huge alumni resource through aggressive fundraising.

However, more aggressive fundraising will not help unless the regulatory regime changes. It is difficult, if not downright counterproductive, for public colleges and universities to tap private resources or seek to leverage old school ties with alumni to raise funds because of the University Grants Commission's practice of deducting such philanthropic contributions from a university's grant-in-aid. It leaves little incentive for these institutes to conduct aggressive fundraising campaigns. A more enabling regulatory regime would surely help.[6]

A major difficulty in putting private investment to good use is the trouble in distinguishing real philanthropic activity from masked profit making since, by definition, all Indian universities and private colleges are 'non-profit' organisations. Unless there is some clarity on this issue, the abuses may continue.

In addition, the government must tighten licensing standards, improve quality assurance, put in place a rating framework which emphasises student learning outcomes and research—not facilities and infrastructure—and, finally, develop a regulatory mechanism in consultation with private players to oversee all educational institutions—public and private.

In conclusion, since education has always attracted philanthropic capital, and since the government alone cannot ensure the finest education to the growing numbers who seek it, every effort should be made to stimulate the nascent shoots already visible, and to channel them in the right direction.

◆

*This article is an abridged version of a chapter in a forthcoming book by the author, *Giving with a Thousand Hands: The Changing Face of Indian Philanthropy*.

NOTES

1. See Sundar (2000), chapter 4, for a more extensive coverage of this period.
2. World Bank data: http://data.worldbank.org/indicator/SE.XPD>TOTL>GD>ZS
3. Ernst & Young. 2012. Ernst & Young, FICCI, and Planning Commission of India. 'Higher Education in India: Twelfth Five Year Plan (2012–17) and Beyond', November.
4. Reported in *The Times of India*, 'Panel Wants Capitation Fees under Anti-graft Law', Delhi, 25 July 2015.
5. 'Higher Education in India: Vision 2030', FICCI–Ernst & Young Report for FICCI Higher Education Summit. 2013. New Delhi.
6. See *Indian Express* edit. 1 February 2014.

REFERENCES

Kapur, Devesh and Pratap Bhanu Mehta. 2004. 'Indian Higher Education Reform: From Half-baked Socialism to Half-baked Capitalism', Working Papers, Center for International Development at Harvard University, September.

Sundar, Pushpa. 2000. *Beyond Business*. New Delhi: Tata McGraw Hill.

Wolpert, Stanley A. 1999. *India*. US: University of California Press.

◆◆

RIGHT TO EDUCATION

KISHORE SINGH

There is growing recognition of the centrality of education in peoples' lives today. Education enables the acquisition of knowledge, values, competencies and skills that every individual needs. Parents put a premium on education for their children for a better future. Demands for the provision of education from the elementary level to the tertiary have been growing. Low-fee private schools have been mushrooming in some developing countries, including India. One can also witness the surging demands made upon higher education.

Educational systems are being expanded with a diversified range of education providers, driven by different motives and objectives, ranging from public education systems to religious institutions. Education is also provided by non-governmental organisations and community-based groups as well as foundations and trusts.

All such non-state providers in education are being overshadowed by enterprises and individual proprietors with an almost free hand, making education a 'for-profit' pursuit. Taking advantage of the inability of an inadequate public education system to cope with rising demands, private providers have been making inroads in education at all levels, making it a lucrative business. Education is being increasingly opened up to profit making and trade, and to agendas set by private commercial interests in India as well as in many developing countries.

This has profound implications for the right to education—as an internationally established right, the exercise of this right, and all its benefits. Among key challenges are the mitigation of growing disparities in access to education, bringing about equality of opportunity, safeguarding education against the forces of commercialisation, preserving it as a public good with its humanistic mission, and reversing the trend of deteriorating quality.

In the face of these challenges, our approach and policy should be guided by some 'perennials' embodied in norms and principles as well as concepts underlying the right to education as an internationally established right. Such principles and concepts are also reflected in India's Constitution.

In developing legal and policy responses to address these challenges, the framework of the right to education as an internationally established right is of paramount importance.

RIGHT TO EDUCATION AS AN INTERNATIONALLY RECOGNISED RIGHT AND INDIA'S INTERNATIONAL LEGAL OBLIGATIONS

The moral foundations of the right to education are laid down in the *Universal Declaration of Human Rights (1948)*, which proclaimed that everyone has the right to education. Based on the Declaration, education as a fundamental human right has been established in a number of international human rights conventions. States are obliged to respect, protect and fulfil the right to education under these conventions. State obligations, which remain even in case of the privatisation of education, must be incorporated into domestic legal order. Policy and programme measures should be in conformity with their international obligations.

For example, India is an original signatory to the *Declaration* in which Article 26 provides for the right to education. India is a State party to the *International Covenant on Economic, Social and Cultural Rights* which comprehensively establishes the right to education. India is also a State party to other United Nations human rights conventions, such as the Convention on the Rights of the Child, which contain provisions on the rights of the child, including the right to education. It is incumbent upon India under international human rights conventions to provide primary education, free of cost. This is the *core* obligation. India is also obliged to make secondary education, including technical and vocational education, generally accessible; higher education, too, should be made progressively accessible, based on merit or capacity.

In a landmark judgement, the Supreme Court of India took into account India's obligations under the international treaties, viz., the right to education under Article 13 of the International Covenant.[1] This article draws extensively upon UNESCO's Convention against Discrimination in Education (1960), which comprehensively covers the right to education. Although India has not yet acceded to this Convention, its obligations under the International Covenant are interrelated with those under the Convention which, in turn, relate to India's obligations as a Member State of UNESCO, with its institutional mission to ensure 'full and equal opportunities for education for all'. It is also important to recall that the fundamental principles of social justice and equity, which are key pillars of the United Nations system for peace and development, are also reflected in India's Constitution.

MITIGATING GROWING DISPARITIES IN EDUCATION AND BRINGING ABOUT EQUALITY OF OPPORTUNITY

These principles are compromised by growing disparities in education, with the persistent challenge of bringing about equality of opportunity in education. India has the largest primary school education system in the world, but also has the world's largest number of children who do not meet basic learning levels.[2] Indians figure prominently amongst the richest people in the world, but India is also a country where more than 300 million people remain victims of poverty, and millions of children still remain deprived of education.

Poverty is an affront to humanity and the greatest obstacle to realising the right to education. Educational policies in India need to give utmost importance to the critical need of educating the poor, the excluded, and the disadvantaged—the rural poor, and children and youth in teeming urban slums. Education is one of the key instruments for putting an end to the inter-generational transmission of poverty. Public policies need to be devised to provide financial and pedagogic support along with positive measures to all those who remain deprived of their right to education, the poor in particular, in an endeavour to mitigate inequities based, inter alia, on social origin, wealth, etc.

It is imperative to expand the opportunities for better public education with an enhanced budget for education if we have to mitigate growing disparities in education. The education budget is consumed by recurring expenditure with scant resources for quality. The government must devote maximum public funds to education as a matter of norm. This is the responsibility of States under international human rights law. Accordingly, some countries have provisions in the Constitution or Education Law for financing education. This provides a firm and enduring basis for budget allocations for education and guarantees sustained investment by the State. India should devote maximum resources to education, recognising its importance in generating intellectual capital.

We must also (re)build trust in the public education system regarding the maintenance of quality standards and provision of quality. Expanding an excellent public education system is essential to nurture talent and creativity, as emphasised by Azim Premji (2015) while addressing senior officials in India on 'How to make India Great: our systems, particularly public education, must empower people at the bottom'.

The fundamental principle of equality of opportunity is enshrined in India's Constitution. A Constitution Bench of the Supreme Court in *Km. Chitra Ghosh vs. Union of India and Others [(1969) 2 SCC 228]* stated:

> [...] the primary imperative of Article 14 is equal opportunity for all across the nation for education and advancement (...). What is fundamental, as an enduring value of our polity, is guarantee to each of equal opportunity to unfold the full potential of his personality. [...] The philosophy and pragmatism of universal excellence through equality of opportunity for education and advancement across the nation is part of our founding faith and constitutional creed. [...].

It is incumbent upon the Government of India to raise the profile of the right to education on account of its political commitments to the 2030 Agenda for Sustainable Development, adopted by the United Nations Summit (July 2015). Goal 4 of the Agenda stipulates: 'By 2030, ensure that all girls and boys complete free, equitable and quality primary and secondary education leading to relevant and effective learning outcomes.' Moreover, following the Incheon Declaration (May 2015) and the adoption of the Education 2030 Framework for Action on 4 November 2015 on the occasion of UNESCO General Conference, countries from all over the world, including India, have reaffirmed their commitment to the provision of quality education for all, free of cost.

The 2030 agenda for education has significant implications for India's Right of Children to Free and Compulsory Education Act (2009), which not only was enacted rather late but is limited in scope, especially as regards elementary (basic) education that is merely of eight years' duration. In today's world, such limited entitlement to education reveals the extent to which India lags behind many other developing countries, where the duration of basic education is of 12 years. The modernised Education Law of 2006 in Brazil provides for the universal right to a basic education of 12 years, as does South Africa. Recently, China amended its law to provide for 12 years of basic education. In the Russian Federation, the Education Law of 2013 guarantees that education upto secondary general education and secondary vocational education is publicly available, free of cost; higher education provided on a competitive basis is also free.

India needs to review and broaden the scope of its Right of Children to Free and Compulsory Education Act so that every child is entitled to, and benefits from, 12 years of publicly-funded superior education, free of cost. This would add strength to the *Rashtriya Madhyamik Shiksha Abhiyan* (National Secondary Education Movement). India, like China, can elaborate a set of laws covering various areas of education. Whether there is one comprehensive education law, or a set of laws addressing various key areas, this should be accompanied by rules and regulations necessary for effective implementation.

SAFEGUARDING EDUCATION AGAINST COMMERCIALISATION AND PRESERVING IT AS A PUBLIC GOOD

The disparities in education are exacerbated by privatisation, which is mushrooming because of the lack of sufficient public provision of education or underperforming public schools. Funded and managed by individual proprietors or enterprises, privatisation in education is fuelled by false propaganda and publicity. As a result, education is being commercialised and for-profit education is flourishing as an attractive business. Low-fee private schools in India are a glaring example of the commercialisation of education, characterised as 'edu-business'.[3] Private providers in education find the inadequacies of the public education system fertile ground for reaping uncontrolled profits.

The negative impact of the commercialisation of education has been brought into focus both in scholarly writings and well-documented reports. A potentially large proportion of these schools are unregistered. Private providers in education escape unscathed despite corruption, which is hidden, because of the lack of financial regulations, of scrutiny of their operations, and of control mechanisms. Driven by business interest, privatisation by definition is detrimental to education as a public good and sacrifices social interest in education for the sake of private profit.

The right to education in the field of higher education faces enormous challenges, where disparities and quality concerns are more pronounced. The uncontrolled and unregulated growth of higher education to meet rising demands is leading to the deterioration of quality and standards. A range of entities, such as individual proprietors or profit-seeking corporate houses, are spreading their businesses by providing higher education. As a result, privatised higher education has become the fastest-growing segment of higher education. Access to these establishments based upon the capacity to pay, which in many cases can be exorbitant, defies prohibited grounds of discrimination based notably on 'social origin', 'economic condition', 'birth' or 'property' in international human rights conventions. Moreover, this undermines the social function of universities, and their very mission as moral seats of learning, as they are made subservient to corporate interests.

The euphoria over Massive Open Online Courses (MOOCs), Open Educational Resources (OER) and other methods of e-learning, portrayed as an alternative path to access higher education, must be seen in the light of norms and principles underlying the right to education. Costs involved relate not only to buying modern ICTs and digital devices, but also to technical support by private providers such as digital network operators, content providers and other stakeholders, in addition to infrastructure and capacity building (especially teachers) and support for open licenses.[4] This concern with the 'digital divide' is being articulated. Moreover, campus-based face-to-face learning and teaching is being undermined by MOOCs and other networks, and web portals operating without human contact.

In light of such developments, we must recall the State's international obligations according to which access to higher education should be merit based and freely accessible. The Constitutional law's obligation to control an unregulated free market in higher education has been commendably articulated by the Supreme Court of India:

> [....] when the State Government grants recognition to private educational institutions, it creates an agency to fulfil its obligation under the Constitution to enable the citizens to enjoy the right to education. Charging capitation fee in consideration of admission to educational institutions is a patent denial of a citizen's right to education under the Constitution.[5]

The privatisation of education and its commercialisation is a severe blow to the principles of social justice and equality of opportunity which are key pillars of India's Constitution. Safeguarding education against the forces of commercialisation and preserving education as a public good are legal responsibilities of the government. It is also a moral imperative.

RESPONDING TO QUALITY IMPERATIVES

The entitlement to education in terms of universal access is inextricably linked with the empowerment in terms of quality to impart knowledge, values, competencies and skills.

The deteriorating quality of education is a widespread concern. Public authorities seem to be allowing quality to deteriorate; school inspections to investigate teacher absenteeism are slack. The greater part of teacher training in India is provided by private establishments, the poor quality of which compromises the fate of future generations and indeed that of the country as a whole.

There is a misconception that the quality of education is better in private schools. The findings of the OECD show that private schools do not provide better quality education as compared to public schools; what matters is the socio-economic background of parents.[6] In fact, the quality of education is compromised by the predominance of under-qualified and under-paid teachers, employed by low-fee private schools. Besides, in many cases, private schools employ teachers on a temporary basis, with no consideration for their career development.

Skill development is an indispensable component of the drive towards quality education. It is a high-priority area in India, as demonstrated by the National Skill Development Mission and National Skill Development and Entrepreneurship Policy, which emphasises the need to revamp vocational education and training (VET) programmes in India. The elaborate legal and regulatory framework governing the institutionalised collaboration between VET institutions and enterprises is required in India for mitigating prevalent weaknesses in this area. Instead of remaining a separate stream, VET should become an integral and respectable part of general secondary education, with pathways to higher technical education. This requires developing standards in higher education and VET quality assurance, not only with respect to the technical requirements of occupational sectors, but also for developing social skills and critical thinking. States must lay emphasis on the importance of high-quality VET and should adopt necessary quality norms and standards, along with national qualifications framework and assessment systems for VET, applicable uniformly throughout the country.

In order to meet quality imperatives, India needs to set common standards and norms conducive to building professional excellence, accompanied by instruments for monitoring and assessment of the quality of education. India's concept of knowledge as power—*gyanshakti*—deserves to be elaborated by relevant programmes for the promotion of quality education. This is especially important as in 'neoliberal methods of evaluating competitiveness of higher education institutions in the academia', introduced by the academic rankings, 'social function' of higher education institutions for 'human development' is not taken into consideration in academic rankings.[7]

Considerations of excellence are especially important with respect to the recognition of studies and qualifications in higher education institutions. A policy framework which seeks to stringently regulate a large number of private providers operating in various technical areas such as management, marketing, accountancy, communication, etc., and which award the diplomas and degrees devoid of recognition in terms of equivalence or validity, is necessary. Public authorities must find ways of preventing fraudulent providers from masquerading as universities and from issuing worthless qualifications, especially when they are based overseas and operate via the Internet. Modernised education law(s) in the field of higher education should seek to foster professional excellence as well as to introduce the rigorous assessment of quality for the recognition of degrees and diplomas.

The Global Initiative of Academic Network (GIAN) launched in India for inviting leading academicians from across the world to take short courses in Indian universities and technological institutions, where costs are met by the government, must be reviewed: GIAN must be redefined as a reciprocal exchange programme in which India does not remain merely at the receiving end. We must be inspired by the conviction expressed in the Delhi Declaration, resulting from the BRICS Summit (March 2012), that there is a 'storehouse of knowledge, know-how, capacities and best practices' available in our countries that can be shared 'for the mutual benefit of BRICS as well as other developing countries'. There is no dearth of professors, scholars and researchers of eminence in India and they must benefit equitably in all possible ways in the context of exchange of scholars and researchers.

REGULATORY AND CONTROLLING MEASURES

A comprehensive and sound regulatory framework with a system of sanctions is necessary for ensuring that 'edu-business' has no place in the education system. Such a framework should be prescriptive, prohibitive and punitive. Prescriptive regulations clearly establish conditions under which private providers may be permitted to operate, as well as minimum norms and standards with which educational establishments must comply. Prohibitive regulations are necessary to outlaw 'for-profit' education and curb false, commercial propaganda. Nationally designated authorities should undertake full-scale investigations of fraudulent practices in education, including tax evasion by private providers. Punitive measures with sanctions are crucial in order to deal with cases of fraudulent and corrupt practices.

Singapore provides a laudable example of how States can effectively regulate and control private education providers. The Private Education Act in Singapore sets very strict standards of excellence and norms with which a private educational establishment must comply. It can be refused permission to operate if it is not in public interest. The Act establishes duties of its educational management and their accountabilities. It provides that 'any registered private education institution which contravenes any requirement or restriction imposed ... shall be guilty of an offence' and it makes acting 'fraudulently or dishonestly' or 'misleading' the public punishable by law. The Act contains comprehensive provisions on inspection and enforcement, with a detailed section on offences by corporate bodies, including unincorporated associations which, when found guilty of an offence, are liable to be prosecuted and punished.[8]

PUBLIC–PRIVATE PARTNERSHIPS: PRESERVING SOCIAL INTEREST IN EDUCATION

Today, there is growing interest in seeking partnerships with multi-stakeholders in education. A differentiated approach with respect to this is necessary, discarding any partnership with private providers of education that commercialises education. We need to foster genuine philanthropy, which is not business driven, and which is infused with education as a social good. Genuinely philanthropic foundations are invaluable for supporting public investment in, and provision of, education. So are community organisations pursuing social interest without any commercial interest. All those valuing education as a public good and a social cause against 'for-profit' education must be encouraged with an 'enabling environment' to contribute to the development of education.

Governments, and through them, all providers of education whether operating independently or jointly with governments, remain accountable because of State responsibility for the right to education. Narendra Modi, in an address in 2013 before becoming the Prime Minister of India, underlined the need to move forward from the 3 Ps: public–private–partnerships to 4 Ps: people–public–private–partnerships, necessary to bring about good governance, in which people with a sense of ownership remain centre staoge and the government becomes accountable.[9] Partnerships with the private sector are not always in public interest. At times, these may act as an indirect mechanism to serve private business interest. While entering into such partnerships, the government must ensure that the right to education is respected, protected and fulfilled.[10]

FOSTERING A HUMANISTIC MISSION, NOT A UTILITARIAN ROLE

The complete development of the human personality is an essential objective of education, laid down in international human rights conventions. Education can create a better world by enabling children and adults to develop attitudes and behaviour patterns so that they are enthused with the spirit of mutual respect and solidarity, and become respectful of one another's ways and culture. Four pillars of education—learning to know, learning to do, learning to live together, and learning to be—propounded by the International Commission on Education for the Twenty-First Century (1996) in its Report, *Learning: The Treasure Within*, are of perennial importance.

Interfaith and intercultural dialogue can provide precious leverage for fostering and learning to live together with respect for the richness of cultural diversity. Universally recognised human values and ideals must inspire educational systems, making them a unifying force. Universities as moral seats of learning must foster common human values that are much needed today to give a human face to globalisation.

Education, of which both the individual and society are beneficiaries, is a foundation of human development. As such, preserving education as a public good and safeguarding it against its commercialisation must be intertwined with the pursuit of the humanistic mission of education for common well-being. Fundamental principles of social justice and equity, which are the key pillars of the United Nations system, and which are reflected in India's Constitution are invaluable in guiding our action. India's rich jurisprudence on the right to education deserves to be given prime consideration in advancing in that direction.

Mahatma Gandhi's saying that for a person to be truly educated, you had to have a united approach—by training the mind to think, the hands to acquire skills, and the heart for human values and ethics—which embodies the mission and holistic concept of education.

Fostering the humanistic mission of education is of paramount importance to counter the trend towards the pursuit of material values and the mere instrumental role of education. Ancient India's civilisational values and teachings like those of Swami Vivekananda for the common benefit of humanity should become the bedrock of India's educational system.

Nicholas Carr provides profound insights into the deleterious impact of the use of digital devices on our mind and spirit, and sheds light on how this is destroying humanist values in education.

> How sad it would be, particularly when it comes to the nurturing of our children's minds, if we were to accept without question the

> idea that 'human elements' are outmoded and dispensable (....) 'meditative thinking,' as the very essence of our humanity, might become a victim of this (2010: 87).

Education as a noble cause has its moral foundation in India's ancient culture and philosophy. This must be central to India's policy and legal approaches in meeting the challenges of education for building a better world for the present and future generations.

◆

NOTES

1. *M. C. Mehta vs. State of Tamil Nadu and Others* (1996, 6, Supreme Court cases, 756).
2. India's Twelfth Five-Year-Plan, 2012–2017 (volume III, 2013).
3. *State Responsibility for Regulating Private Providers of Education and Preserving Education as a Public Good.* Report by the United Nations Special Rapporteur on the Right to Education (A/69/402), 24 September 2014.
4. Report of the International Conference on ICT and Post-2015 Education, UNESCO, 2015, p. 5.
5. *Ms. Mohini Jain vs. State of Karnataka and Ors, AIR 1858, 1992 SCR (3) 658.*
6. http://www.oecd-ilibrary.org/education/education-at-a-glance-2014_eag-2014-en (p. 410).
7. *BRICS as New Form of Multilateral Relations: A Report of the Global University Network*, Moscow, 26–28 October 2015.
8. Private Education Act No. 21 (2009) of Singapore.
9. Address by Narendra Modi to Network 18. Think India Dialogue, 8 April 2013 https://www.youtube.com/watch?v=GAyhWgthmpg
10. *Public–Private Partnerships and the Right to Education.* Report by the United Nations Special Rapporteur on the Right to Education (A/70/342), 26 September 2016.

REFERENCE

Carr, Nicholas. 2010. *The Shallows: What the Internet is doing to our Brains.* New York, London: W. W. Norton & Co.

Premji, Azim. 2015. 'How to Make India Great.' *The Times of India* (Ahmedabad). 22 December. http://epaperbeta.timesofindia.com/Article.aspx?eid=31805&articlexml=How-To-Make-India-Great-22122015012028

◆◆

'WEAK' STUDENTS AND ELITE INSTITUTIONS

The Challenges of Democratisation in the Indian University

SATISH DESHPANDE

> It will never happen again. This is the first and only generation of South Africans that would have lived through one of the most dramatic social transitions of the twentieth century. Nobody else would be able to tell this story with the direct experience of having lived on both sides of the 1990s, the decade in which everything changed (Janson, 2009).

These are the words with which Jonathan D. Janson, the first black Dean of the Faculty of Education in the previously whites-only University of Pretoria, begins his book on life after apartheid in South Africa. This moving book describes a historical moment, and Janson's claim that it represents 'one of the most dramatic social transitions of the twentieth century' requires no justification in the South African context. But most educated Indians, especially academics, would be offended by the suggestion that, with a little bit of exaggeration, these words could well apply to the Indian university in the early 21st century.

Unsettling though it may be, there is little doubt that Indian higher education, and especially its elite segment has, until recently, functioned under a kind of caste apartheid. Of course, unlike the classical apartheid regime, there have been no formal or legal proscriptions based on caste—if anything, quite the opposite, given the new republic's commitment to the principle of equal citizenship. It is true that university education (like other state services) has been formally available to all Indians at least since the 20th century and, arguably, even before that, ever since the advent of Western-style universities in 1859. However, despite the absence of legal

Winter 2015–Spring 2016, Volume 42, Numbers 3 & 4

proscriptions, higher education has been, in practise, the virtual monopoly of a privileged minority of Hindu upper castes.

Although India at independence had initiated the world's largest programme of compensatory discrimination through caste-based reservations, elite segments of Indian higher education were exempted from this programme. It is only in later decades that the uneven process of instituting reservation for Scheduled Castes (SCs) and Scheduled Tribes (STs) in elite institutions began to take effect. The final stages of this process were enacted in 2006 with the 93rd Amendment to the Constitution, which introduced reservation for the Other Backward Classes (OBCs) in hitherto exempt elite institutions such as the IITs, IIMs and all Central Universities. These provisions were implemented from 2008, effectively raising (in a phased manner) the potential representation of the lower castes to nearly 50 per cent. In effect, therefore, the process of integration that started in South Africa after the defeat of the apartheid regime in 1994 took a decade-and-a-half longer to begin in elite Indian institutions.

To get a sense of how exclusive the elite sector has been in caste terms, we may turn to the most recent (finalised) edition of the All India Survey of Higher Education (AISHE), conducted by the Department of Higher Education of the Ministry of Human Resource Development (DHE–MHRD), published in 2015, which provides data for the year 2013–14. If we include the Central Universities, which number 42 (and their affiliated colleges), as well as 68 Institutions of National Importance (which include the IITs, IIMs, among others), we get a rough measure of the 'elite' sector. Enrolment in this sector is about 18.4 lakh students, which is roughly 5.4 per cent of total enrolment in all universities, deemed universities, and other such institutions enumerated in AISHE.[1] Within this elite sector, enrolment data is provided separately for SCs, STs, OBCs, Persons with Disability (PWD), Muslims and Other Minorities. By subtracting the various caste categories, Muslims and Other Minorities from total enrolment, we can estimate the enrolment share of Hindu 'upper castes' (HUCs).[2]

Five years after the implementation of OBC reservations (in addition to the SC–ST reservations already instituted), the share of the HUCs stands at 70.2 per cent, i.e., for 2013–14. It is reasonable to assume that this share would have been even higher in the past. Given that (Hindu) upper castes account for roughly 15–20 per cent of the population, it is not much of an exaggeration to say that the elite sector of Indian higher education has been, until recently, segregated in an apartheid-like manner.[3]

The point of this extended comparison is to highlight the under-appreciated fact that we in India are also living through a revolution in higher education, one that dwarfs the South African case in sheer scale. Indeed, it can be said without any hyperbole that India (along with China) is currently witnessing the largest such revolution in human history—never before has access to higher education been widened so quickly to include such huge numbers. Another aspect of this gigantic revolution is that, despite the centrality of caste in determining access to higher education in India, class, too, has been no less crucial. Broadly, caste has functioned much as a necessary but insufficient condition for access—within the cluster of the so-called 'upper' castes, there is a significant section that is too poor to afford a college education. Conversely, a tiny minority of the affluent, or otherwise privileged, among the lower castes has also managed to access tertiary education.

As the statistical database on higher education has been enhanced relatively recently, there is no reliable data on these intersections of caste and class. However, overall figures do give us a sense of the phenomenal growth of higher education in the past quarter-century. Between 1991 and 2014, the total enrolment in higher education has increased six-and-a-half times (from 49 to 323 lakh); the number of universities has nearly quadrupled (184 to 723); and the gross enrolment ratio for the 18–23 age group has almost tripled (from 8.1 to 23.9 per cent). The bulk of the expansion has been in private colleges, which now account for 65 per cent of the enrolment and 75 per cent of the institutions at this level.[4] Despite this breakneck expansion, only one of every four young Indians reaches college. However, the most important aspect of this expansion is a huge variation in the quality of the education on offer, something that really cannot be captured by statistics. It is a known but unprovable fact about Indian higher education today that the majority of institutions, especially the new privately owned ones, offer substandard training, and sometimes no training at all.

CONTEXTUALISING THE 'QUALITY OF EDUCATION'

Concerns about the quality of higher education have been frequently written about. But unlike the case of school education, where some rigorous attempts have been made to measure quality in a reasonably transparent way,[5] no comparable benchmarking exercise has been undertaken for higher education. What we have are private employment agencies or employers' organisations that produce estimates of the 'employability' of Indian graduates;[6] or the indirect effects of governmental accreditation or ratings agencies such as AICTE (All India Council for Technical Education) or NAAC (National Accreditation and Assessment Council). There are unresolved (and, perhaps, unresolvable) conflicts of interest involved with the former, because a for-profit entity has a direct stake in the variable ('employability') that it claims to measure. As for the latter type of agency, the problem is that their coverage is not comprehensive, and it is precisely the institutions of dubious quality that will evade evaluation. Unless certification is made mandatory and is backed by strong, independent verification and oversight, there will always be scope for (at best) variation in standards or (at worst) widespread corruption.[7] In short, there is no reliable macro measure of the quality of higher education, whether by type of institution, by discipline or faculty, or by state or region.

While the problem of quality manifests itself in every aspect of education—under-qualified or unmotivated teachers, ill-prepared students, institutions lacking basic resources, and lax or absent regulatory bodies—the specificity of higher education imposes further constraints. The most important of these emerges as three interrelated features or, rather, one basic feature with two contradictory consequences. The basic feature of higher education is that it is a 'downstream' phase: in fact, the closing or final stage of the educational cycle before 'educated' students exit into the job market and, more generally, into adult life. In other words, it is the payoff stage of education, the final three or five or more years that will, at long last, enable the long-term investment in the 15 or 20 years of continuous education to begin bringing in returns. This means that the stakes in higher education are very high because it is viewed as an asset that may be quickly encashed.

Being a final stage implicates higher education in two contradictory developments. First, the 'input' into this final stage of education—the already schooled student—has to be taken 'as is' by higher education. If upstream stages of education have not performed their job, and the system allows students to acquire entitlements (minimum qualifications) to higher education without being prepared adequately, then higher education has to bear the brunt of this educational deficit. Given the accumulated nature of the deficit, it is usually impossible to make good within the time and resource constraints of the higher education phase. In brief, the college or university is often asked to do what it simply cannot, viz., compensate for the lack of proper training and skilling at the school level. Of course, it does not mean that this is always the case, or that higher education itself is not to blame, but it does point to the specific predicament of this sector.

On the other hand, because it is the penultimate stage prior to the encashment of a lifetime's investment, higher education can command an irrationally high price. This, in turn, means that higher education can become—and is now established as—a lucrative industry in itself. Expectations of high profits lure powerful players into this arena, with all the attendant consequences. The most visible of these is the politician–higher education nexus that is especially strong in the most lucrative professional–technical fields. As they are able to manipulate the levers of state, politicians are the logical group to emerge as educational entrepreneurs. Not only can they manage the necessary certification and clearances, they are also ideally situated to handle the inflow of black money into the institutions they set up. This creates a sustainable spiral: access to legislative power enables ownership of educational institutions, which enables huge cash earnings, which in turn helps to finance political manoeuvring (including ever more expensive election campaigns) required to stay in power.

Nonetheless, the flourishing of clearly substandard higher educational institutions cannot be explained by politicians and entrepreneurship alone—consumers, too, play a crucial role in reproducing this corrupt system. The market for higher education or, more accurately, for educational credentials, is an abnormal or distorted version of its well behaved theoretical counterpart. In theory, the marketing of recognisably substandard products is supposed to force its producer out of business because consumers will refuse to buy the product. But in India, a credential is valued more for its legal form than its educational content. As long as an 'inflated' degree or certificate (i.e., one that greatly exaggerates the level of competence of its holder) has the same legal status as a more 'genuine' credential, it meets the needs of particular kinds of buyers. These buyers have other resources or entitlements, which will make the true value of the credential irrelevant as long as it is legally recognised.

For example, doctors, lawyers, architects or other professionals, who wish to pass on the 'family business' to their progeny, are happy to use substandard degrees to achieve this objective, confident that their children can be trained 'on-the-job' after acquiring the legal entitlement to practise a profession. Another category of willing buyer comprises those who can acquire jobs through 'influence' (i.e., nepotism of various kinds), as long as they have the legal credentials. A substantial segment of the Indian credential market consists of corrupt buyers who support corrupt producers who are protected by corrupt politicians. Educational 'quality' is undermined by the collusion of the very agents who are required to promote it.[8]

THE 'WEAK' STUDENT

The preceding discussion of the question of the quality and overall context of Indian higher education is necessary in order to understand the phenomenon of the 'weak' student. To begin with, we must carefully distinguish the 'weak' student from the 'bad' student—two very different categories that are often conflated because they are both marked by poor academic performance.

The 'bad' student is an agential and individualised category; it arises from the choices made by the agent or his/her personal attributes, e.g., the refusal to put in the requisite work, or a lower-than-average level of intrinsic ability or intelligence. By contrast, a 'weak' student is a structural category that has little do with agency, personal choices or individual attributes. The 'weak' student is one whose educational training has been deficient, and who does not have access to the forms of social or cultural capital that can offset these deficiencies. Therefore, the student's 'weakness' is not due to any individual traits, but to the educational and social milieu to which he/she belongs. The 'weak' student is thus the individualised bearer of systemic and social deficiencies, and deficits. Of course, the distinction between 'weak' and 'bad' is conceptual and not empirical:

any concrete individual could embody aspects of both categories. Nonetheless, the distinction is an important one because it is critical for grasping the true nature and scale of the challenges facing higher education today.

For the sake of simplicity, let us construct a basic two-sector model of higher education comprising an elite and a mass sector, while deliberately postponing definitions for the moment. Since mass-sector institutions are themselves weak, the 'weak' student is the ubiquitous rule rather than the rare exception. Precisely because of this ubiquity, the 'weak' student cannot be seen as an anomaly, but must be considered an inevitable norm. This, in turn, implies that the phenomenon of the 'weak' student does not appear as itself in the mass sector, but as what it really is, viz., the natural product of *weak institutions*. The focus of attention is rightly shifted to substandard institutions rather than substandard students, and thus to the quality of education rather than the quality of students.

The insight offered by this simplistic model is that the 'weak' student appears as such only in the elite sector of higher education because it is here that this category is juxtaposed to the 'strong' or 'well-prepared' student. In fact, this contrast gives meaning to the category of the 'weak' student. But, because in this case the context is an elite rather than a mass institution, the phenomenon of the 'weak' student tends to be seen as an individual rather than an institutional problem. Even when the institutional contribution to the making of the 'weak' student is recognised, it is attributed to *other* institutions at the school or undergraduate levels. The point is that elite higher educational institutions see the 'weak' student as an unfair burden imposed from the outside and, therefore, as a burden that it can legitimately refuse to bear.

The perception of an unjust imposition is greatly magnified because of the role of 'politics', understood here in its popular pejorative sense. From the point of view of the elite institution, it is political pressure that has produced interventions, such as the 93rd Amendment, opening the floodgates of reservation and swamping previously vibrant institutions with an unmanageable influx of 'weak' students. While the interpretation of causal factors and processes may be debated, there is much that is undeniable in terms of sheer empirical fact. Although the 'weak' student has been a longstanding presence in elite institutions, this category has been a marginal one in every sense. Not only has it been neglected and is powerless and peripheral, it has also involved a numerically small minority. Today, the 'weak' student is at least a substantial plurality, and often a large majority. One crucial aspect of the multidimensional crisis that besets elite institutions today is that they are being forced to deal with a type of student that they were never designed to handle.

Contrary to the dominant view, it is not true that the 'weak' student is an exclusively lower caste, or caste-based reservation phenomenon. However, it is true that lower castes are greatly over-represented among 'weak' students. But while a significant proportion of 'weak' students is also from upper-caste, first-generation learners, the proportion of lower-caste students among 'well-prepared' students is still very small. It is also important to note that caste-based reservations are not the only form of reservation and, sometimes, they may not even be the most important. Various forms of explicit (as different from implicit or defacto) reservation exist for the already privileged: prominent examples being reservation for own-institution graduates/alumni, and the infamous 'management quota' in private institutions and 'self-financing' segments of public institutions. The contribution that these types of quotas make to the 'weak' student population is usually ignored, while that of caste-based reservation is made to bear the burden of all evils.

The elite university has responded in different ways to the situation of the 'weak' student being the majority of its student body. The first is, of course, sheer inaction, which results in raised drop-out and failure rates as ill-prepared students fail to cope with the level and amount of work expected from them. But because high failure rates eventually invite pressure from above (politicians, higher administration) as well as below (students), most institutions tend to gravitate towards the path of least resistance, which is to 'pass' students by relaxing the standards they are required to meet. This is not explicitly discussed or decided, but begins to take place 'spontaneously' as a logical consequence of the balance of forces as it is the path of least resistance for all involved. Simply passing students is much easier for teachers than the tougher option of going above and beyond the formal requirements of their job in order to spend extra time and effort to address educational deficits. For most students, being passed is the preferable way out rather than putting in the very hard work of trying to compensate for the deficiencies in training they have accumulated over the years. Finally, parents and administrators are also happy because everything seems to be proceeding smoothly.

It is also true that numerous efforts are continuously being made to tackle the problem head-on by mobilising resources for 'remedial' efforts of various kinds. These include special mentoring and tutoring sessions; help with the translation of materials from English into Indian languages; formal and informal peer-to-peer learning groups; and, confidence-building measures of various kinds. Official committees appointed to address the post-admission requirements of beneficiaries of reservation have made suggestions along these lines, and there also exist formal UGC guidelines for the creation of these support systems. The creation of resource materials in Indian languages is one concrete option that will have a massive impact and is also amenable to easy institutionalisation. However, this is deceptive because what is actually needed is not just the passive translation of texts, but the active cultivation of demand, and the ability to engage with them. This requires much more than just funds.[9]

However, for the most part, such efforts are voluntary initiatives undertaken by teachers and students, with or without formal support from the administration. As such, they pay the price for not being institutionalised because they run out of steam eventually, as the individuals involved move on (students) or become exhausted (teachers). Nevertheless, such efforts do have a significant impact on the university community, and need to be sustained and nurtured. For this, institutionalisation is a necessary first step, but insufficient in itself without the commitment of a critical mass of teachers, students and administrators.

DEMOCRATISATION AND ELITE INSTITUTIONS

At this historical moment, the phenomenon of the 'weak' student raises two important questions that need a lot more attention than they have received. The first question concerns the nature and role of 'elite' institutions. There are two popular definitions of such institutions, and dominant common sense tends to conflate the two. In a given society, one perceives elite institutions in intellectual terms as centres of excellence and thus superior to similar, but 'ordinary', institutions of the same kind. The other definition emphasises a social perspective, and recognises elite institutions as exclusive in the sense that their membership is restricted to the wealthy and/or powerful minority of society. The natural tendency in most societies is for the two definitions to converge or to at least overlap significantly. The 'best' institutions are the most coveted, and the powerful have better access than average citizens to what is coveted; hence, institutions that are elite, in the intellectual sense, would tend to be dominated by those that are elite in the social sense.

There is no doubt that the advent of modernity requires not only the separation of the two definitions (so that the one need not imply the other), but that the intellectual sense takes precedence over the social as well. After all, this is what meritocracy implies, and modernity, at least at the formal level, is firmly committed to meritocracy. But tradition has found many ingenious ways of deceiving modernity and getting its own way, with elite education being an obvious example. Historically, centres of excellence have never been democratic in any easy or natural way—they have had to be forced to open their doors to the non-elite.

This brings us to the second question posed by the category of the 'weak' student: How is this democratisation to be achieved, i.e., how do we kill the elite higher educational institution as a monopoly of the social elite, while keeping it alive as a site for the training of the intellectual elite?

History teaches us that this is a formidable challenge, because it involves 'capturing' an institution without harming its intellectual health or its institutional stability. This is almost impossible to do precisely because democratisation necessarily involves large numbers of 'weak' students entering elite institutions. Such situations tend to invite a decline in intellectual standards because this is the easiest option for all the main stakeholders, viz., students, teachers and the state. The temptation to follow a 'scorched earth' policy is very real and very strong, as is demonstrated by many historical examples. It has often been argued that the destruction of institutions is a necessary price—collateral damage—to be paid for the greater good of a more egalitarian society. China's Cultural Revolution in the mid-1960s is probably the best-known example. But there is also one closer to home—Bihar of the 1980s, presided over by Laloo Prasad Yadav. It is said that Yadav admitted to deliberately allowing the universities of Bihar to decay because they were the strongholds of his arch enemy, the upper castes. Now into his third innings as one of the most astute politicians of our times, Yadav has assuredly realised the shortsightedness of his former strategy. Higher educational institutions are surprisingly vulnerable entities—they can flourish only in a limited range of environments and are rarely resilient enough to recover from serious damage. That is why the means and the methods used in the struggle to democratise them are as important as the goal. Democratising our universities without destroying them is the almost impossible task that we must collectively undertake, with our hopes pinned to the word 'almost'.

On the other hand, the elite public university is today the most likely site where democratisation could actually occur. The best students and teachers congregate in institutions with the best facilities. These are also the institutions with the most autonomy, although the space for this has been shrinking in the past decade. Regional universities are today far too constrained by funding and political interference to play a leading role. And private institutions will not be hospitable to such efforts because of the nature of the business model they embody. Thus, it is not accidental that the most productive efforts for empowering 'weak' students have been located in elite institutions such as some of the IITs, IIMs and Central Universities. Our task, then, is to sustain existing efforts, and to create conditions for the imagining of more and better ways of democratising the one resource that can make a significant impact on social inequality.

◆

NOTES

1. 'Stand-alone' colleges, which are not affiliated to any university, and mostly grant vocational or professional diplomas, are excluded from this estimate, mainly because a large proportion of such institutions have not participated in AISHE.
2. Since the PWD category cannot be subdivided by caste and community, it is left within the Hindu upper caste. Given its size, the number of non-upper caste (or non-Hindu) persons who might be miscounted as Hindu upper castes because of this assumption is going to be extremely small.
3. As caste has not been counted in the Census since independence, there is no authoritative data on the population of upper castes, but since most other groups have been counted at one time or another, the estimate of 15–20 per cent is

likely to be correct. Just by way of comparison, racially 'white' South Africans constitute about 9 per cent of the total population, though there are significant differences across age groups—whites are more than 20 per cent of the above-65 and less than 5 per cent of the under-5 age groups.

4. The 2001 figures are from the Report, *Educational Statistics at a Glance*, Bureau of Planning, Monitoring and Statistics, MHRD, New Delhi, 2014. The 2013–14 figures are from AISHE, 2013–14, published in 2015.
5. For example, the benchmarking studies associated with the World Bank-supported Sarva Shiksha Abhiyan.
6. The most cited (at least in the media) example is the 'National Employability Report' produced by a private company called Aspiring Minds, which describes itself as 'India's leading employability solutions company'.
7. As in the infamous instance of the Medical Council of India (MCI), whose former chairman was convicted of taking bribes to certify private medical colleges, yet was re-nominated to the executive council of the IMC, and may even be in the running to head the World Medical Council! More generally, the widespread involvement of politicians in the private education sector ensures that dubious institutions flourish under political protection and patronage.
8. See Deshpande (2012) for more on the 'distorted credential market'.
9. For a detailed discussion, see the Report, *Social Science Teaching in Hindi*, available at: http://cscs.res.in/dataarchive/textfiles/social-science-teaching-in-india. inventory-and-analysis-of-current-curricular.pdf/

REFERENCES

Deshpande, Satish. 2012. 'Social Justice and Higher Education in India Today: Markets, Ideologies and Inequalities in a Fluid Context', in Martha Nussbaum and Zoya Hasan (eds.), *Equalizing Access: Affirmative Action in Higher Education in India, United States and South Africa.* New Delhi: Oxford University Press.

Janson, Jonathan D. 2009. *Knowledge in the Blood: Confronting Race in the Apartheid Past.* Stanford: Stanford University Press.

◆◆

FREE TO CHOOSE OR FREE TO LOSE?

Debating 'Ability to Pay' for Education

MANABI MAJUMDAR
SANGRAM MUKHERJEE

INTRODUCTION

This is the age of privatisation in, and of, education. Across the globe there seems to reverberate a zealous admiration for rising private aspirations for schooling and growing private efforts for their fruition. Indeed, the family strategy approach to education seems to overshadow the alternative view that public vision and action are critical factors to secure social opportunities and conditions for universal schooling. To be sure, there is no ineluctable trade-off between collective endeavour and private enterprise in education and, hence, there is no reason why we should be forced to choose between the two. Disconcertingly, however, there is a growing tendency amongst scholars, policymakers and even amongst sections of the community to view anything 'public' as wasteful and irretrievably impaired, and to then use that already 'opinionated' opinion to posit a false binary between public and private educational initiatives. What is more, there is an attempt to nudge or even force the public to rely more and more on their individuated and isolated efforts to actualise their educational goals, thereby allowing private responsibility to 'crowd out' collective culpability for educational progress.

Foregrounding family obligations for educating children is often couched in the idiom of 'choice', the family's 'ability' and 'willingness' to pay for their children's education, and even in bold terms such as 'parentocracy' (Nogueira, 2010), to convey the idea of parents being in the driving seat. Admittedly, the educational activism of upper- and upper-middle-class parents suggests a model of middle-class control of both educational imagination and practice, which more often than not zeros in on fierce competition for educational credentials and excessive examination orientation. Indeed, we can ill afford to ignore the role of educational preferences and educational strategies that privileged sections of parents pursue in shaping the very contours of educational thinking of our times. To borrow from Lareau (2003), the 'concerted cultivation' by have-enough parents of schooling and skilling opportunities for their children unmistakably reveals the force of the idea of parental choice. This acknowledged, excessive focus on individual educational 'choice', however, tends to obfuscate the utter centrality of the 'voice' of a collective, whose network of collaboration and cooperation is essential to inspire public solutions to public educational deficiencies.

FREE TO CHOOSE OR FREE TO LOSE?

The choice versus voice debate, however, is not the central concern of this paper. Rather, we aim to complicate the notion of choice itself by underlining its class-differentiated nature. More concretely, we focus on private/household expenditure on schooling, which is routinely and straightforwardly taken to be the 'revealed preference' of parents, signifying allegedly both their willingness and ability to pay for their children's education. To problematise this rather benign, social division-blind, notion of parental ability, we closely examine widespread inequalities in private expenditure on education across various social classes to then find out whether, for certain sections of parents, the so-called ability is actually a burden and whether for them the 'freedom to choose' is, for all practical purposes, a 'freedom to lose', as Roemer (1988) argues.

In highlighting inequality in household spending on education our aim here is not to diminish the importance of parental striving, including that of indigent parents, for the educational progress of their children. It would be unacceptably patriarchal to do so. But, since unequal private investments can hardly level the educational playing field, their effects need to be factored in for any debate on parental choice.

It is well to acknowledge that the involvement of private actors, let alone of households, in education is not new. Also, it is unhelpful to start with a view that the idea of the private is necessarily bad (Macpherson, *et al.* 2014). What is new, however, about the privatised model of education in recent times is its '....scale, scope and penetration into almost all aspects of the education endeavour' and its predominantly commercial ethos which conceptualises the learner as a consumer and education as a consumer good (ibid.). Our discussion on private spending on education is set within this larger laudatory climate in favour of private, even for-profit, educational pursuits, to the relative neglect of their onerous effects on some sections of the population. Two examples, presented below, set the tone of our discussion that follows.

It was sometime in 2012. One of our colleagues was interviewing an urban family of three in a district of West Bengal, which was surviving on the meagre income of a single daily-wage earner. Yet the family strove hard to pay for supplementary private coaching of their school-going daughter; at the time of this interview they reported skipping dinner for two consecutive days in order to arrange for her coaching fee. This hardship—this 'well-being compromising ability'—forces one to revisit the notion of purchasing power, since in situations like this it is rather disempowering. It makes us question the virtue of a system in which unless one has a certain amount of resources to simultaneously hone one's core capabilities, one is only 'free to lose'.

Let us turn to another example of the 'ability' to make an ad hoc purchase of education as a commodity which entails the accompanying incapacity to continue schooling on a sustained basis. A student studying in an Omega school in Ghana that functions under the system of paying on a daily basis (part of the Omega Schools Franchise—a Low Fee Private School [LFPS] chain) said, 'I sell water on the streets one day so I can go to school the next' (Riep, 2014). For reasons like this, a sizable section of the student body is absent every day. The LFPS advocates claim that these schools have both efficiency and equity advantages. However, the so-called equity advantages will materialise for this Ghanaian girl only if she is able to participate in 'school life' in a regular and sustained manner and thus improve her 'school life expectancy'. It is time, therefore, to probe deeper into the patterns of private spending on education.

More specifically, the focus of this paper is on school education, and our analysis draws on calculations of unit level data of 2014 culled from the 71st round of the National Sample Survey Organization (NSSO, 2015).

Ideally, a comparison of household and government/private management expenditure on schooling would have revealed more in order to learn whether public expenditure support (or even investment on the part of private school management) could ease the family burden and costs of schooling, especially of disprivileged families. Some recent studies compare the per student government expenditure incurred on children studying in government elementary schools and per student expenditure by households on students attending private elementary schools and conclude that government schools are 'very inefficient' in that they produce 'such low levels of learning at such high cost' (Pritchett and Aiyar, 2014). Bhatty, *et al.* (2015), however, make a powerful counterargument by showing basic methodological and conceptual problems that beset the former class of analysis. They compellingly argue that public expenditure on education caters to broader, and systemic, functions and tasks that shape the contours of the entire system of education (including a considerable share—17 per cent—of governmental educational expenditure on non-government schools), and that its efficiency and equity effects need to be assessed with respect to such broader objectives. The present paper is limited in its scope in that it does not delve into comparisons of public versus household expenditure on education. Our focus is restricted only to asymmetries in household spending on education.

WHEN 'ABILITY TO PAY' IS STARKLY UNEQUAL

It is a truism worth repeating that the size of the purse matters as far as family expenses on education are concerned, and that some people are far less able to pay than others. This is by no means surprising; but because we remain unsurprised we seldom step down from the generalities of lopsided spending patterns to probe deeper into the actual spread and depth of such asymmetry. This paper aims to cull out and analyse available data on household educational expenditure in order to build up an evidence-based account of the yawning gap that exists between household investments of parents from different class backgrounds, who are vastly 'differently able' to privately finance their children's schooling. These micro-details, we hold, are important to infer the macro-picture of educational opportunity, or its lack, in the country at a time when the education system itself is becoming increasingly market-oriented.

Such marketisation, some scholars argue, enables poorer parents to buy 'quality' education at affordable costs, and hence is not only efficient but also equity-enhancing. And this so-called 'win-win' situation happens mainly through the workings of the LFPS. Kingdon (2016), in a recent essay, shows that according to the National Sample Survey 2014, for all the high- and low-fee private unaided primary schools taken together, the median fee in rural India was ₹300 per month and the corresponding figure was ₹416 in urban India. This amount, many would think, is affordable by large sections of parents. Two concerns may be voiced here, though. One, the median monthly per capita expenditure (MPCE) in rural India in the same year was ₹1,166, and the corresponding figure in urban India was ₹2,000. This means that a little over 25 per cent of the median monthly per capita expenditure was used up for primary schooling in the so-called low-fee unaided schools in rural India (a little over 20 per cent in urban India). Two, apart from school fees that this study refers to, households need to spend significant amounts on books, stationery, transport and privately paid coaching. Taken together, the household burden, therefore, becomes heavier, which in turn raises the question of how 'low' is the low level of spending, just as it is apt to ask how 'free' is free schooling (Tilak, 1996).

Furthermore, aggregated measures of household spending hide more than they reveal; mean educational expenditure masks distributional inequalities across social classes, while median expenditure provides only a partial picture of the same. But inequality in private spending by both the indigent and affluent is huge, and it is this stark disparity that contributes to the reproduction rather than reduction of inequality in their children's educational participation and progress. Therefore, it is hardly surprising that the children of these two unmatched sections of parents are unequally socially positioned. We set out to probe deeper into the patterns of such inequality.

Members of households—individuals—are grouped into the MPCE quintile classes, ranging from the poorest (first) to the richest (fifth), in order to then furnish details of the quantum of their educational spending and the inequalities therein (Figure 1). Educational expenditure itself is classified under various heads to include school/course fees; transportation costs; payments on books, uniforms and other stationeries; and expenses on paid coaching as well as 'other' costs. It is obvious that the household expenditure on children studying in government schools is much lower than the corresponding figure for those studying in private aided or private unaided schools. This result is true for every level of school education, both in rural and urban areas, using whichever statistical measure we consider for comparison—mean or median. The highest gap across quintile classes is observable in the case of course fees/ school fees—ranging from ₹63 per student from the poorest households to ₹846 per pupil from the richest families in a month. This once again appears to be obvious, and this gap is consistent, although not in magnitude, across almost all the heads under which NSSO provides information on household expenditure.[1]

Figure 1. Distribution of Students by Type of School Attended and Reliance on Private Coaching Cross-classified by Quintile Class of Monthly Per Capita Expenditure (MPCE)

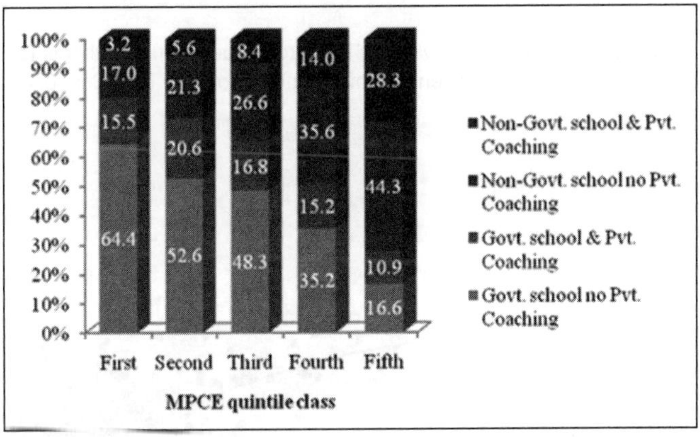

Importantly, the proportion of students of government schools availing of private coaching (26.2 per cent) is marginally lower than that of private school pupils availing of extra coaching (28.1 per cent); this indicates that the need for private coaching is felt equally amongst students of government and non-government schools.[2] The expenditure on transportation varies across MPCE classes, perhaps for expected reasons—from ₹22 per month per student from the poorest expenditure class to ₹248 per student per month from the richest economic class. Children from deprived sections mostly attend government schools for obvious cost implications; and government schools outnumber private schools by a great margin. The relative abundance of government schools ensures that these schools are within the reach of their pupils, and their comparative physical proximity helps lower transportation costs of their pupils. There is indeed clear evidence that private schools tend to undersupply services in difficult-to-access areas in the country that suffer from a scarcity of amenities and sparse population; these are often the areas that are peopled by those from disadvantaged socio-economic backgrounds. As Figure 2 shows, the district-wise share of private schools declines as the share of rural schools increases. It also declines as the percentage of schools with less than 50 students increases; similarly, the share of private schools drops with the declining share of schools with an all-weather approach road. All this implies that children attending private schools usually need to travel long distances in comparative terms, leading to a higher household spending on transportation.

Figure 2. Distribution of Districts by Percentage of Rural Schools to Total Schools and Percentage of Private Schools to Total Schools

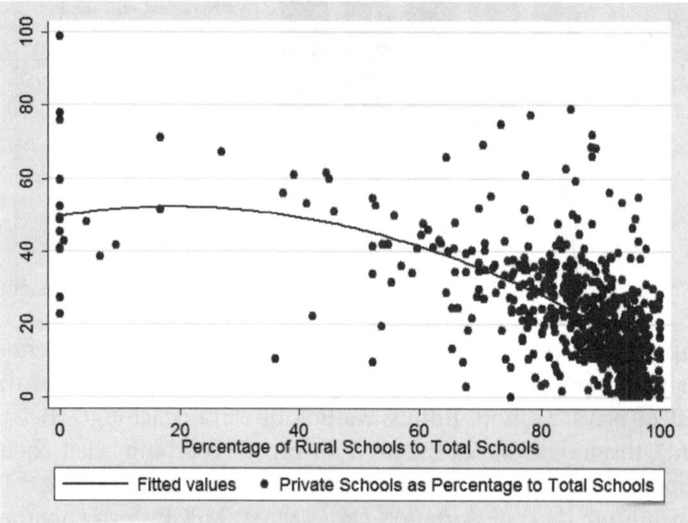

Source: Calculated from District Report, 2013–14, NUEPA.

In a nutshell, the economically disadvantaged expenditure groups—a proxy for low-income classes—have two available ways by which they can somewhat reduce the burden of private expenditure for their school-going children: first, by skipping private schools and thereby reducing school fees; and, second, by foregoing, in a relative sense, private coaching. Both these family strategies are clearly deducible from Figure 1. Similar averting is noticeable among various social categories, STs, SCs and OBCs in the same order. In recent times, not much variation is observed in terms of per capita private expenditure on the education of girls and boys. Privately paid supplementary coaching appears more and more as an inevitable correlate of schooling expenses in contemporary India and across its constituent states. Importantly, patterns of spending on extra tuition across expenditure classes do not yield any unequivocal verdict in favour of the argument that it is only those who need extra help who reach out for it, either because of their own shortcomings or because of quality deficits in schools they attend. On the contrary, students of all abilities—mediocre to meritorious, and from all types of schools—elite to low-fee to government, avail of, and spend on, private coaching. This certainly complicates the notion of 'affordable' private education. From Figure 1, it is evident that in any particular monthly per capita expenditure quintile class, almost equal proportions of students across government and non-government schools avail of private coaching, although this proportion increases from 18.7 per cent to 39.2 per cent across these classes, further corroborating our claim made earlier that not much variation in the pattern of availing of private coaching is observed across school management. The quantum of household spending on supplementary private tutoring, however, varies significantly in the country, from a monthly per capita payment of ₹404 in the most well-to-do families, to the corresponding figure of ₹59 in the least advantaged families.

WHEN THE COST OF SCHOOLING IS PROHIBITIVE

In the discussion on household spending on education, the sections that usually remain outside the purview of analysis are of those children of school-going age who do not attend school. The NSSO 71st round data reveals that amongst the children aged 6–14, an overall 4.79 per cent never attended a school of any type; in addition, 2.96 per cent of children of the same age group were not going to school at the time of the survey. This suggests that 7.75 per cent children in the 6–14 age group were out of school at the time of the survey. If we look at the distribution of these children across expenditure classes, we find the expected but extremely dispiriting pattern: the percentage of school children for the first, i.e., the most poverty-stricken MPCE quintile class, is 13.56 per cent, which rapidly tapers down to 8.8, 6.7, 3.8, and only 1.2 per cent for the second, third, fourth and fifth MPCE quintile classes, respectively. It is well to point out that financial constraints feature as one of the main reasons (20.5 per cent) for children remaining out of school. Some of the other reasons cited also allude to financial hardship faced by these children, as 10.84 per cent reported being engaged in domestic activities, whereas 3.85 per cent were directly engaged in economic activity at such an early age.

If, for some children from poorer families, joining school itself remains an unaffordable luxury, for others from similar socio-economic backgrounds staying in school beyond the elementary level becomes increasingly onerous largely because of considerable private costs of schooling at the secondary level and beyond. For certain sections of students, therefore, it becomes hard to improve their 'school life expectancy' by making a successful transition from the elementary to the post-elementary level. In more concrete terms, e.g., from the most impoverished households in rural India, secondary school participation is only 8.9 per cent, whereas it is 17.5 per cent from the richest households. In urban India, the corresponding figures are 9.4 per cent and 16.3 per cent, respectively. The much lower rate of secondary school participation amongst economically deprived sections of society, in contrast to their privileged peers has, surely, many reasons. Undoubtedly, one of them includes the cost burden that households have to put up with. We try to infer the disproportionate weight of such costs that fall on the bent shoulders of indigent parents by making a comparison with the relative ease with which the privileged meet such costs (Table 1). More elaborately, we look at the range or the band of household per capita schooling expenses—from the minimum to the maximum spent by the least and the most solvent classes, respectively, at elementary and secondary levels—and then ask whether expenses that poorer households have to inescapably bear at either elementary or secondary level is modest in comparison to what the most affluent spend at these levels of education.

Table 1. The Disproportionate Burden of Secondary Schooling on Indigent Families, India, 2014.

	Rural			Urban		
	Monthly Per capita Expenditure (Mean) ₹	Monthly Per capita Expenditure on Education ₹		Monthly Per capita Expenditure (Mean) ₹	Monthly Per capita Expenditure on Education ₹	
		Elementary	Secondary		Elementary	Secondary
The Poorest Quintile MPCE Class	525	92	292	909	296	509
The Richest Quintile MPCE Class	2391	649	941	5407	2438	2881
The Ratio of Spending by the poorest to that by the richest	0.26	0.14	0.31	0.17	0.12	0.18

Source: Calculated from NSSO, 2015.

The figures presented in Table 1 suggest that at the elementary level the expenditure band is comparatively broad, i.e., poorer households can get by with lesser payments in comparison to those made by affluent parents. This is perhaps due to the expansion of public provisioning of education under the aegis of the newly introduced Right to Education Act. In contrast, at the secondary level the expenditure band enveloping the most impoverished and the most solvent classes is much narrower. This implies that the essential expenditure that indigent families cannot help making, to make sure that their children continue secondary education, is substantial. And this is particularly the case in rural India (although the same pattern also holds true for urban India), where the ratio of what the most impoverished classes need to pay to buy secondary education to what the richest classes pay for the same services is the highest. Put another way, the inadequacy of affordable secondary schooling facilities in rural areas makes it extremely difficult for the poorer children to complete secondary schooling. It is hardly surprising, therefore, that participation at the post-elementary level is extremely limited among disprivileged children. Therefore, blanket advocacy in favour of parental choice along with vociferous claims about their ability to pay, irrespective of their social position, may not take us far in achieving wider secondary school participation from all sections of society. A quick analysis of NSSO 2014 data on the expenditure class-wise distribution of grade repeaters in schools of rural India shows that about 24 per cent of them belong to the lowest expenditure class, whereas the corresponding share is only 15 per cent for the highest quintile class. For disadvantaged families, therefore, there is a higher risk of bearing a double burden which makes school completion that much more difficult for their children.

What remains unaddressed in this paper is the broader question of the quality of the 'commodity' that parents find and select in the education bazaar. This question is utterly germane to any discussion on parental choice. In theory, the expansion of consumer choice is likely to bring about improvements in the quality of the goods and services in question. But the private domain of educational provisioning, especially the sector that ostensibly caters to the children from poorer families, is a 'territory of informational limitation and asymmetry'. Thus, impoverished parents are mismatched with their well-heeled cohorts not only in terms of their ability to pay, but also in terms of their informational grip on the quality and relevance of educational services that are on offer in an excessively commercialised education market.[3] For a more rounded analysis of the right to educational choice, the entanglement of issues of ability and quality deserves greater scrutiny.

CONCLUSION

This paper is a preliminary and necessarily limited analysis of widely yawning inequalities in household educational expenditure. Such disparities are part of common knowledge, part of a normalised reality, but not part of an inclination to carefully collate evidence on the scope and depth of the asymmetries in the spending power of families, so that in the light of such credible information remedial action can be taken in order to better equalise educational opportunities for children of all classes. We try to argue that we need to pay heed to the class-differentiated pattern of household educational spending, and acknowledge that some people suffer more than others when they are driven to rely more and more on their personal wherewithal at the expense of social spending on user fees at the expense of tax-financed public expenditure. If we fail to accept and act on this simple but profound truth, in the name of advocating parental autonomy and choice, we may end up ensuring for a large section of parents only the freedom to lose. This by no means suggests that private actors, especially family members, have no role to play in educating the country's boys and girls. Nor is it an attempt to posit a false dichotomy between individual preference and public action. Rather, our aim here is to counter the concerted advocacy, in recent times, of an evidence-indifferent conviction that public education is doomed to fail and that the only redemption is through atomised, individuated and isolated private efforts. This line of thinking, however, glosses over the fact that individual families are very 'differently abled' to single-handedly take care of their children's schooling; some of them are in a vastly better position than others to buy education for their children and hence to secure their position of advantage in future. The converse of this relative advantage is, of course, the relative deprivation of the children of other hapless families.

The broader argument, if only implied in this paper, is about the need to concede that individual freedom is, essentially, a social commitment (Sen, 1998). Whether parents have the freedom to choose or lose with respect to educational fortunes of their children depends, crucially, upon the presence or absence of enabling social conditions. The right to educational choice, unavoidably, requires collectively nurtured conditions that allow parents to choose.

◆

NOTES

1. NSSO procures information regarding expenditure on course fees, books, stationery and uniform, transport, coaching and other costs, separately.
2. Non-government schools include private aided and private unaided schools.
3. Some of these questions have been raised in Majumdar (2014).

REFERENCES

Bhatty, Kiran, Anuradha De and Rathin Roy. 2015. 'The Public Education System and what the Costs Imply', *Economic and Political Weekly*, vol. 50, no.31.

Kingdon, Geeta Gandhi. 2016. 'Schooling without Learning', *The Hindu*, 8 February.

Lareau, Annette. 2003. *Unequal Childhoods: Class, Race and Family Life*. Berkeley: University of California Press.

Macpherson, Ian, Susan Robertson and Geoffrey Walford (eds.). 2014. 'Introduction.' *Education, Privatisation and Social Justice: Case Studies from Africa, South Asia and South East Asia.* Didcot, Oxford: Symposium Books.

Majumdar, Manabi. 2014. 'The Shadow School System and New Class Divisions in India', TRG Poverty and Education Working Paper Series, paper 2, Max Weber Stiftung.

NSSO (National Sample Survey Organization). 2015. *India: Social Consumption–Education Survey, 2014*, NSSO 71st Round, New Delhi.

NEUPA (National University of Educational Planning and Administration). 2013–2014. *District Report Cards.*

Nogueira, Maria Alice. 2010. 'A Revisited Theme: Middle Classes and the School', in Michael W. Apple, Stephen J. Ball and Luis Armando Gandin (eds.),*The Routledge Handbook of the Sociology of Education*. New York: Routledge.

Pritchett, Lant and Yamini Aiyar. 2014. 'Value Subtraction in Public Sector Production: Accounting Versus Economic Cost of Primary Schooling in India', Centre for Global Development, Working Paper 391, December.

Riep, Curtis B. 2014. 'Omega Schools Franchise in Ghana: "Affordable" Private Education for the Poor or For-profiteering?', in Ian Macpherson, Susan Robertson and Geoffrey Walford (eds.), *Education, Privatisation and Social Justice: Case Studies from Africa, South Asia and South East Asia.* Didcot, Oxford: Symposium Books.

Roemer, John E. 1988. *Free to Lose*. Cambridge, MA: Harvard University Press.

Sen, Amartya. 1998. 'Individual Freedom as Social Commitment', *India International Centre Quarterly*, volumes 25&26, Winter 1998–Spring 1999.

Tilak, J. B. G. 'How Free is "Free" Primary Education in India', *Economic and Political Weekly*, vol. 31, 1996.

◆◆

PARENTING AT SCHOOL

A Case for Re-imagining School Spaces

SALAI SELVAM
V. GEETHA

In 2012–13, we undertook a study that started out as an interrogation of parenting practices amongst different social segments. However, it did not remain that. Instead, the study metamorphosed into one showing how parents from extremely marginal communities view and engage with the school, both as a normative entity and a specific institution. The content of that study forms the basis of this article.

Disparate reasons came together to focus our attention on parenting practices. One set of reasons has to do with the pervasive violence that marks adult–children interactions in particular contexts that border on the abusive, suggesting levels of dysfunctional behaviour that have not been addressed or probed. For instance, shocking revelations about how care homes are run have featured in the news for some time now, prompting the Tamil Nadu government to get stricter with permissions, monitoring and general surveillance. Children have been starved, made to labour at tasks not suitable for them and, in some instances, subjected to sexual abuse. There are stories of children being locked up in rooms for days, as punishment.[1] Less dramatic, but equally shocking, is the psychological violence that children experience at home in families beset by unstable conjugal arrangements. While this does not make news, listening to children refer casually to various incidents at home has been a sobering experience.[2]

If hurting children appeared worrisome, the adult inability to communicate with them seemed an equally pervasive problem. For instance, there has been an increasing number of teen suicides in Tamil Nadu, usually around the time exam results are announced.[3]

Many of these take place at home and have never failed to shock parents, who cannot understand how their child had arrived at this decision. Likewise, parents are clueless when it comes to their children making 'adult' decisions—for instance, they continue to be in denial about the so-called 'runaway' marriage phenomenon, when girls from Class 8 upward are lured by older men, often in their 20s, or even 30s. On the other hand, parents are known to marry off girls early to prevent such an eventuality. When the former comes to pass, parents are indignant and inclined to blame school authorities for not being sufficiently vigilant, rather than turn the searchlight on to their own parenting practices.[4]

Side by side with these realities exist others: for one, more than at any other time in the recent past, parents are vocal about 'parenting'. This is evident by their interest in 'parenting' manuals, counsellors, and their contribution to sophisticated 'advice' columns, which speak a new language of caring and raising children. Mainly from the middle and upper middle classes, and mostly from the so-called dominant castes, parents from this segment appear to want to do the right thing by their children, not only to encourage them to 'achieve' things, but also expand their experiences through arranging their leisure time, so that children play, swim, dance, learn an instrument or sing. Yet, this is not as straightforward as it seems: there is an anxiety that drives these parenting efforts, which can be as punishing for the child as direct violence. For, the child becomes an object of intense attention and even surveillance; she is disciplined into a mode of existence that she cannot entirely protest against, resist or transform. Clearly, violence and obsessive care mirror each other in complex ways, and embody the adult inability to engage imaginatively with the messy richness of childhood.

Both these responses appear to be signs of the times, with children embodying hope as well as helplessness. Attempts to discipline, punish and mould them have as much to do with adult modes of living through changes that are at once economic and social: recasting of livelihood, labour, familial and social relationships and, importantly, practices of the state, whether through the school or the punitive justice system, which impinge on the experience of childhood.

In order to make sense of this contradictory reality, in our context, we decided to undertake a study of how parents image their hopes, fears and plans for their future, with respect to their children. We chose the context of education to examine these emotions and ideas by means of which we would try and grasp how parents view learning, the school—both as a normative ideal and a specific institution—their relationship to the school, their expectations from it, and their own role in the schooling process. We started out by evolving a detailed questionnaire in discussion with a group of teachers, education rights activists and interested parents. The questions were straightforward and based on the criteria parents employ when it comes to selecting schools for girls and boys, and if different concerns guide them in doing so; their involvement in their children's school life, including attendance at parent–teacher meetings; their unease about specific practices in their children's schools, or, alternately, their approval of existing arrangements; and their expectations from schools, which were not at present being fulfilled, both with respect to the curriculum as well as caring for the children in a more fundamental sense. Once the questions were in place, we identified particular social segments to which we would take the questionnaire: specific peasant and artisanal communities, especially those that occupy the lower rungs of rural society; state employees, particularly district and *taluq*-level workers; professionals, including teachers and lawyers; and working-class people who labour in factories or in the non-formal sector. We wanted also to ensure that we covered dominant 'backward' as well as Dalit families. Being feminists, deploying a gender lens to what we expected to find was central to our method and understanding.

While the questionnaire seemed easy enough to use, we were dismayed by the responses after a few rounds of soliciting information. The parents we approached initially were mostly from lower-middle-class families, resident in medium-sized towns, clearly belonging to an aspirational class of professionals such as teachers and government employees, and mostly from the backward and most-backward castes. We spoke to a few Dalit families as well, from the same aspirational class of families. Perhaps this influenced their responses as, whether Dalits or others, parents saw themselves as being swept away by the momentum of 'development' and, therefore, did not wish to discuss further the contradictions that lie at the heart of this process.

In effect, these parents 'performed' for us, in that they represented themselves as ideal care-givers, and even when they voiced demands, did so in a register that was both appropriate and politically correct. Thus, they would express their doubts about the usefulness of a given school practice, and wonder about the arbitrary, disciplinary methods that schools used or, alternately, lamented the absence of such methods; but they did not offer us what we expected: their sense of uneven, unequal relationships in which children were placed at school, the pressure exerted on them at home and, further, the many inadequacies of the school system. Nor did they speak of their dilemmas as parents in a fast-changing world.

Not satisfied with the monotonous responses that our questionnaires elicited, we decided to change track. We wondered if we ought not to, in free-wheeling fashion, speak to parents whom we could meet directly, rather than through questionnaires. We decided also to speak with teachers and hostel wardens to get a sense of their interactions with parents. When we began identifying parents, and parent groups to this end, we decided to start with those from marginal social groups—even within the spectrum of families whose children go to government schools—and then go on to talk to others. We broadly defined the term marginal to include within that category Dalit and Adivasi families; households comprising parents who worked for nearly 14 hours a day, being engaged in either construction work or sanitary labour; those from nomadic and semi-nomadic communities, who did not speak the local language, and who did not have a permanent dwelling place; and parents who undertook work under the Rural Employment Guarantee scheme, who, we realised, had become a visible social category. We spoke to teachers from state-run schools, including Adi-dravida welfare schools, government-aided schools, those run by Chrisitan missions or trusts, and non-formal education centres. In all, we spoke to 17 teachers and over 50 parents from diverse backgrounds, including a group of fathers. The information and ideas that we gleaned through this process proved startling and, in the event, we never got around to the other social classes that we wished to make part of our study.

Yet, our exercise, limited as it was, proved fruitful in unexpected ways: we realised that for this set of parents their own role in shaping their children's future, with respect to education, was contingent upon their relationship to the school—and this, we thought, was an important factor as it pushed us to rethink fundamental questions with regard to child-rearing, so that we do not imagine these practices as anchored merely in the household and family, but also in the school and its environs. Interestingly, while studies exist of parental attitudes to schooling, teachers' roles and performance, and the government's duties and responsibilities in providing for the education of the poor, there are not many of how parents think or feel about acts of care in the school context.[5] To be sure, studies have pointed out how parents use the word 'care' to call attention to how teachers ought to behave and function.[6] But there is another level of caring that parents from specific contexts imagine schools can offer: this pertains to everyday acts of nurture and understanding, which take into account their own situation as working-class adults whose lives are difficult, unstable and precarious. While neither the parents nor teachers to whom we spoke voiced this in as many words, we sensed that both conceded that schooling had to necessarily involve the 'raising' of children as well.

◆◆◆

The headmistress of a state-run primary school in the Pudukkottai district of Tamil Nadu, famous for the work undertaken in the 1990s during the heyday of the National Literacy Mission, had much to say about the conditions in which girl children negotiated learning. She gave us two examples, one of which was that of an 8-year-old girl who would come to school with her 4-month-old brother and stand outside the classroom. Their parents went to work leaving her in charge; she wanted to be in school, but was not sure if she could bring the baby along. Eventually, the school arranged for her to keep her brother in school, and for her to feed him from time to time throughout the period she was in primary school. The second story concerns an even younger child: a 7-year-old who would ask permission to go home every afternoon at 2:00 p.m. to collect water from the pipes on the street, since there was no one else at home to do so, with her mother being away at work for the better part of the day. She, too, was allowed to do this and then come back to school.

Another teacher from Thanjavur district spoke of girls in her school whose parents worked on construction sites and would leave home very early, returning late at night. The oldest girl child was entrusted with cooking rice, feeding herself and her siblings, putting away food for the night, and then ensuring that every one of them got to school. Teachers, in turn, accommodated the needs of these children and did not penalise them if they were late or stayed on longer than others, and made sure they ate their free afternoon meal.

Where there are no sensitive teachers, children simply do not go to school regularly. An entire neighbourhood of children, we discovered, remains at home in a Dalit hamlet in western Tamil Nadu, because there are no adults around during the day. Being sanitary workers, adults in this community leave before dawn and return later in the evening. It is the oldest child in each family or street that literally takes charge—and it is entirely up to her whether she can get the other children to school.

These are neither new nor startling facts. However, we wish to draw attention to how teachers who recognise the social conditions in which their wards come to school can, and do, make a difference, and how parents, who are not present to supervise their children's learning, rely tacitly on such teachers and the school as a space to not only teach their children, but also nurture them in a quotidian sense: make sure the children eat, and that their younger siblings are taken care of. The teachers who do this also know that unless the school assumes this role and becomes that space, the children will not remain in school. While these expectations are not loudly voiced, the presence of an enabling school environment defines the parents' own approach to taking school seriously.

The question is, of course, if schools are organised to be the kind of spaces expected by parents. Whatever individual teachers do, or not do, the school is yet to emerge as a community space which serves multiple purposes. Subject to a strict administrative regimen, teachers' tasks are defined by what the state expects from them not only by way of teaching, but record-keeping as well. This makes the school day a fairly inflexible one, and while teachers do adapt in any number of ways in keeping with their sense of vocation, such adaptation does not always mean that teachers can consistently pay attention to home conditions and ensure that learning allows a negotiation of these as well. Sadly, parents whose conditions of existence require this from the school are not in a position to argue their case—their work conditions do not permit this; besides, unless they feel empowered to do so, either on account of their public-spiritedness or education, they are not likely to push their case.

Ironically, discussions that concern parenting and childcare seldom address these realities. The only other register to address them has been that associated with the socialist school and care system, where children were subjects of state care in the former Soviet Union and several countries in Central and Eastern Europe. These debates have been renewed after the collapse of state socialism, given the challenges faced by societies where state provisioning of care, in whatever form it existed, with all its problems, has ceased to exist. Clearly and unequivocally gendered, the concerns that are expressed in such debates—including those to do with care work, women's responsibilities and the nature of state care—are yet to be seen in tandem with debates on state schooling in countries like ours.

◆◆◆

A state-run or state-supported school stands a better chance of working productively with communities in two ways: first, when its functioning is defined by an older educational history, especially that of mission-inspired schooling, which was directed at children from underprivileged backgrounds and came with the assurance of basic education, and sometimes more; second, when it is part of the Sarva Shiksha Abhiyan (SSA) initiative of the Government of India. We had the opportunity to record the work of two such initiatives: the Seva Mandir School in Parangipettai, not far from Puducherry; and the Vanavil School in the Nagapattinam district of Tamil Nadu. We spoke to teachers of the former, especially those familiar with hostel conditions, and who, therefore, interact with parents, and parents and teachers of the latter. We also spoke to a group of parents whose children go to Vanavil School.

Seva Mandir is a nationalist-inspired girls' school, established in the 1920s by Anne-Marie Petersen, a Danish woman who wished to take Christian education forward, but within an indigenous framework. She was inspired by Gandhi's educational ideas, in addition to Denmark's folk-education movement in the early 20th century. The school was an experiment, in every sense of the word, and over the years emerged as a residential and day school for hundreds of children from nearby villages, many of whom were, and are, from peasant, fishing and Dalit communities. The school's residential system, being a mixture of firmness and flexibility, has rendered it a favourite with parents of the region. We had the opportunity to learn much about the status of the school as a 'second home' in the memories of past students. Speaking to teachers, we discovered that the nature of challenges in the present day was very different from the times of older generations of students.

Currently, and this is corroborated by wardens of several government residential schools as well, children are sent away to hostels, either because the school, as in the case of Seva Mandir, is seen as a place that will foster 'good' values, and as enabling children to 'learn a thing or two'; or they are placed in hostels, because familial relationships are unstable. The perception of an unstable home may be summarised by disclosures made by teachers at Seva Mandir and others from state-run schools who have also been hostel wardens: A home has been rendered unstable because a parent has either left, or taken up with another partner; the father drinks incessantly; the mother is the head of the household, and is insecure keeping a girl child at home; both parents are dead or have committed suicide; or one of them is in jail. Another reason, though not widely voiced, but perhaps as important, is that the parents fear their child will 'run away' as soon as she comes of age, and so want her in a 'safe' place.

For the teachers to take on board these contexts and reasons while admitting children poses a set of challenges that is not easy to resolve. For one, the parents cannot be counted upon to keep children in school, since their exigent situations do not always allow for that or, in their reasoning, schooling does not occupy as important a place. Second, schools have to reckon with the fact that when the children go home during holidays, they step out of the disciplinary regime of the school, and that freedom sometimes results in the children not wanting to come back. In such situations, the parents are either helpless, or unhelpful. Third, the teachers professed bewilderment at parental attitudes to raising children—clearly, these fell outside the norm of what most considered acceptable parental behaviour. For instance, the parents were open about their extramarital relationships; further, rather than disciplining children, they tended to indulge them, which probably stemmed from guilt at sending them away to a hostel.

As hostel wardens or caregivers in schools, the teachers pointed out that they had to walk a fine line between nurturing and being firm. Further, they had to be constantly aware of the fact that the children in their charge were 'not their own', in a biological sense, and they could not easily reprimand them or direct their lives beyond what was required by the school system. We were astonished by this confession of limits to authority, since one had heard rumours and instances of authority exercised with impunity in schools and hostels. Those we spoke to said that they could only speak for themselves, but added that as much as some teachers and wardens exercised authority in an unaccountable manner, many remained indifferent and disinterested, leaving children to their own devices, which was irresponsible.

This model of engaging with children from marginal backgrounds gives us room for pause: its moral earnestness is of a kind that belongs to another time and place, whereas its current dilemmas demand action that is not served by earnestness alone, requiring robust engagement with the overall school system on the one hand, and with children's realities on the other—these latter being shaped by the media, peer pressure and major transformations in adolescent cultures. The appropriateness of the school as a place for nurturing children, not only in terms of learning, but of ethical growth and development, is a subject that has to stretch beyond the singular idea of the right to education and include a redefinition of the schooling ideal itself.

In this context, the experiment that is the Vanavil School seems an instructive example. Set up in 2005, in the wake of the damage wrought by the tsunami in Tamil Nadu's Nagapattinam district, Vanavil is a residential school under the aegis of the SSA. Essentially, it is a school for children who do not enrol in government schools, or drop out very soon if they do. The children are from nomadic and semi-nomadic communities—*Adiyan, Narikuravar* and *Boom-boom maattukarar*. Associated with small-game hunting, itinerant trading and soothsaying, these communities are, needless to say, poor and, worse, have been pushed into begging for a living. This is a profession that is widely practised around the three major pilgrimage sites of Christianity, Islam and Hinduism in the region. The tsunami destroyed the fragile seaside homes of these communities, which could not avail of relief since they could not provide proof of long-term or permanent residence. In this context, some relief volunteers came together to set up the school. Today it is a residential campus, with its own farm, where rice is grown to cater to the school's needs. Financed by public funding, including the support of a software major as part of their employees' support programme for education, the school is home to over one hundred children.

Having been in contact with Vanavil from its inception and observed the attitudes with which parents from the communities in question had initially approached the school and schooling, it is fascinating to see how, in less than a decade, communities suspicious of learning and education have come to accept and even begun to think of their own future in terms of what their children would do in the years to come. We spoke to over 30 parents, including grandmothers, and they charted their own growing interest in the school. Putting together their views and our observations, we have pieced together an extraordinary story.

Initially, children did run away from school, going back to their parents and the streets, and school volunteers would have to bring them back. Parents, too, were not particularly convinced of the need for their wards to attend school, or the good this would actually achieve. This was not difficult to understand, considering these children's experience of state schooling had been uniformly unpleasant and disempowering—other children teased them, teachers did not quite take to their rather free ways of speaking and behaving, and some openly discriminated against them. Ideally, while the children qualify under the Scheduled Tribes and Nomadic Communities category, as in Maharasthra, the communities they belong to have not been able to define their claims to state support on this ground in an unequivocal fashion. Vanavil School addressed this issue fairly early on and this won them the trust of the community.

Over a period of time, the Vanavil school population has stabilised and this is in no small measure attributed to the school's functioning. Since it comes under the SSA, it is assured of some resource support from that body. There has also been support from other donors, which has enabled the school to provide nutritious and healthy food all year round, and to maintain rather large, and imaginatively designed, school premises. Further, apart from the regular curriculum, children learn to draw, make sculptures, participate in theatre, and play music, among other activities. The teachers, particularly the warden, have been receptive to the community and its concerns with regard to the children. Regular meetings are held with the community and community elders are brought into the foreground when it comes to school-related celebrations. For instance, on 8 March 2015, the occasion of International Working Women's Day, women within the community were upheld as models of labour, enthusiasm and strength. On the other hand, it has not always been easy to work with the state system. Since Vanavil is officially a residential school for dropouts, children cannot treat it as a permanent educational space. After a point, particularly once they finish the primary stage, they have to be enrolled in a local state school, though they are permitted to stay in Vanavil. This has not always worked to the children's advantage, since regular schools continue to be spaces of disquiet and torment. Yet, some of the children have succeeded in completing Classes 10 and 12, and today two of them are in college.

As far as parents are concerned, they would like their children, at least one of them, to find a place in the local administration, in addition to wanting them to be artists, engineers, etc. Some of them have started planning for the day their children would go to college, or to other schools, by saving money. Many find it curious and interesting that children talk to them animatedly about school, things they have learned, invoking worlds and contexts that are removed from the imaginative worlds they have known. There are concerns about behaviour, watching television in particular, and chewing betel nut (*paan*). Teachers have to reckon with an easy attitude to sexuality and with early adolescence, and while this necessitates engaging with what parents say and do, it is not clear how best this may be done. Parents, however, did not bring these up as matters that bothered them.

What is evident though, from what parents said and what the Vanavil teachers know from speaking to their children, is that government schools remain unresponsive and unreceptive to the children's needs, and to engaging with their obviously different cultural context. Not just teachers or students, but the local educational establishment does not also seem open to thinking of imaginative ways to integrate schools such as this one within the overall educational scheme. While this may require policy changes within the SSA's own framework, there are decisions that can be made locally, especially flexibility in enrolling children in state schools—but these do not seem possible, given the social stigma attached to these communities, and the fact that they are electorally insignificant.

Vanavil's exceptional work came home to us in another context while speaking with parents of another nomadic group who whip themselves in public and earn a living by calling attention to what they do. This community has its own designated residence in Madurai city and the SSA has made pointed references to the need to engage with them. Yet there is a marked reluctance on the part of these parents to send their children to school. Some parents had tried to persuade their children, but their experience has been that the latter invariably come back very soon. For others, it is not viable since the children are part of their performance on the street. Yet others point out that the school remains an alien space for their children, since they are not used to being confined within four walls for over eight hours a day. A more generalised problem in the community is a feeling of neglect, because they have not been able to obtain a caste certificate that would enable them to access government aid—and it appears that this is also one reason why education does not seem an attractive option, without adequate state backing in the form of scholarships, etc. Vanavil's approach is instructive in this regard, considering that the parents they now work with are not all that different from those of the early days of the school's existence. Yet sustained work with the community by creating a sense of ownership in them with respect to what the school does, and an open and non-judgmental attitude towards social values that are not normative, has made a fundamental difference to how children and parents view school.

◆◆◆

Apart from these obviously marginal groups, we spoke also to parents and teachers of government schools, where children from peasant, Dalit, and small trading communities study. Dalit marginality emerges as an important concern in all schools, pointed to by both teachers and parents. While much has been spoken and written about Untouchability-related concerns in education, not much has been done or is known with respect to everyday interactions in the schoolroom, not just between the students, but teachers and parents, especially of Dalit children. Caste feelings run high amongst children, according to teachers from government schools that we spoke to, particularly in the southern districts of Tamil Nadu. Such feelings, pointed out one of the teachers, are accentuated when a parent demands to know why her son or daughter was made to work with a Dalit student, or why their wards should have to study under Dalit teachers. Teachers also tend to ignore poorer parents, we were told, and if the latter happened to be Dalits, they were seldom granted the respect they deserved. Worse, a Dalit parent could be put to work inside the school premises by being made to shift furniture, sweep, clean up, etc.—and all this, while waiting to meet with the headmistress or a teacher.

In such a context, Dalit parents point out, they do not feel confident of going to school and confronting teachers: the latter's education and the fact that they are salaried employees of the state make it difficult for Dalit parents to question them or, even if they do, secure a dignified hearing. So, unless their children are particularly troubled or hurt, parents rarely go to school to speak to teachers. But, it was also evident that notwithstanding this expression of helplessness, Dalit parents, particularly Dalit mothers, invested a great deal in education: they were insistent that their children should complete school, and put up with whatever inconveniences there were, for that was the only guarantee that they would get beyond a wage labourer's job or employment mandated by their caste status, such as sanitary and graveyard labour, and leather work.

We discovered, too, that where there is a receptive teacher, that teacher can actually create precedents for Dalit parents to visit school regularly and remain involved with their children's education. In this context, a Dalit teacher noted, it is not always easy to remain in touch with parents as in many families the men drink and squander away their earnings, and women bear the burden of worrying about their children. For children, the teacher added, the home atmosphere becomes stifling, with an anxious mother and a violent father, and we often have to keep this in mind when we see that children remain listless even after we have given them a lot of attention.

◆◆◆

This is a short description of the manner in which school and home spaces intersect with respect to parenting practices, and of what schools are capable, or not, what they are organised to deliver, and what is beyond their ken. Some of these are familiar themes to do with the connection between deprivation and schooling; other concerns, to do with how schools have to converse with marginal communities, are yet to be richly debated, although we have done some work in this regard with respect to involving young people from communities as mentors in primary education. But what we are highlighting has as much to do with redefining the functions of a school in specific contexts and the role of the teacher. Clearly, he, or she, emerges as a caregiver as well, but with this difference: that he, or she, does so as part of a continuum of tasks that help the child mature into an observant learner. Here, we now return to that with which we started out: the nature of adult–child interactions, and the authority and violence that structure this relationship, in many instances.

A difficult home situation is often mirrored by an indifferent one at school and children either withdraw into their own worlds, or find other malcontented children with whom they share experiences and develop ways of dealing with their own angst, unease, anger and confusion. Where the school is enabling, the children find it easier to tolerate the limits of a desperate home situation. Where the home is familiar and a source of comfort, even if children tend to take on adult roles, negotiating the school is less burdensome. Yet, in all cases, if a school space is disrespectful of the child, her background and her ways of being, she has no desire to continue her education. The violence of the school space is, therefore, a matter of concern, and it is not only corporal punishment or sexual abuse—both of which are more widespread than we can imagine—that makes for a culture of hurt, but also everyday abusive behaviour of children towards each other, and adults towards children.

In all this, parents are left with fairly limited options: they can cajole their children to go to school, or not mind if they do not wish to go. They can, and do, take children along when they go out to work.

Children grow up watching parents work, getting drunk, quarrelling, leaving each other for other partners, without actually marking the situation as exceptional in any manner, although when they repeat stories of violence to which they are witness, or are victims of, to receptive teachers, the magnitude of what they endure is evident.

At a time when child-rearing and care are visible aspects of an obsessive discourse which dominates social media and alternative educational practices, it is sobering to think of what it means to be a parent, when one is poor, female, Dalit or Adivasi. It is also sobering to ask ourselves: What are the implications of such an understanding of parenting for the way we think of education itself, in terms of state policy and practice, and for teacher education?

◆

NOTES

1. See, for instance, http://timesofindia.indiatimes.com/city/chennai/Tamil-Nadu-failed-to-protect-rights-of-children-in-homes-says-plea/articleshow/40841890.cms (accessed on 15 September 2015). See also, http://www.newindianexpress.com/states/tamil_nadu/article478334.ece (accessed 15 September 2015).
2. Interview with Christy Subatra, Correspondent, Crea Matriculation Academy Higher Secondary School, Trichy, Tamil Nadu. 23 July 2013.
3. The AASRA Suicide Prevention Blog notes: 'It is observed that 11.7 per cent (355 out of 3,035) of children (upto 14 years) who committed suicide belonged to Tamil Nadu.'
4. Many parents that we interviewed displayed their anger at these marriages thus—they could not concede, or were willing to accept, that their children could be emotionally intimate or sexually aware at that age.
5. Studies of this kind have been conducted chiefly with respect to parents from tribal communities in so-called backward states such as Orissa. See, for example, Samal (2012).
6. See, for example, 'Parents Perspective on Schooling of Children in Andhra Pradesh'. UK: Young Lives/Save the Children, 2014.

REFERENCE

Samal, Rojalin. 2012. 'Parents' Attitude towards Schooling and Education of Children.' Unpublished project report. Submitted to the Department of Humanities and Social Sciences, for the partial fulfilment of the requirement in Master's Degree in Development Studies. Rourkela: National Institute of Technology.

◆◆

DRAWING PICTURES

A Review of the Policy and Action on 'Adolescent Girls'

DIPTA BHOG, DISHA MULLICK

> Girlhood is made up and girls are brought into existence in statements and knowledge about girls, and some of the most widely shared or commonsensical knowledge about girls and feminine adolescence provides some of the clearest examples of how girls are constructed by changing ways of speaking about girls (Driscoll, 2002: 5).

Catherine Driscoll begins her engaging and provocative book, *Girls*, with memories of interactions with her grandmother at the time she began menstruating, and the oral and written literature that was handed over in this highly charged phase of her life. She talks about instructions this literature provides in terms of seeing herself as a girl:

> [I]t tells me that I am now a young woman. It tells me to be proud of that in the rather ominous context of warnings about the physical and emotional distresses of being a girl-becoming-a-woman, as well as the difficulty of successfully getting through girlhood as the right kind of woman. The point at which I will stop being a girl is even less clear to me, but I know it has to happen. Girls should grow up (ibid.: 1).

If the idea of girlhood was always significant, it has taken on more visible and tangible import than ever in the last few years. In 2015, in recognition of increased national and international attention on 'adolescent' girls, in the language of policy and development rhetoric, funding and programmes, we undertook a research study on the nature and strategies of work in which adolescent girls in India were engaged. This study involved a mapping, and subsequent analysis, of the policies on girls' development—the language and imperatives it drew on—to see the action, and politics it allowed (or not) on the ground. A reflection on the policies creating and perpetrating the category of the adolescent girl, both nationally and internationally, forms the basis of this article.

HIGH RISK, HIGH POTENTIAL: THE GIRL CHILD REPRESENTED IN POLICY

In a speech in 1992, the vice-president of the World Bank, Lawrence H. Summers (1994), underlined that the cycle of female deprivation could only be broken through investing in girls' primary education. At a *modest* cost, the benefits of reduced child and maternal mortality, the birth of healthier children, lower fertility, control over the spread of AIDS, and environmental benefits could be achieved. The girl child became the key target group to map the success of governments in achieving gender parity; over time, education was articulated as a right. The World Conference on Education for All in 1990 declared 'improving access to quality education for girls and women as "the most urgent priority"'; by the end of the decade, in April 2000, at the Dakar World Education Forum, the UN Girls' Education Initiative (UNGEI) was launched.[1] This was a 10-year initiative in which 13 UN entities, led by UNICEF, agreed to work together to help governments meet their commitments to ensure quality education for all girls.

The success of efforts to universalise education in different developing nations, initially for primary, and then elementary, education at the turn of the century dovetailed with two of the eight Millennium Development Goals (MDGs) introduced in 2001. As secondary education became the new frontier, development policy and programming, especially over the last five years, has been witness to a proliferation of programmes that focus on girls, especially adolescents. A statement released by the Director of UNFPA in 2011 declared adolescent girls to be the 'unexpected solution to the world's most pressing problems', and explained how investing in adolescent girls results in much wider benefits:

> When she is educated, healthy and skilled, she will be an active citizen in her community. She will become a mother when she is ready and who will invest in her future children's health and education. She will be the entrepreneur discovering solutions that breaks the cycle of poverty, one girl at a time.[2]

This provides the framing for a dedicated 'Action for Adolescent Girls', which comes into effect with the UNFPA's strategic plan for 2013–2017. The Action broadly aims to 'protect adolescent girls' rights, in particular delay the age at marriage and childbearing, and empower the most marginalised girls.[3] The inter-sectoral (health, environment and social) benefits that Summers had set out over two decades ago have thus been expanded marginally to include early marriage for this age group. The vulnerability of the adolescent girl to early marriage and early pregnancy is part of the powerful logic to ensure her continuation in schooling.

Policy and data reinforce each other when it comes to constructing adolescent girls in development discourse. Research reports published by agencies spanning the World Bank, the International Council for Research on Women and more recent reviews of organisational programmes, provide numbers and voices that corroborate the rationale for focus on this specific age group of girls. One interesting illustration is 'Girls Speak', from the Girls Count (2010) series of reports put out by the Coalition for Adolescent Girls. Here, adolescent girls, in a sense, speak to the policy priorities and strategies set in place to empower them: not surprisingly, they strongly agree with the perspective that investing in their education, livelihoods and freedom to delay marriage will be transformative to their lives.

> Girls say: Give us the choice to put off marriage and childbearing until we decide that we are ready.... I don't want to be like another girl I know who is 13 years old and already pregnant...I just want to get a job of my own and help my parents, who looked after me when I was young. (Greene, *et al.*, 2010: xxii).

These 'girls'-eye perspectives are a persuasive, neat fit into the global discourse and advocacy around the aspirations and needs of adolescent girls.

The financial data/narrative is endlessly fascinating: a working paper by the World Bank (Chaaban and Cunningham, 2011) from data collected in 14 countries across Asia, Africa and South America details the nature of dividends when girls are invested in—in terms of their education, their health and the delay of marriage. The analysis is based on the concept of 'opportunity costs', not secondary or inter-generational impact. It therefore sees 'inactivity' and 'joblessness' among adolescent girls as lost wages and lost opportunities. Targeted programmes that bring girls into school, for instance, could drastically increase opportunities: the Report uses a study by Levine (2002) to argue that primary education increases girls' earnings by 5 to 15 per cent; for boys it is 4 to 8 per cent; and secondary education increases earnings for girls by 15 to 25 per cent. Further, the Report places the cost of early pregnancy as the greatest in India, Brazil and Bangladesh. In India, 67 out of 1,000 girls marry early; yet in terms of the sheer volume of population, it is high—four million girls. The loss, as assessed in terms of lifetime opportunity costs, is as high as 12 per cent of the annual GDP. These figures highlight the stark economic gains to be made when '600 million' of a thus far unproductive population of adolescent girls is 'empowered' to play a healthy and productive role in society.

While the advantages of investment in adolescent girls has led to the mushrooming of various initiatives, both at the governmental and international level, one key idea to entrench itself is 'The Girl Effect', as it is popularly known. The Girl Effect is a movement that was launched by Nike Foundation, in collaboration with NoVo Foundation, United Nations Foundation and other partners, in 2008. Nike's belief in human potential, according to the Foundation's website, has led to its focus on investing in girls: 'Change the world for girls and enable girls on their unique capacity to change the world.' As of 2015, the Girl Effect is an independent charitable organisation.[4]

The process of working on the welfare of adolescent girls and their rights has, while advocating for gender equality and gender mainstreaming, completely ignored the gains of social and political movements of the last few decades. In Latin America, Africa and Asia there have been popular local women's movements that have criticised oppressive political structures and inequalities. The discourse and programmes with girls seem to forget this past and present struggle, focusing instead on creating a new class of productive, knowledgeable and skilled labour to participate in a market economy.

A CONTINUUM OF CARE: ADOLESCENT GIRLS IN INDIAN POLICY

In Indian policy, the focus on girls emerges in tandem with the international push towards universalising education. At the start of the 1990s, a diversity of strategies marked educational initiatives that engaged adult women in processes of learning. The Total Literacy Campaign, launched nationwide in 1988, saw poor rural women actively participate in large numbers, much to the surprise of policy planners and implementers. They constituted 70 per cent of learners in literacy centres. The New Education Policy (1986) was envisioned as playing a positive, interventionist role in empowering women, with the ultimate objective of achieving a change in the status of women.[5] The Mahila Samakhya Programme was another initiative across five states that defined itself as Education for Women's Equality. This required a collective voice, action, and an understanding of education's potential as a vehicle of change. However, by the mid-'90s, the focus had shifted from women to girls, with the launching of the District Primary Education Programme (DPEP) in select districts in 1994, which later transformed itself into the national Sarva Shiksha Abhiyan (Education for All Mission) in 2001, that set access to elementary education, along with gender equity in enrolment, as its goal.

By 2000, youth figured as a prominent group across sectors—health, sports, women and child development, and human resources—connecting to the international discourse on adolescents. India was slated to become the youngest nation, with an average age of 29 years (Basu, 2007)—this was 'the demographic dividend' that would pave the way to India's economic growth. A Ministry for Youth Affairs was set up to drive policies on youth, adolescent health and livelihoods. The recent National Youth Policy borrows, too, from the language of investing in the health and productivity of youth, focusing on education, entrepreneurship and skill building—all towards higher GDPs. Partnerships between youth, training institutes and labour markets—public and private—are sought to be forged. The youth policy is largely gender blind. Drawing on previous discourses, it reflects the classic gender divide, with boys selected for skills and livelihoods development and girls located in their reproductive role.

> There is a need to pay special attention to health issues concerning women youth. This would entail greater pre-natal and post-natal care for women in the vulnerable age group of 14–18 years, [the] need to bring down maternal and infant mortality rates, [and] campaign against female feticide to improve [the] child sex ratio.[6]

The focus on the adolescent girl child ties educational access to health (primarily reproductive) as the instrumental strategy to 'empower' India's onward march to economic prosperity. As a result, the 'Sabla' scheme for 'empowering' girls between 11 and 18 (located in the Ministry of Women and Child Development), states that,

> Adolescence represents a window of opportunity to prepare for healthy adult life….Adolescent Girls (AGs) need to be looked at not just in terms of their own needs as AGs but also as individuals who can be productive members of society.[7]

The scheme is meant to provide inputs and resources for young girls in selected districts in matters of nutrition, reproductive health counselling, vocational training and leadership building through the formation of, and capacity building with, collectives of girls at the village level. Although conceptually, and in terms of structure, the Sabla scheme holds potential as an empowering programme, its focus on health (especially sexual and reproductive health) and nutrition is far greater than the inputs both on accessing public spaces and entitlements, and vocational training. The definition, too, of 'productive' in the context of adolescent girls is telling:

> The module developed for training AGs will include issues pertaining to home maintenance, budgeting, saving, running the household, gender sensitivity, schooling of children, etc. [The] AGs will be advised on these issues to orient them to become more productive members of society.[8]

Recent health policies for adolescents move from the language of fear and risk towards the need to create strong and healthy youth. The National Adolescent Health Programme (2014), part of the National Health Mission, echoes the emphasis of the National Youth Policy in determining its focus areas:

> Investments in adolescent reproductive and sexual health will yield dividends in terms of delaying age at marriage, reducing the incidence of teenage pregnancy, meeting unmet contraception needs, reducing maternal mortality, reducing STI incidence and reducing HIV prevalence.[9]

The programme claims to be making a 'paradigm shift' from clinic care to 'reaching adolescents in their own environment, such as in schools, families and communities'. Reducing infant and maternal mortality rates is also at the heart of the recently launched integrated approach to reproductive, newborn, maternal, child and adolescent health care. It is here that the link between women and adolescent girls is seen as a continuum—the 'continuum of care'.

> The health of an adolescent girl impacts pregnancy, while the health of a pregnant woman impacts the health of the newborn and the child. As such, interventions may be required at various stages of the life cycle, which should be mutually linked.[10]

In policy, the link between the empowerment of women and its relationship with young, adolescent girls has come to roost in their present and future roles as mothers and pregnant and lactating women/girls.

Indian agencies that are bridging the role of advocates and funders seem to draw on the neo-liberal narrative of productivity and benefit in constructing the focus of programmes on youth and young girls. Social and economic potential, imminent risk, and a focus on building the aspirations of young girls echo through these programmes. 'Owning Her Future', a report that advocates investing in empowering adolescent girls in the Indian context, and provides a glimpse into some organisations working on the ground in India, makes a strong point about the '100 billion dollars' that could be added to the Indian GDP over the lifetimes of adolescent girls if they had

> the opportunity to stay in school and delay early marriage and pregnancy.... Adolescence is the last chance for interventions that would continue to have a positive impact through subsequent life stages.[11]

In a throwback to the '80s, the burden of ensuring appropriate reproduction and control over fertility has now shifted to adolescent girls, just as it was earlier placed on women (Sen and Grown, 1988).

THE PARADOXES OF ABSENCE: MAKING WOMEN INVISIBLE

International developmental discourse in the past three decades—also leading to the framing of MDGs—has been greatly impacted by the power and transformation by grassroots popular movements for political and social change. These struggles and movements have involved both men and women of many categories of marginalised people. Women have been at the forefront of many of these collective actions for change: they have imagined, worked and fought for new futures, and built diverse collective forums and structures. However, in the programmes designed for the development or empowerment of adolescent girls, gender equality has emerged as a concept disassociated from movements for women's rights, or from concepts and theories emerging through research and feminist scholarship.

The shift from the experience of forming collectives with women and girls/youth to the existing neo-liberal preoccupations with mapping, and quantifying the benefits of investment is a shift from a concern with the present—that which is contextual and experienced—to that which is harvestable in the future. Katie MacDonald makes this observation while addressing the question regarding the pride of place adolescent girls occupy in today's development discourse. In her view, the current focus is based on prioritising a notion of futurity and potential, rather than the present lives and aspirations that girls may have.

> Through the positioning of girls as future mothers and dedicated community members, and as in need of investment to make this transition to good and productive future mothers, they come to represent a possible future. This future is created through their commitment to bettering their community, the workforce, and their qualities as future women. Girls are an emblem for an imagined future the organizations are able to usher in through the Western support (2016: 12).

MacDonald's work, as well as that of others, points to the limitations of targeted work with girls in a way that either focuses on a cost–benefit analysis, or sees girls as mere tools in a process of economic or social change. The shift in language also points to the significant shift in context, to one decreed by the economic paradigm and the dictates of public and private global capital. More important, adolescent girls across the developing world are viewed as vulnerable, where their voices come to merely reiterate the developmental benefits sought by state and international agencies.

CONCLUSION

Policy and advocacy documents and research on the status of adolescent girls are marked by 'paradoxes of absence' (Manzo, 2008) in their representation of adolescent girls: women and their struggles for gender equality find hardly any reference. While adolescents are increasingly being viewed as potentially empowered women of the future, they must, however, continue to bear the burden of bettering family and community and producing able, healthy children. International and national advocacy briefs on adolescent girls often focus excessively on individual growth, identity and the filling in of the 'lack' or 'denial' they experience in their families. Projections of girls as role models is part of a narrative that promotes the idea of 'agency and motivation against all odds', often sidelining the deep structures and hierarchies that determine girls' choices. Existing knowledge, the experience of collectivising women, and the hard-fought gains for women's rights are seen to be of little consequence to how work with adolescents is imagined and positioned.

However, in primary research for this study, from visits to organisations working with young girls in various contexts, we did find that on-the-ground interventions, both conceptually and in practice, challenge the discourse set out by the policies reviewed earlier. Many organisations came to work with young girls, as they organised women and worked on their rights and entitlements. Their work is part of a deepening engagement with gender issues across different age groups. Their understanding of the adolescent girls' situation is located in a larger framework of structures, and institutions of power and control, through which they can view long-term objectives of working with girls in challenging patriarchy as an institution to achieve gender equality. Others have come to this group through their work with marginalised communities and within these groups they focus on the emerging generation of young boys and girls, in terms of how they are excluded from mainstream development and the erasures of their cultural, social world. This translates into interventions emphasising access to existing schemes and developing interventions affirming their own lived world.

If women are absent in policy-speak on adolescent girls, there exists at the grassroots level a symbiotic relationship between women's collectives and adolescent girls' groups and forums, which creates the enabling environment for girls' collectives to grow. They also share common long-term objectives of gender equality. The existence of women's collectives provides an important buffer to grassroots organisations to take on issues related to girls vis-à-vis the community. Be it getting girls to school/residential centres or even complex issues of sexuality, women's collectives are a space where these efforts or issues can be discussed and negotiated. There is clarity that within the family structure, the adolescent girl is lower in the power hierarchy than women, and there are limits to what can be achieved in the mother-daughter relationship. However, the relationship with women's collectives draws on a more shared vision of claiming citizenship and space in the public realm. We see girls' collectives aligning with and supporting campaigns on sexual harassment, right to public spaces and equal wages, to become part of processes to claim citizenship.

Women mirror what the future holds for girls, and adolescent girls provide women a sense of the possibilities of change. By isolating them, or then fracturing this continuum, existing policies are merely claiming a commitment to 'transforming' the lives of young women. The future and present are inextricably linked, just as girls and women are.

◆

NOTES

1. UNGEI. 2002. 'The Millennium Development Goals and the United Nations Girls Education Initiative: A Guidance Note to UN Country Teams.' UNGEI, April. Accessed on 12 April from http://www.unesco.org/education/efa/know_sharing/flagship_initiatives/ungei_guidance.pdf
2. UNFPA/ ED statement http://www.unfpa.org/news/putting-girls-first
3. UNFPA. 2014. 'Action for Adolescent Girls.' Accessed on 12.04.2015 from http://www.unfpa.org/sites/default/files/resource-pdf/UNFPA%20AAG%20programme%20document_25july2014.pdf
4. 'The Girl Effect', girleffect.org
5. Government of India. 1992. 'New Education Policy.' Accessed on 28.06.2015 from http://www.ncert.nic.in/oth_anoun/npe86.pdf
6. Government of India. 2011. 'National Youth Policy.' Accessed on 14.04.2015 from http://www.jnu.ac.in/Students/National%20Youth%20Policy%202014.pdf See also Sen and Grown (1988).
7. Government of India. 2010. 'Rajiv Gandhi Scheme for Empowering Adolescent Girls.' Accessed on 14.04.2015 from http://wcd.nic.in/SchemeSabla/SABLAscheme.pdf

8. http://wcd.nic.in/SchemeSabla/SABLAscheme.pdf
9. Government of India. 2014. 'National Youth Policy.' Accessed on 14.04.2015 from http://www.jnu.ac.in/Students/National%20Youth%20Policy%202014.pdf See also Sen and Grown (1988).
10. Government of India. 2013. 'A Strategic Approach To Reproductive, Maternal, Newborn, Child and Adolescent Health (Rmnch+A) in India.' Ministry of Health and Family Welfare. Accessed on 22.06.2015 from http://nrhm.gov.in/images/pdf/programmes/rmncha-strategy.pdf
11. Dasra. 2012. 'Owning Her Future—Empowering Adolescent Girls in India'. Accessed on 14.04.2015 from http://www.dasra.org/pdf/Dasra-Empowering-Adolescent-Girls-OHF.pdf

REFERENCES

Basu, Kaushik. 2007. 'India's Demographic Dividend.' *BBC News*. 27 July. Accessed on 28.06.2015 from http://news.bbc.co.uk/2/hi/south_asia/6911544.stm

Chaaban, Jad, and Wendy Cunningham. 2011. 'Measuring the Economic Gain of Investing in Girls: The Girl Effect Dividend.' Policy Research Working Paper. Washington, D.C.: World Bank.

Driscoll, Catherine. 2002. *Girls: Feminine Adolescence in Popular Culture and Cultural Theory*. New York: Columbia University Press.

Greene, M. E., L. Cardinal and E. Goldstein-Siegel. 2010. *Girls Speak: A New Voice in Global Development*. Washington D.C.: International Center for Research on Women.

Levine, Ruth, Cynthia Lloyd, Margaret Greene and Caren Grown. 2009. *Girls Count. 2010. A Global Investment and Action Agenda, Coalition for Adolescent Girls*. Washington D.C.: The Center for Global Development and International Center for Research on Women.

Macdonald, Katie. 2016. 'Calls for Educating Girls in the Third World: Futurity, Girls and the "Third World Woman"', *Gender, Place and Culture*, volume 23, issue 1, pp. 1–17, January.

Manzo, K. 2008. 'Imaging Humanitarianism: NGO Identity and the Iconography of Childhood', *Antipode*, volume 40, issue 4, pp. 632–57, September.

Sen, G. and C. Grown. 1988. *Development, Crisis and Alternative Vision*. US: Earthscan Publications.

Steady, Filomina Chioma. 2006. *Women and Collective Action in Africa— Development, Democratization, and Empowerment, with Special Focus on Sierra Leone*. NY: Palgrave.

Summers, Lawrence, H. 1994. 'Investing in all the People: Educating Women in Developing Countries.' EDI Seminar Paper. Washington D.C.: World Bank.

◆◆

A SILENT REVOLUTION?

Gender, Sexual Harassment and the Democratisation of Higher Education

MARY E. JOHN

Those of us who work in colleges, universities and research centres are only too painfully aware that we are witnessing an extraordinary time in the life of higher education in India, perhaps even globally. We are just as painfully aware of how little we really know of what is happening. The pace of change has been immense, whether it be within the life of a particular university or in the realm of government policy. Indeed, it is at the level of the state's relationship to education that recent developments have been the most bewildering. Barely a decade ago, the UPA government in power at the time announced a dramatic reform of higher education in the Eleventh Plan (2007–12), a plan which gave so much emphasis to education and to higher education in particular (with a nine-fold increase in outlay from the previous plan) that it was popularly called the Education Plan. What made it so unprecedented was the Indian state's intention to actually invest further in higher education and recognise that, even in neo-liberal times, the expansion of public universities is crucial to the future of the nation. That this was not a simple act of state support became evident when much else was sought to be achieved, and at a frenetic pace. Various commissions and committees provided their recommendations, and a host of bills were summarily introduced into Parliament without any prior discussion.[1] Today, with a new government in power at the centre (one of its achievements has been to dismantle the already much-weakened institution of planning), all that is palpable is an onslaught on university autonomy, the increasing marginalisation of the functions of the University Grants Commission (UGC), and unexpectedly large cutbacks in funding.

Winter 2015–Spring 2016, Volume 42, Numbers 3 & 4

Given this volatile scenario within which, it is believed, the basic structures of higher education are being drastically undermined, I would like to reflect on questions of gender. Such a choice might seem quite odd, since gender issues have not been seen as a priority in this crisis-ridden situation. Nonetheless, I would like to ask whether recent years might be witnessing a 'silent revolution' where gender is concerned, replete with its own contradictions and distortions. I proceed to suggest that while some aspects of this gender revolution have been unobtrusively in the making for quite some time now, there are dimensions that are no longer even particularly silent.

◆◆◆

Perhaps because the very educational institutions we inhabit have hardly appeared on our agendas, we do not appreciate sufficiently the sense of the uniqueness of the composition of our student bodies. One of the most remarkable characteristics of the present-day educational system is the sharp contrast between the growing costs of education, on the one hand, and processes of democratisation, on the other. On the eve of independence, there were barely one lakh students enrolled in our colleges and universities at a time when all Indian universities were state-run and charged practically no fees. According to the most recent All India Survey of Higher Education (AISHE) Report, 2013–14, this number now stands at a staggering 3.23 crore, with over one lakh students at the PhD level alone. With 723 universities, 36,634 colleges and 11,664 stand-alone institutions, India now has the largest system of higher education in the world, and is second largest in terms of the sheer number of students enrolled. The emergence and growth of privately-run higher educational institutions, predictably in professional courses, began in the 1970s in several south Indian states. Subsequent expansion through privatisation (a complex phenomenon since this includes private aided as much as unaided institutions) has been surging ahead by leaps and bounds. According to the AISHE figures for 2013–14, 75 per cent of India's colleges are now private, as are 233 of the 723 universities. But what is remarkable is that just 10 per cent of students at the time of independence were women. Yet, by the year 2000, this figure had jumped to 40 per cent, and by

2013–14 had inched its way further upwards to 46 per cent. Being an average number covering every kind of institution that offers a degree after Class 12, it hides those sectors with relatively low female enrolments, such as our institutions of national importance (which include the prestigious IITs and IIMs), BTech and engineering courses, and state private universities. But we would be quite wrong to think that young women are simply crowding into the countless, but relatively small, BEd colleges and other teacher-training shops that have mushroomed all across the country. There is no getting away from the overall fact that what was, till a few decades ago, an elite male bastion has now decisively given way to a situation close to gender parity. This paper will assess this peculiar 'revolution' in a country where gender inequalities are otherwise so rife, but about which so little is known.

It is not easy to make sense of the rapidity with which the most recent expansion in higher education has taken place, as is evident from various data sources. According to the National Sample Survey Organisation (NSSO), which conducts major surveys every five years, and smaller ones in between, gross enrolment ratios (GERs) of all Indians in the age group 18 to 23 years (which measures the proportion of this age group in higher education), stood at just 7.7 per cent in 1983—thus, only a small proportion of our youth was attending any kind of higher educational institution at the time. Disaggregating this figure, however, we find that 22 per cent of urban men, 12.4 per cent of urban women, and barely 1.8 per cent of rural women were enrolled in higher education. Within two decades, the overall average had risen to 12.6 per cent, according to the NSS round of 2004–05 (14.4 per cent men and 10.6 per cent women). These are the decades when democratisation could be said to have made some headway. Interestingly, there was not much of a change in the enrolments of urban men in 2004–05 (25 per cent), but urban women were catching up (22.6 per cent), and rural India was beginning to make its presence felt (5.7 per cent rural women in 2004–05, when compared to the minuscule number of 1.8 per cent in 1983). It is the huge increase from 2004 to 2014 that is harder to fathom. Even allowing for differences because of alternative data sources, according to AISHE, the gross enrolment in 2013–14 (across both urban and rural sectors) stands at 23 per cent overall (23.9 per cent men and 22 per cent women), i.e., almost doubling in a span of less than 10 years. By any account this is extraordinary, even if we allow for the OBC-led expansion in public universities that followed the implementation of what is commonly referred to as Mandal II (vide the promulgation of the 93rd Constitutional Amendment in 2006), and growth by private players in a burgeoning educational market. Moreover, being very close to gender parity is now an all-India phenomenon.

This picture acquires a different perspective when we look at proportions of different categories of students based on caste and religion. According to AISHE data for 2013–14, 32.4 per cent of students are from the Other Backward Classes (OBCs); 13.1 per cent, Scheduled Castes (SCs); 4.6 per cent, Scheduled Tribes (STs); 4.3 per cent, Muslim; and 2.0 per cent, other religious minorities. The balance of 43.6 per cent, amounting to close to half of our student body, are upper castes. In other words, while there has been democratisation across caste and religion, these processes of inclusion have only been partial. The benefits of reservations appear palpable in the case of the OBCs and SCs, although they continue to be under-represented, while the most marginal groups are Muslims and STs. By way of comparison with the situation a decade ago, a very mixed and troubling picture of recent shifts emerges. The dominance of the upper castes, in terms of their proportion, has been slightly mitigated over this decade because of the growing presence of OBCs and SCs; increased enrolment among STs, however, has been much slower, while Muslims have actually lost out in the last 10 years, as comparisons with NSS data for 2004–05 show.

When it comes to gender, AISHE figures for 2013–14 would have us believe that women are approximately 46 per cent across all categories. By comparison, a decade ago, going once more by NSS data in 2004–05, the picture was much more uneven in gendered terms (John, 2012). Women lagged behind men to a certain degree among all disenfranchised groups and had only reached parity levels among upper castes (while also overtaking men among Sikhs and Christians, which continues to be the case today). All these shifts and developments call for much closer scrutiny than I can offer here. They speak of a very significant process, whereby an elite upper-caste student body has had to make room for greater heterogeneity, albeit one that has yet to adequately reflect the social composition of the nation. With reservations, groups such as SCs and OBCs are gaining some kind of space within higher education today in a way that simply did not exist before. Of course, much more needs to be said about this kind of space, as is brought home by the recent suicide of Rohith Vemula. At the same time, cutting through all these fluctuations, there appears to be the growing presence of women across every group. In other words, while some aspects of democratisation may be enforced and backed by mandated reservations in our public universities (although, here, there are clear gaps in implementation), the entry of women speaks of another kind of democratisation process. My question is: How should we view this? Is this simply a 'normal' development, as families aspire for upward mobility for their daughters as well as sons? Or could there be something taking shape here that is potentially more 'revolutionary'?

◆◆◆

In order to take these questions forward, let me switch gears and approach the sphere of higher education from within. After all, even at their best, enrolment numbers are only the beginning of the story and tell us nothing about the experience of being a student. What the numbers do say—and this is, surely, very important in the context of the much-cited demographic dividend that characterises India's population structure—is that so many young women are going to a college or university for several years (the bulk being in institutions offering an undergraduate degree), sometimes at considerable cost to their families, in the hope of a new and better future.

The gendered nature of everyday life in a higher education institution became newly visible in the wake of the unprecedented waves of protest against the 'Delhi gang rape' of 2012. It is surely not an accident that the victim Jyoti Singh was a student. She was studying to become a physiotherapist and was the first in her family to go beyond school. The horrific, and fatal, nature of the gang rape undoubtedly played a large part in the national, and international, outcry that followed, including the state's response in setting up the Justice Verma Committee, and the rapid enactments of the Criminal Amendment Act (2013) and the Sexual Harassment at Workplace Act (2013). For women's organisations and feminists who, since the late 1970s, had made issues of violence one of the springboards of a new movement, this critical event of the 21st century has been a somewhat mixed blessing. On the one hand, it brought issues of sexual violence into public discourse in a way that decades of agitation had not been able to achieve. At the same time, it required considerable effort in the midst of all the clamour to address the commonsense perceptions that the Delhi rape case was dangerously close to cementing, viz., that the greatest danger to women is the stranger lurking in the streets after nightfall, and that the only way to curb such crimes is through the death penalty. Feminists from the women's movement found themselves thrust into the media glare in the months that followed, becoming spokespersons for alternative visions of justice and freedom.

One of the institutions to respond to the moment was the UGC, which set up a Task Force in January 2013 'to review the existing arrangements that have been put in place on the campuses ... to ensure the freedom, safety and security of girls and women in particular and of the entire youth population in general' (UGC, 2013: 95). As a member of the Task Force, I had the opportunity of being a part of the investigations into how universities were tackling sexual harassment and enabling gender sensitisation that resulted in the UGC Report, 'Saksham'. We conducted Open Forums in a number of universities and were able to get a broader glimpse of the state of affairs in many more institutions by sending out questionnaires to all the constituent colleges and universities under the UGC's jurisdiction. If we had to sum up our findings as briefly as possible, they would be thus: The subject of sexual harassment is, at best, a matter of considerable confusion and, more frequently, one of outright denial, especially among administrators and teachers, while the weakest aspect of institutions of higher education turns out to be their lack of gender sensitivity. We repeatedly heard about the pervasive vulnerability to forms of sexual harassment that constitutes the everyday life of women students on our campuses. It is exacerbated by the lack of basic facilities such as transport, lighting, hostel accommodation, health care and counselling. And, it is compounded when gender is reinforced by other structures of discrimination and disadvantage such as rural location, caste, class, minority status, disability and sexuality. In peri-urban and rural areas, there were women students who could only get to college by tractor; but even in the heart of our metros, the lack of public transport within a sprawling campus made many women dependent on male students with motorbikes for their 'little daily needs', who then expected 'favours' in return, in a classic quid pro quo mode. Women students wearing the *hijab* were recipients of frequent comments and taunts, while those from the North East were considered morally loose and subjected to propositions if they ventured out for a walk in the evenings.

Very few members of higher educational institutions took the need for gender sensitisation seriously, even though it is, arguably, the most critical input for creating an atmosphere on campus that is conducive to gender equality and freedom from harassment. Moreover, given the heterogeneous nature of student populations, who not only study but often live together for many years, it is not just experiences of discrimination but different ideas about 'appropriate' behaviour that create confusion and alienation among students, which must be explicitly addressed. The university or college—precisely because their purpose is education—should be places that are especially well placed to think further about equality, to enable students to take risks and to experiment, to learn how to not just tolerate but to also live well with others who are different, whether these differences are social, economic, religious, or related to caste, sexual orientation or ability. The Saksham Report attempted to capture the views of students who strongly, and repeatedly, articulated that a university 'should help women transition from the protected atmosphere of the home into a real life situation where she had to be independent' (ibid.: 37).

The greatest obstacle to gender sensitisation was the administrative approach employed to deal with the presence of significant numbers of women students, viz., protectionism and policing. In the wake of the Delhi gang rape, while students took out marches and held vigils for greater freedom and justice, authorities in many parts of the country responded by making their rules for women students even more stringent than they had been before the incident. Hostel timings were curtailed and 'night outs' cancelled. Most poignant of all is the exposure of the most effective method for silencing students: in undergraduate colleges and privately managed institutions, in particular, there appears to be a kind of pact or contract between the administration and parents, whereby discriminatory rules must be tolerated if not respected, even though they are oriented towards blaming the victim. If students speak up or act against such rules, they could well be asked to leave. Here again, it was only too obvious as to which students would be most vulnerable to this kind of threat—those already battling 'conventional' family backgrounds, those with limited economic resources or from marginal communities. In such a situation, many students said that it would be better to quietly endure the daily humiliations and constraints than risk giving up these precious few years.

At the same time, the last two years in particular have also seen many moments of open protest against sexual harassment and gender discrimination on our campuses. #Hokkolorob' ('let there be noise', in Bengali) became the tag of a student movement that began in Jadavpur University, Kolkata, in September 2014, when their gherao of the Vice Chancellor for not responding to a case of sexual molestation resulted instead in police brutality. This police action, in turn, triggered widespread student support not only in Kolkata, but in several other Indian cities and even among alumni abroad, and used popular music (it is also the title of a Bangladeshi pop song) to great effect. Interestingly, these protests invited a range of responses from other activists and intellectuals, including the accusation that this was an elite protest by a newly articulate middle-class student body, but was devoid of social content, since it did not make common cause with 'inarticulate' poor students elsewhere (Samaddar, 2014). It is not my intent to enter into this particular controversy here, especially given the enormously complex political scenario at this time in a state like West Bengal, except to say that I find it odd that a matter of sexual harassment is thought of as being outside the frame of social equality. (However, the fact that Vemula's death in Hyderabad Central University in January 2016 resulted in unprecedented waves of solidarity across so many universities in the country, but found no echo from #Hokkolorob leaders so far, may be an indication that Samaddar has a point after all.)

In August 2015, women students across various campuses in Delhi came together under the banner #PinjraTod (Break the Hostel Locks, Break the Cage). Here was a campaign exhorting everyone to oppose 'big walls, huge hostel gates, locking of gates at night, numerous security guards, constant checking of Id-cards, a plethora of arbitrary and regressive restrictions'.[2] Students pointed to the arbitrariness, if not hypocrisy, in the avowed claims of 'safety' on the part of Delhi University authorities, given that the various women's hostels under their jurisdiction—including one for SC students, a special one for students from the North East, and an international hostel for foreign students—all had variable timings. Needless to say, in the case of the last two, students were permitted to stay out till much later. Interestingly, this was a campaign that not just focused on college hostels for women, which after all cater to a minuscule proportion of outstation students in the city, but also on the huge service industry of PG accommodation that has quite transformed the residential areas surrounding Delhi University, in particular, with their spiralling rental rates and unregulated modes of functioning. Most recently, #PinjraTod has made a video, uploaded on YouTube, on the dismissal of 10 *safaikaramcharis* who worked in one of the undergraduate women's hostels, because they had been protesting against caste discrimination by the hostel provost. In so doing, they hope to bring student residents closer to the highly exploitative nature of the labour contracts of those who keep their hostels clean.[3]

These are but two examples of protests that have struck a chord amongst students on issues relating to sexual harassment and gender discrimination. There are many more: the social media network 'Hyderabad for Feminism' (Madabhushi, *et al.*, 2015); the Mumbai-based #Why Loiter (Phadke, 2015); and numerous 'take back the night' campaigns, all of which directly address students' and youth experiences and fears of sexual violence, and not just in public spaces. Others have directly countered the *Hindutva* fabrications of 'Love Jihad', and right-wing attacks on young couples, more generally. The data of the National Crime Records Bureau (which provides annual information on crime rates as collected from police stations) has been put to productive use as well. Public lectures and classroom interactions have drawn on such data to demonstrate how exceptional the stereotypical stranger rape actually is, and to further provide concrete evidence of the much higher incidence of cases of abduction and rape lodged by parents against the boy in a consensual sexual relationship, and the vastly greater number of cases of domestic violence that are registered with the police.

I have been further struck by women students' strong participation in a rather different movement: #Occupy UGC.

Here was a campaign that began in November 2015 in response to the sudden UGC directive to cancel non-NET fellowships given to research students, from the forthcoming academic year. In ways that the Ministry of Human Resource Development surely never anticipated, students have been 'occupying' the entry to the UGC offices in the heart of Delhi's ITO area right through the winter months, demanding not only the unconditional rescinding of the order but the enhancement of research fellowships. At the time of writing, the movement has called for the renewal of the campaign, with the additional demand that the upcoming Union Budget allocate 10 per cent to education. In several pamphlets and public statements, the gendered quality of the financial constraints on research students was emphasised, alluding, among other things, to the role that a fellowship, even a modest one, can play in staving off parental pressure for marriage. Students in this movement have been grappling with the ways in which current financial cutbacks in education are threatening the fragile and incomplete democratisation process that has been underway, of which the cancellation of non-Net fellowships is a symptom. As it happens, women's investment in higher education beyond the undergraduate level is often greater than that of men. The proportion of women at the postgraduate level stands at 51 per cent, and actually increases to 55 per cent at the MPhil level, before dropping to 40 per cent at the PhD stage, according to AISHE, 2013–14.

To return to the initial question: What kind of revolution, if any, does all that has been discussed so far portend? We have seen near parity in terms of enrolment among women students at a time of galloping expansion in higher education, coupled with growing privatisation. Over one-fifth of young women in the age group 18–23 go beyond high school, and the vast majority of these are in college, as are their male peers. This growth towards parity has been proceeding relatively silently, and has hardly garnered any public attention. Much less silent, especially in the aftermath of the Delhi gang rape, has been the question of sexual harassment, which has been taken up not just by student-led campaigns, but the UGC as well. This ought to be a source of hope as students seek to make their lives on our campuses more genuinely fulfilling and less humiliating. And yet, I have to pause and wonder why all this churning appears incomplete to me, if not distorted. It is one thing for young women to claim the space of higher education in which they wish to transit from the protected sphere of the home to one of greater independence. But is this in fact the case? What happens afterwards? Are these figures of gender parity mirrored in any other public institution beyond education, such as the workplace? Unfortunately, if we now look to the NSS for a statistical picture, the figures that emerge are truly shocking. Barely 15 per cent of women in India in 2009–10 had any kind of paid work, and this is a figure that has been stagnating, if not declining, in recent years, the very years of the highest levels of economic growth that the country has ever seen (Mazumdar and Neetha, 2011). Moreover, if we disaggregate this figure, we find that the vast majority work in agriculture in rural India, while only a small proportion accounts for the urban female work force, the bulk of which is engaged in primary-school teaching and paid domestic work. This means that while more women are gaining entry into higher education than ever before, declining proportions of these women will be employed, no matter how accomplished and well educated they might be. But where does the demand for economic independence through paid employment figure in contemporary campaigns and demands for greater freedom and equality? These must become integral to student campaigns, so that questions of freedom from violence and greater sexual autonomy do not remain circumscribed within the years of student life alone, but are part of a larger vision for alternative gender-just futures.

Just as I look to conclude this paper comes a small news item. Three girls—E. Saranya, V. Priyanka and T. Monisha, aged 18–19 years—studying naturopathy at a private yoga medical college near Villipuram in Tamil Nadu, committed suicide by jumping into a well.[4] According to their suicide note, they blamed the head of the institution, where 'they learnt nothing', but were subjected to 'torture'. All three had sold their land and taken educational loans of several lakhs, hoping to find employment in the world of alternative medicine. We might simply want to wish away this terrible tragedy as a by-product of corruption-ridden commercialised private education, rendered immune through political connections.

I would like to think that something like a revolution is underway. But unless there is as much noise about these young women's shattered dreams as about everything else that is bringing us out into the streets, we are falling short severely of the potential for radical change that characterises this critical moment in the history of higher education.

◆

NOTES

1. See *Seminar*. 2011. Special issue on 'Democratizing Knowledge: A Symposium on Reforming Higher Education in India', no. 624, August.
2. See *Indian Express*, 22 September 2015.
3. See youtube.com: 'Caste Away: The Story of Dalit Women Sanitation Workers in a DU Women's Hostel.'
4. See *Indian Express*, 28 January 2016.

REFERENCES

Department of Education, Ministry of Human Resource Development. 2013–2014. 'All India Survey of Higher Education Report'. New Delhi: Government of India.

John, Mary E. 2012. 'Gender and Higher Education in the Time of Reforms', *Contemporary Education Dialogue,* vol. 9, no. 2, July, pp. 197–222.

Madabhushi, Tejaswini, Grace Maranatha, T. Wahlang and Gitanjali Joshua. 2015. 'Locating "Hyderabad for Feminism" in the Present Struggle against Violence', *Economic and Political Weekly*, vol. 50, no. 44, pp. 38–46.

Mazumdar, Indrani and N. Neetha. 2011. 'Gender Dimensions: Employment Trends in India, 1993–94 to 2009–10', *Economic and Political Weekly*, vol. 46, no. 43.

Phadke, Shilpa. 2015. 'Risking Feminism? Voices from the Classroom', *Economic and Political Weekly,* vol. 50, no. 17, pp. 63–70.

University Grants Commission. 2013. 'Saksham: Measures for Ensuring the Safety of Women and Programmes of Gender Sensitisation on Campuses.' New Delhi: UGC.

◆◆

MAJORITY IN THE MARGINS?

A Case for Bilingual Pedagogy

TEJASWINI NIRANJANA

In 2011–12, during the last days of the UPA Government's second phase, I had joined other academics and activist–scholars in attending numerous Planning Commission meetings in the hope that we would have some impact on the priorities for the allocation of funds for the higher education sector. We were seeking infrastructural support for the majority of students in state-aided institutions for tertiary education. Those were the days, barely four years ago, when the model of the university, and its affiliated colleges, was the prevailing norm, with postgraduate and undergraduate education distributed between these. I refer here to the institutional pattern for the arts, sciences and commerce education that has been the staple of the Indian tertiary sector for the best part of the 20th century. (Professional institutes for the study of management, architecture, engineering and medicine are not included in the sweep of this remark, and neither are the stand-alone science institutes opened in the last decade or two.) Enrolment patterns are still skewed in the direction of the traditional arts–science–commerce streams (with 60 per cent undergraduates enrolled in these streams), although these figures are likely to change in the present decade.[1]

Today, the field of higher education is crowded with well-funded private universities, which appear to have abandoned the affiliating college model and its division of pedagogic labour. With two interesting exceptions (Ashoka University and Azim Premji University [APU]), these private universities have, at their core, a set of professional and vocational programmes, with add-on courses in Economics and English. This dizzying proliferation of new courses does not, however, indicate that knowledge fields have increased exponentially; it may only mean new ways of slicing the pie, with on-campus recruitment opportunities included in the educational promise. Eighteen-year-olds, who did not want, or could not get, admission to the IITs, and whose parents are willing to invest more than a lakh per annum in the expectation of a new-economy job, are beginning to throng these institutions in significant numbers. While the disaggregated statistics for student enrolment are currently not available, it is apparent that nearly one-third of the degree-granting institutions, which number over 700, are now in the private sector. While the 'private' phenomenon has been part of the college system since the beginning of modern general higher education—with colleges that are over 100 years old in Mumbai, Kolkata, Bangalore, Delhi and other metros such as Jaipur, Agra, Patna, Indore, Mysore, among others—the idea of the private university is relatively more recent, having emerged as a significant feature in the last five years or so. The figures for the Ministry of Human Resource Development (MHRD) indicate that from a total Gross Enrolment Ratio (GER) of 20.4 per cent of the 18–23 age group, 91 lakh students are in private institutions and 58 lakh in government colleges. Of these, 12.5 per cent are from the Scheduled Castes (SC), 4.2 per cent from the Scheduled Tribes (ST), 31.6 per cent from the Other Backward Class (OBC), 4.5 per cent are Muslim, and 2.1 per cent from other minorities. However, we don't know how these categories are represented across public and private institutions, or across the college–university spectrum.[2]

In this article, I look back on attempts over the last few years to address the issue of Indian languages in the higher education classroom, and speculate on what might lie ahead. At the time of writing, in late 2015, we are at a juncture where the consultations to draft a new National Education Policy (NEP) are ongoing. While there is some evidence of regional consultations with experts,[3] the bulk of the discussions appears to be in the social media format[4] with all the rant-or-praise structure and opinions, without the evidence that such a format involves. Nevertheless, the webpage on the Promotion of Languages under this NEP discussion asserts the following: 'A multi-lingual society recognises the importance of education in languages', and comments are invited for the formulation of a language policy in education. To date, there are

1,102 submissions (accessed on 20 October 2015). A random sampling indicates that there is overwhelming support for education in the mother tongue at the school level, to be supplemented by English and Hindi, with some even advocating the addition of a fourth language in schools in so-called backward areas. Strikingly, the advocates of linguistic plurality do not clarify whether they are referring to instruction in multiple languages or simply the teaching of several languages to school children. The comments, several of which are copied verbatim from a template, tend to veer implicitly towards the latter, a situation familiar to some of us from our own school days. The uploaded PDFs are mostly handwritten reports of Mandal-level meetings in which the participants unanimously propose education in the mother tongue, while admitting that there is a universal aspiration to acquire 'English'.

Alongside this ongoing 'curated' national discussion, we should read the figures put together for 2013–14 by the District Information System for Education of the National University of Education Planning and Administration (NUEPA), covering 14.5 lakh schools in 35 states and union territories.[5] The survey indicates the rising enrolment of students in English-medium schools since 2008–09, with Bihar (4,700 per cent increase) and Uttar Pradesh (1,000 per cent increase) topping the charts. Taken together, the purported national discussion on the MHRD website and the NUEPA study can only reaffirm what we have seen since independence: claims about language standing in for claims to a national/subnational identity, and the rights that flow from such a claim through the logic of the welfare state.[6] Unsurprisingly, there is no apparent tension between the claims and the desire for the aspirational horizon of 'English'.

It must be noted here that the emphasis should not be on how many languages the student learns but on whether s/he is developing cognitive capabilities. This has been a serious blind spot in modern Indian education over the decades, right up to the recent May 2014 Supreme Court judgement on the non-enforceability of instruction in the mother tongue.[7] The Court invoked the right to freedom of speech and expression, in this instance, to say that children and parents could choose the language in which the child would be educated, thus separating the language question from the right to education. If exposing a child to English at a very young age is dictated either by opportunism or a desperate bid for social mobility, this choice flies in the face of language and education research as well as the most enlightened pedagogic practices available. If the mother tongue or Indian language education is not practical today, it is because of the enormous lack of good educational resources in those languages, another need that state initiatives have failed to address adequately. We see an oblique reference to this failure in the Supreme Court's judgement, which holds that 'prescribing English as a medium of instruction in subjects of higher education for which only English books are available and which can only be properly taught in English may have a direct bearing and impact on the determination of standards of education'.

THE LANGUAGE DIVIDE

Given the scenario to which I refer in the opening paragraph of this article—a scenario we believed is a persisting aspect of the higher education sector—my colleagues and I had offered a diagnosis around 2008: The language divide in Indian higher education, where the default language of instruction is the local language, despite the mandated English medium, is an indicator of a deep-seated problem. It suggests that the majority of tertiary education students in India and often their teachers, too, are unable to comprehend knowledge systems and conceptual frameworks that do not resonate with their own experience. Much of state intervention, as well as a public understanding of the problem, tends to read it simply as one more indication of social backwardness, to be remedied by the most obvious solutions.

Beginning in the 1960s, the Government of India established four Regional Institutes of English (RIE) to enhance English-language skills, especially for schoolteachers, and, simultaneously, supported the translation of standard textbooks into Indian languages, culminating in the establishment of the National Translation Mission (NTM) in 2007.[8] However, this latter idea goes back 150 years. In the Education Despatch of 1854, translations from English were made a priority as a way of making European knowledge available to the general public. Despite these strategies, a high failure rate and poor employability continue to haunt the higher education system. The improvement of English skills has no effect when attention is not paid to the relevance of the curriculum to contemporary needs, or to clarifying the larger objectives of higher education. Similarly, translating large amounts of material into Indian languages has little impact because attention is not paid to the effectiveness of the materials produced for higher education.

As an alternative approach to the language divide, we had argued for bilingualism in teaching and research, without either jettisoning English altogether or abandoning the local language. Further, we had contended that the preconditions for bilingual pedagogy need to be actively created, since they did not obtain in our universities and colleges, and that a significant precondition would be the production of new critical resources in Indian languages. A further step would be to translate these resources into English so that they could help raise new questions in the English-only classroom as well.

These suggestions were made by a group of scholars, drawn from a number of institutions across India, in Bangalore, in 2008, to discuss the modalities of intervention in the bleak higher education scenario. So that our proposed interventions were not based only on our intuitions about the scale of the problem, we decided to put together some data about language use in higher education. Following the meeting, a few of us took up the task of designing and conducting scoping studies so that preliminary diagnoses could be made and suggestions put forward. It was felt that a systematic survey of existing resources would facilitate the planning of future initiatives to address the problem of quality teaching materials and research resources in Indian languages. Described briefly below are two such studies, one focusing on Kannada and the other on Hindi.

MAPPING INDIAN LANGUAGE RESOURCES

In 2009, a mapping exercise was undertaken by the Department of Translation Studies, Kannada University.[9] This study was intended to collate the available resources for higher education in Kannada and provide an assessment of past strategies in addressing the linguistic divide in higher education with reference to Karnataka. The findings were disturbing: approximately 96 per cent of the local language books used in higher education are translations and only 4 per cent are original resources. The report also drew attention to the severe scarcity of locally relevant materials for higher education.[10]

The Kannada study pointed out that from the 1980s onwards, in a majority of the universities in Karnataka, the most widespread language of examination has become Kannada, even though the language of instruction is still supposedly English. A fair amount of teaching takes place in Kannada, even in postgraduate courses, especially in the humanities and social sciences. Increasingly, students are also choosing to write their research dissertations in Kannada. But even as the number of students pursuing higher education through the resources available in Kannada is increasing, this is not matched by a corresponding increase in the availability of quality materials in Kannada that can be put to use in higher education.

Interestingly, even with all the state resources being poured into the development and propagation of Hindi, the situation there is not very different from that of a much smaller language like Kannada, which does not have the same national aspirations. An inventory and review of the quality of curricular resources in Hindi in three social science disciplines—History, Political Science and Sociology—at both the BA and MA levels was taken up in 2010 by a group of scholars from New Delhi.[11] Six major universities in five states of north India were considered: Patna University, Patna (Bihar); Allahabad University and Banaras Hindu University (Uttar Pradesh); Barkatullah University, Bhopal (Madhya Pradesh); Maharshi Dayanand University, Rohtak (Haryana); and Rajasthan University, Jaipur (Rajasthan). The textbooks were evaluated for their coverage of course content, the academic quality of content, their suitability for the relevant educational level, and production quality. Since Hindi is used in 151 universities and deemed universities in the 10 Hindi-speaking states, it is likely to occupy a key position in any initiative dealing with Indian languages in higher education. This inventorying exercise helped us understand that students use whatever textbook material there is, irrespective of whether that material belongs to the very small category described in the study as 'excellent', to the moderately large 'reasonably competent' category, or to the very large 'deficient' category (Deshpande, 2010: 100).

I describe the findings of this study in some detail because it provides comprehensive parameters by which we could conduct similar exercises across languages. The main reasons why the evaluators classified material as deficient included

> incomplete or 'gappy' coverage of the topics specified; factual errors; biased or one-sided treatments; oversimplification of explanations;

> outdated or obsolete treatment; insufficient differentiation between different levels (e.g., BA, MA); absence of citations, references; lack of guidance for further reading; bibliographies; poor language (i.e., cliché-ridden, jargon-filled or otherwise obscure) (ibid.: 100).

An even more serious issue could well be the absence of a scholarly or critical approach:

> ...[T]ext books generally tend to convey information rather than encourage students to think critically or to consider an issue from different standpoints. The lack of scholarly orientation is felt most acutely not only in the absence of bibliographies or suggestions for further reading, but in the absence of even references and citations. The failure to cite material available in Hindi is another issue (ibid.: 100).

The Hindi textbooks study concluded with the following suggestions, and the admission that it would require a high level of intellectual and financial investment:

> *A series of course-specific 'Readers' at the MA level, containing a mix of existing, newly translated, and newly written materials; a similar series of short monographs on key topics with extensive bibliographies* [italics mine] aimed at BA Honours students; strategic, discipline-specific 'gap-filling exercises' that will produce new translations or original texts to plug holes in available curricular material; 'inspirational' general introductions to disciplines designed to exploit and extend the momentum provided by the new NCERT Class XII textbooks in the hope of weaning fresh undergraduates away from the temptations of the guide book genre; and sustained efforts to ensure that good textbooks are updated regularly, both to drop obsolete material and to include new perspectives (ibid.: 101–02).

Thus far, impressionistic understandings of other linguistic contexts indicate that these suggestions could well be generalised to all Indian language initiatives.

A special feature of both the Kannada and Hindi studies was the focus on social sciences. This stemmed from our shared analysis, forged at the 2008 meeting, that it was by creating a social science vocabulary in the Indian languages that we would be addressing a number of problems unique to that domain of higher education.

CREATION OF NEW RESOURCES

As an initial step towards making good intellectual resources available in Indian languages we, at the Higher Education Innovation and Research Applications programme (HEIRA), worked with J. Devika at the Centre for Development Studies (CDS), Thiruvananthapuram, to design and create a history of gender in Malayalam,[12] which was developed through discussions with the Kudumbashree government programme workers.[13] This project was taken up to see what kinds of innovative resources could be developed to teach complex subjects in regional languages. Another project, which has had an extended impact, was the set of readers in Marathi on women's studies produced by the Krantijyoti Savitribai Phule Women's Studies Centre at the University of Pune,[14] and another set of anthologies, published in 2011, drawing on the special issues of the Marathi social science journal, *Samaj Prabodhan Patrika*. These included volumes on critical historiography; energy: issues and challenges in India; and international relations—these topics being identified by the journal's then executive editor Mahesh Gavaskar as being directly relevant to postgraduate courses in several Maharashtrian universities. Alongside, we incubated a curricular intervention in research training in 2009–10 using bilingual bridge materials at Kuvempu University in Karnataka. This project was designed as a pedagogic intervention in teaching advanced research in the social sciences to students from rural areas. It provided research training to undergraduate and postgraduate students through four week-long workshops spanning a year, with the assumption that the crisis of education in rural India was not one of service delivery (i.e., the lack of linguistic resources to deliver already available content), but one of relevance (in other words, designing the curriculum in such a way as to incite in students a spirit of critical enquiry regarding the world around them).

More recently in 2014–15, I helped design and conduct a series of workshops for postgraduate students along with colleagues in Jadavpur University, Kolkata; Savitribai Phule University of Pune; Tata Institute of Social Sciences (TISS), Mumbai; English and Foreign Languages University, Hyderabad, and TISS–Hyderabad;

and Tumkur University, Karnataka. The focus of these workshops was to generate born-digital resources in Indian languages, using the Wikipedia platform. Working their way through exercises on denotation and connotation, on demarcating the meanings of concepts, and on translation, the participants created new encyclopedic entries for Wikipedia in Kannada, Marathi, Hindi, Bangla, Assamese, Gujarati, Telugu and Malayalam.[15]

In the area of resource creation, TISS supports its faculty's work at the Centre for Indian Languages in Higher Education in a number of disciplines. In the last two years, projects on biodiversity (Marathi), human rights (Telugu), women's studies (Hindi, Marathi), literature and the conditions of writers in the North-East (translation of North-Eastern poets into Hindi), and collections of annotated writings on the feminist and Dalit movements (Telugu) are being readied for publication. They will be available by 2016 on the portal of the TISS Research Council.[16]

PRIVATE UNIVERSITIES AND THE LANGUAGE DIVIDE

In the second scenario sketched in the opening section of this article, I touched upon the new private universities which have become visible on the Indian higher education scene in the last few years. We don't as yet know, except in an impressionistic way, the kind of students entering these private universities, especially those for liberal arts/liberal studies. However, we can guess their economic background from the kind of fees charged in these institutions, many of which claim to be non-profit.[17] While all the private universities promise scholarships, we have no idea of the percentage of students that obtain them. An examination of the curriculum may give us another insight into what might be happening to the language question in the private universities: e.g., a BSc in Art and Design (the course closest to a humanities degree that I could find in a non-liberal studies university in northern India) offers Soft Skills, Foreign Language, English, Manners and Etiquette. O.P. Jindal Global University, yet another non-profit private institution, offers a liberal arts degree in conjunction with Rollins College, USA, promising a 'liberal arts education which transcends cultures', in which the languages we can glimpse are Sanskrit, Mandarin and Spanish, in addition to English. At Azim Premji University, substantial support is provided to undergraduates of liberal studies seeking to improve their English skills. They don't learn any other language, although they are encouraged to work in an Indian language under the mentorship of a faculty member for the study or research of topics in their for-credit Understanding India courses.

Has the language divide problem disappeared in the new institutions? Another improbable thought: Have the students been so thoroughly filtered that they all appear at these institutions fully formed by English and without any mother tongue impediments? What new challenges do we face in such classrooms? Have the old challenges disappeared? Are we observing a new segregation in higher education, such as air-conditioned buses for 'international school' students? If all the readings on Indian society and history are in English—as is evident in the liberal studies syllabi of leading private universities—are students encountering an India already processed and pre-digested?

That we may be witnessing, in at least some examples, iterations of the old problem is evident from the graduate studies student intake of Azim Premji University (e.g., Development Studies), where I have been told by reliable sources that less than 50 per cent of the students comprehend the English-language course readings. For the rest, APU has set up a unit which is hiring commercial translators to translate select readings into Hindi and Malayalam. When asked how this initiative differed from that of the National Translation Mission, the person in charge of the unit could not offer any satisfactory answer.

At this crossroads in Indian higher education, it may be worth asking whether we should persist with the effort to advocate bilingual teaching and research. My answer would be that we need to think both about the student disadvantaged both for lack of English and knowing only English. I cannot emphasise enough that bilingual education is not about addressing only those who are struggling with English—it is about fomenting a crisis in English education by bringing in material with which the English curriculum is not designed to deal. While we know that most of our languages cannot sustain teaching and research in the context of the modern university and its disciplines, we should also be aware that enforced monolingualism in English will make higher education unsustainable. We need to create critical vocabularies across several conceptual domains to feed into the creation of relevant knowledge. Students need to learn the ability to distinguish between levels of meaning, to contextualise/translate, and to create new concepts that capture the life of our societies and our institutions. And in doing this, they have to learn to draw on multiple linguistic resources. To include bilingual pedagogy in our horizon of aspiration for higher education would be to ensure that bi- and trilingualism are not seen only as the situation of everyday interaction in India, but also as an important feature of knowledge production and dissemination.

◆

NOTES

1. All India Survey on Higher Education, published by the Ministry of Human Resource Development, New Delhi, 2013. Available at aishe.gov.in
2. Ibid., p. 10.
3. http://www.thehindu.com/opinion/op-ed/the-new-education-policy-still-stuck-in-the-old-school/article7781017.ece?homepage=true
4. https://mygov.in/group/new-education-policy/
5. Reported in http://timesofindia.indiatimes.com/india/Number-of-children-studying-in-English-doubles-in-5-years/articleshow/49131447.cms
6. See Ashwin Kumar (2014) for a concise presentation of this problem.
7. http://supremecourtofindia.nic.in/outtoday/41504.pdf. Accessed on 21 October 2015.
8. See, for example, the 'About Us' section of one of these institutes: http://www.riesielt.org/. See also the website of the National Translation Mission: http://www.ntm.org.in/
9. The principal investigators for the study were V. B. Tharakeshwar and M. Usha of Kannada University. The project was in partnership with the Higher Education Innovation and Research Applications (HEIRA) programme at the Centre for the Study of Culture and Society, Bangalore. Available from the HEIRA webpage at cscs.res.in
10. The Federation of Indian Publishers Annual Report (2006) shows that the per capita book production in Kannada is 5 per cent (as against English, which is 23 per cent), a figure indicative of the general lack of resources in Indian languages.
11. See Deshpande (2010).The principal investigator was Satish Deshpande, Department of Sociology, Delhi University. Available from the HEIRA webpage at cscs.res.in
12. Available at https://ml.m.wikisource.org/ if one looks for the title *'Kulastreeyum' 'chanthapennu' undayathengane?*

13. http://www.kudumbashree.org
14. http://www.unipune.ac.in/snc/womens_studies_centre/wsc_webfiles/publications.htm
15. http://www.tiss.edu/TopMenuBar/academic/centres-of-schools/centres-of-school-of-education/centre-for-indian-languages-in-higher-education
16. http://www.tiss.edu/TopMenuBar/research/office-of-the-dean-of-research-and-development
17. A sample of fees for an undergraduate course at Ashoka University, a private non-profit institution, in 2015: tuition, ₹5,70,000; hostel fee, ₹1,25,000, mess charges extra; security deposit, ₹50,000, etc. At JNU, a central university, the tuition fee for the postgraduate course is around ₹1,350. At SNDT, Mumbai, it is about ₹14,000. An MA programme at TISS, a deemed university, is approximately ₹2 lakh inclusive of the hostel. In Mumbai University, a state university, fees for the MA is approximately ₹9,000. While this range is quite varied, the new liberal studies private university is clearly in a league of its own. However, amongst these, Azim Premji University is closer to TISS in the fee structure, with its undergraduate fees amounting to one-fourth that of Ashoka University.

REFERENCES

Ashwin Kumar, A. P. 2014. 'Local Labyrinths: Language as a Problematic.' Unpublished dissertation. Manipal University.

Deshpande, Satish. 2010. 'Social Science Teaching in Hindi: An Inventory and Analysis of Current Curricular Materials at Six North Indian Universities.' Delhi: Institute for Social and Economic Research and HEIRA, CSCS.

◆◆

TEACHING POETRY IN SCHOOL

Literary Common Sense and Prevalent Classroom Practices

MANOJ KUMAR

Ink-blue is the colour which generally represents government schooling in India, the colour of the school uniform in most Indian states. From a remote village in the forests of Bastar to one in the mountains of Uttarakhand, from a village in the deserts of Rajasthan to a coastal one in Karnataka, one finds children of school-going age in ink-blue shirts even after school hours as the school uniform is usually their only clothing in good condition. It appears as if the Indian nation state has successfully colour-coded Indian childhood and has, eventually, got its aesthetic marker right. It has been argued that the aesthetic vouched for by modern nationalism is that of homogeneity in a diverse imagined space (Anderson, 1983; Bhabha, 1990). It appears that with the successful enrolment of most children of relevant age in schools, the Indian nation state has achieved one significant breakthrough.

Under this apparent monochromatic, homogenous childhood lies the multitudinous diversity of cultural tastes, speech verities, modes of cultural expressions and forms of everyday life. In some ways, democracy in India is more alive to this diversity than the Indian educational system. This diversity appears to have stifled Indian education, along with perceived demands of the globalising job market and parental pressure for an education in English. Theoretically, cultural diversity can be accommodated as much in English as it can in any standardised Indian language such as Hindi or Marathi—these Indian languages can promote hegemony in many classrooms just as English might. But beyond this purely theoretical and analytical realm, historical-empirical analyses suggest otherwise. In a recently conducted survey of the learning achievement of students across states and union

Winter 2015–Spring 2016, Volume 42, Numbers 3 & 4

territories by the National Council for Educational Research and Training (NCERT), the only subject area in which children of Class 10 have performed satisfactorily is Indian languages. As reported in *The Times of India*, only 41 per cent of students answered correctly in the English exam, 40 per cent in mathematics and 43 per cent in science, while the corresponding score for Indian languages was 53 per cent.[1] Although the percentage for Indian languages is not impressive and there is no reason to celebrate it—considering the fact that of late the teaching of Indian languages suffers the most neglect by Indian education officials, headmasters and parents—one must reflect in comparative terms on the reasons for this rather satisfactory performance. Notwithstanding all the valid criticism of projects promoting Indian languages such as Hindi or Kannada as mediums of instruction in schools as hegemonic (which delegitimises various cultural expressions), children in Indian schools still find these languages less threatening and more culturally accessible. If this is the case, then genuine criticism regarding the use of standardised Indian languages as mediums of instruction should strengthen the project, rather than declaring it dead. Abandoning this project would be akin to throwing out the proverbial baby with the bath water.

However, one has to accept that the demand of multilingualism posed by almost one hundred per cent enrolment in Indian schools has not been met so far by teachers of Indian languages.[2] The honest admission of this limitation by both the teacher and curriculum planner will lay them open to the criticism of hegemony, and it will certainly help them in reflecting on their pedagogy by taking them through the historical making of their projects.

This is an important moment in the history of Indian schooling when children from various disadvantaged backgrounds are joining schools and bringing different modes of linguistic and cultural expressions into the classroom. Therefore, teachers of Indian languages should be better equipped to respond to those expressions and accommodate those voices. This can happen only if they are made to realise that the linguistic and cultural norms they often try to impose in their classrooms are formed through several historical contingencies, rather than as an outcome of their language being *naturally* superior.

This essay argues that until this kind of reflection and dialogue becomes an integral part of pre-service and in-service teacher education, reform in curriculum and textbook writing will have limited impact. A small exploratory study that I conducted on the teaching of Hindi poetry in New Delhi schools after a new Hindi language textbook was introduced in 2005–2006 identifies the discomfort of teachers, and even some of the textbook writers, with new kinds of demands made by the teaching of poetry. Following a brief account of this study, the essay will examine the historical processes of the making of literary common sense in the Hindi public sphere. Finally, it will point to some of the ways in which critical dialogue can be initiated amongst teachers and educationists, to bring their common sense into the realm of critical consciousness.

POETRY TEACHING IN SCHOOL: AN EXPLORATORY STUDY[3]

I conceptualised a study to attempt to understand the pedagogic shifts proposed by National Curriculum Framework, 2005 (NCF–2005), and NCERT's new textbook vis-à-vis poetry teaching, and the manner in which educators comprehend the place of poetry in achieving overall educational aims. The two questions to be addressed in this study were: first, what kind of treatment of poetry textbooks had the developers of the NCERT Hindi textbook imagined? Second, do teachers understand the place of poetry in curriculum and human life? How do they comprehend the reception of poetry and its manner of instruction? How does their overall view of poetry influence its teaching in class?

DISCUSSION WITH THE TEXTBOOK COMMITTEE

This study in Delhi was conducted with five teachers and five members of textbook committees between 16 September 2010 and 1 October 2010. Textbook writers were asked to describe their experience of the selection and rejection of poems; rationales which were put forth; the engagement with poetry expected in a classroom; and, devices to be used in textbooks to ensure those engagements, etc. The format of the interview, both with teachers and textbook writers, was semi-structured.

Textbooks, which are key teaching–learning material for Kendriya Vidyalayas and a majority of CBSE-affiliated schools from 2006 onwards, were compiled by textbook committees constituted by NCERT for various subjects. Textbooks for primary grades and upper-primary grades were compiled by two different committees.

The teachers interviewed were all working with NCERT textbooks. The NCERT textbooks currently being used were supposed to facilitate the actualisation of the objectives of teaching and learning set by NCF–2005, which makes several recommendations for *language* teaching, but only some general remarks on the teaching of *literature* in school. The Position Paper of National Focus Group on Teaching of Indian Languages makes a total of 22 recommendations, of which only one recommendation is relevant to the compilation and selection of literary texts in language textbooks.

> It is extremely important to produce interesting and challenging textbooks and other books covering a wide range of genres, themes, and registers and to provide for professionally trained teachers to ensure high levels of proficiency in different languages (NCERT, 2006: 31).

As is evident, NCF–2005 documents provide a very general framework for the selection and teaching–learning process of, literary texts. Nevertheless, the members' approach to the selection of poems reflects some key insights into the NCF approach to language. The selection of poetry was made on the following grounds: (i) age-appropriate writings; (ii) playful, hilarious and sensitive use of language; and (iii) poetry which suggests new ways of perceiving things.

SELECTION FOR PRIMARY CLASSES

The committee which compiled textbooks for primary classes showed some consensus within the group. Its poetic sensibility, however, was not as varied as that of the committee for the upper-primary group.

The committees' expectations, vis-à-vis treatments of poetry in classrooms, are also reflected in the exercises they have designed following each poem. One interesting point that emerged in the discussions was that, usually, whenever there was a lack of consensus amongst the members regarding the inclusion of any poem, the proposer was asked to develop exercises on it. The underlying assumption was quite clear—if good exercises could be developed, then there was a rationale for its inclusion in the textbook.

There are mainly four to five categories of exercises following each chapter:

(i) Questions relating to certain aspects of the poem, intended to encourage children to read carefully, closely and repeatedly.
(ii) 'Poem and You' categories of questions in which the text works as a springboard from which children are supposed to delve into their own experiences, reflect upon them, and share them.
(iii) Questions relating to Poetic Language.
(iv) Questions relating to grammar and construction as an inductive method for the identification of grammatical rules.
(v) Factual questions relating to the subject of the poem.

SELECTION FOR UPPER-PRIMARY CLASSES

TEXTBOOK CANON VERSUS POPULAR FORMS

One group within the committee was keen to include more writings from contemporary, popular works to encourage children to connect with the text. The other group possibly felt the need to initiate the children into the 'great' canon of Hindi literature. As a result of this debate and negotiation, Sahir Ludhianvi's *Saathi Haath Badhana* was selected, but several poems and other popular forms of writings were eventually rejected by the in-house faculty members of NCERT.

I sensed that there were members who took fairly unconventional positions by insisting on the inclusion of poetry, bearing in mind the creative use of language and new ways of relating to things. One member told me that there could be poetry in ordinary objects and everyday mundane issues. Children needed to appreciate their surroundings with poetic vision and to know that there was the possibility of poetry everywhere. If that were indeed the objective of teaching poetry and literature, then textbook developers were not required to concentrate only on canons of textbook poetry, and on celebrated Hindi poets. According to him, *Hindiwallahs* (professors, teachers and litterateurs of Hindi literature) were far too concerned with the poets themselves than with their oeuvre. However, members who genuinely felt the need to initiate the next generation into great poetic traditions had their own arguments. Regrettably, these debates were more acrimonious than rational, and it is quite possible that the reason behind these discordant and emotionally charged debates was the fact that some of the changes demanded could potentially unsettle cultural common sense, which constructs, and is constructed by, the culture of nationalism. One member shared his view on the tradition of selecting poetry: 'As Hindi is considered the national language, textual tradition is bit overwhelmed with inculcating nationalist values and providing moral messages through textbooks.'[4]

DISCUSSIONS WITH TEACHERS

The discussions encompassed the following areas:

(i) What if there were to be no poetry in language textbooks?
(ii) What makes poetry different from other forms of writing?
(iii) Teachers' descriptions of their last poetry class.
(iv) Exercises/types of activities that were generally conducted in poetry class.
(v) The selection of poems in NCERT textbooks.

I witnessed verbal expressions of annoyance and outrage in teachers at the prospect of the non-inclusion of poems by curricular planners in language textbooks. The reason probably lies in the belief that the significance of poetry is self-evident. It is not the case that there is no alternate position in history—Plato's disdain for poetry was well known. However, questioning the significance of one of the oldest literary forms known to mankind is a bit unusual.

A teacher from an innovative private school in Delhi tried to articulate the loss by saying that if poetry were not included in textbooks, a certain sweetness would be lost—we would be reduced to tasteless, dry things. Another teacher from Kendriya Vidyalaya equated poetry with the heart, likening it to a human being without one. Yet another equated poetry with heart, and prose with thought. So, teachers generally described their sense of loss by applying metaphors of taste (sweetness) and movement (the pulsating heart).

One may wonder whether the use of these metaphors is arbitrary and therefore viewed as the expressions of individuals, or if their frequent use is the consequence of socialisation in certain cultures. In classical Sanskrit aesthetics, *rasa* (juice/nectar) is the descriptor for aesthetic pleasure. Although there are many rasas, and equating poetry with any one taste (sweetness) would be inadequate even in this tradition, here I am tempted to suggest that the dominant categories and frameworks of Indian classical aesthetics, which have been used for centuries for the analysis of poetry and aesthetic pleasure, have percolated to literary common sense.

The metaphor of the heart is even more synthetic—it contains layers of meaning even though it is frequently used for kindness, empathy and aesthetic pleasure. The comparison of poetry to a pulsating heart might suggest that it is a live entity and not simply an object. The heart indicates the embodied emotional sensation, and its juxtaposition to disembodied thought is quite prevalent. This symbolisation has now pervaded popular culture. It would be interesting to trace this metaphor in Western and Indian cultures, but is beyond the scope of this essay.

Nevertheless, in another formulation, poetry needs to contain some moral lesson, which might very well be dry; but, then, poetic devices could be used to make those teachings more interesting. Eleventh-century Sanskrit scholar, Mammat, uses the analogy of 'preaching by the beloved' to explain the purpose of writing poetry. While preaching by a conventional preacher might not be persuasive enough, if carried out by the beloved/wife, perhaps it could.

A government school teacher in Delhi told me that literature is meant for human welfare (*sa+hit*). In Hindi, 'hit' means welfare, although *sahit* also means 'coordination', 'balance', 'concord and 'coordination'. Pravas Jivan Chaudhury writes:

> The Sanskrit word for literature is *Sahitya*, which etymologically means coordination, balance, concord, and contact. Following one of these several meanings, literature is defined by one school of Indian poetics as the art where the words and sense meet on equal terms and enhance one another's beauty and worth. They are compared by Kuntakal (10th century A.D., Kashmirian) to two close friends, one having powers and virtues equal to the other (1965: 197).

Nationalist literary critics of Hindi literature either interpreted sahit as general welfare, or inclusion. This sense continues to prevail amongst many language teachers.

THE MODE OF INTERACTION IN POETRY CLASSES

Most teachers are of the opinion that rhymes and regular metre distinguish poetic forms from other literary forms, although they accept that most poetry written currently is in free verse. Three of five teachers discount such writings as poetry. One teacher said that she likes to teach some of those 'writings' because of their content and style. Teachers commonly focus more on the emotional or moral content of a poem than its form. Symbols and metaphors are interpreted by either locating the text in a historical context or by taking some clue from the poet's biography.

CLASSROOM PROCESSES

Teachers' descriptions of their poetry class may be divided into three categories. The first category comprises three steps, which include creating an appropriate emotional state before teaching poetry through activity or thought experiment; organising discussions on the 'issue' that has been described; and an eventual interpretation of the poem, with some help from students.

The second category of description involves the recitation of the poem by the teacher with proper intonation and stress. This powerful, live presentation makes its meaning explicit to listeners/ students. This is then followed by providing a brief account of the poet's life, a practice that rests on the belief that the historical milieu in which the poet and poem are located is essential.

The third category involves the introduction of both poet and poem after which the teacher recites the poem stanza by stanza, each of which is followed by an interpretation. These processes are known in Hindi as *satik vyakhya* (accurate meaning) and *saprasang vyakhya* (contextual interpretation, which does not include the readers' context).

Other activities that teachers occasionally, or regularly, use are competitions for painting, posters and elocution, and memorisation and presentation of poetry that is related to the long, cultural association of poetry as a literary form which needs to be sung, recited and heard.

ON TEACHING POETRY

As poetry is one of the oldest literary forms, a teacher's or textbook writer's poetic sensibility is intricately linked to her cultural worldview. It is not possible to change the pedagogy of poetry simply by addressing discrete 'misconceptions' about poetry or by designing good exercises or adding poetic text of a different flavour. A teacher's pedagogy is probably informed by her 'naïve' poetics and not simply by some stand-alone conception or misconception. The teacher who treats poetry as a means of promoting moral lessons for the general well-being of her students adopts the process of teaching, which resembles that of cultural training. Other teachers, who view poetry as a spontaneous overflow of powerful emotions, adopt a classroom process which can bring children to a particular emotional state of mind. Several intermediate positions are possible between these two extremes. In a class, students who get some space try to connect with poetry in a very personal way.

◆◆◆

THE MAKING OF THE HINDI LITERARY CANON AND LITERARY COMMON SENSE

Henry Giroux interprets the Gramscian idea of *common sense* as an uneven intellectual terrain. According to him, ideology operates at three different levels—at the levels of unconscious desire, of common sense, and of critical reflection. In Giroux's words:

> Following Gramsci (1971), I want to argue that human behaviour is rooted in a complex nexus of structured needs, common sense, and critical consciousness, and that ideology is located in all of these aspects of human behaviour and thought so as to produce multiple subjectivities and perceptions of the world and everyday life. The interference of ideology and individual experience can be located within three specific areas: the sphere of the unconscious and the structure of needs; the realm of common sense; and the sphere of critical consciousness (1997: 77).

So, common sense finds a place somewhere between the unconscious and full, critical consciousness. In the realm of common sense there can be elements arising unintentionally from dominant prevailing ideology and also from contesting critical ideologies. However, there can be contradictions and inconsistencies in a commonsensical approach. It goes without saying that language is not merely a medium of communication; it is also an important marker of both social and political identities. Language has a constitutive role; it constitutes forms of subjectivities and socio-cultural locations.

The advent of the print-culture in Hindi in the 19th and early 20th century, and the use of this language in education, facilitated the carving out of a new public space which, in turn, works as an incubator for the formation of new kinds of subjectivities. Communities of readers and writers were formed, and these communities crisscrossed fixed, ascribed identities of caste and gender. It provided newly educated urban and rural youth an opportunity to imagine their life trajectories beyond their caste and gender-ascribed social roles. It was possible to answer the question 'who am I?' in different ways. However, new avenues, which the use of Hindi in print and education had provided to new generations in the 19th and early 20th century, were not totally open for creative redefinitions. Soon after Hindi's use for print communication and education, new norms were set up in terms of the use of language and cultural appropriateness. Hindi as a language of mass contact and public reasoning also became one of markers of national identity. Under the stewardship of Mahavir Prasad Dwivedi (editor of the reputed Hindi journal *Sarasawati*) and also under the guidance of the editors of Narari Pracharini Sabha (an association for the promotion of the Nagari script and the Hindi language), the Hindi literary field increasingly became a space more accommodative of linguistic registers and cultural expressions of high-caste literate Hindus than of masses inhabiting popular space (Kumar, 1990: 1247–49; 1251–55). Along with this shift towards regulation, new forms of patriarchy were instituted with a series of social reforms. These reforms did provide some space to imagine new gender roles such as women in the service of community and nation, etc. But, gradually, it was as if one of the given roles was appropriated rather than fashioning new forms of subjectivities and gender roles. During the same period, Hindi became a subject for higher studies. Banaras Hindu University began a postgraduate programme in Hindi in the early 20th century. The selection of texts and evaluation was needed for which norms were proposed and debated and, in this process, the canon of Hindi literature was formed.

It should be emphasised that the standardised, Sanskritised version of Hindi was constituted as a marker of national identity in opposition to colonial cultural domination, as well as in competition with other lingua francas of that period; those lingua francas, or contact languages, were Urdu and Hindustani. In day-to-day linguistic communication, delimiting Hindi from Urdu and Hindustani was difficult; however, it was comparatively easy to identify literary expressions of Hindi and Urdu because conscious efforts had been made by both sides to transcend immediate linguistic surroundings. The Hindi and Urdu languages for literary expression were created by borrowing directly from the classical literary culture of Sanskrit and Arabic–Persian. This notion of immediate '*folk*' surroundings and medieval India—which had just preceded the modern colonial period—as decadent was consistent with certain ideas of national religious revivalism. However, the problem with establishing the Hindi canon was that it could not avoid medieval literature altogether as the Bhakti movement was located in those centuries. Forms of religiosity and cultural expressions that were established during the medieval period were still prevalent in the Hindi-speaking region until the early 20th century. There was a certain vehemence against the use of *Brajbhasha* for writing poetry in the early 20th century, and an insistence on standardised *Khari Boli* Hindi as best able to represent and express the modern ethos of the time. Nevertheless, the medieval poetry of Brajbhasha, Awadhi and Maithili did get prominent places in the Hindi canon.[5] Although these languages were, and still are, living languages spoken in 'Hindi-speaking' states, they were assigned to the medieval era in the Hindi canon. Thus, it was created by denying synchronicity to languages such as Brajbhasha, Khari Boli, Awadhi, Maithili, etc., as well as by arranging them diachronically by assigning standard Khari Boli Hindi to modernity, and Brajbhasha, etc., to tradition. It is the socialisation of Hindi teachers in this canon which does not allow the use of any of these languages in their classrooms and consciously discourages the use of Arabic-Persian-sounding Urdu expressions. A teacher at Kendriya Vidyalaya in Delhi was quite resentful about the use of Haryanvi and Punjabi versions of Hindi by his students. For him, it was not just about the violation of linguistic norms, but a sign of cultural decadence and ethical–moral permissiveness.

There is hope that intuitive actions on the part of teachers could be brought into the realm of their critical consciousness, which is entirely possible as literary canons and aesthetic standards are precariously poised at any given time. Mahavir Prasad Dwivedi published a Bhojpuri poem written by a Dalit poet, Hira, in *Saraswati* during the high noon of literary canon making. In the early days of the print culture it was possible to use many expressions in Hindi journals (Orisini, 1999: 409–16). The discussion of aesthetic norms to evaluate literature while considering modern values has always been noisy and lively. Hopefully, the memory of these historical debates will still be alive in the minds of Hindi teachers and can be critically reflected upon. For example, the confrontation over the aesthetics of modern poetry among poets such as Surayakant Tripathi 'Nirala' and Sumitranandan Pant on the one hand and Ramchandra Shukla, the established literary critic of his time, on the other, could potentially allow students of Hindi to arrive at an informed opinion. Also, poetic sensibilities in Hindi literature have come a long way from the heyday of romanticism (*Chhayavadi* era) and early days of social reform-induced nationalism. Poetry writing in Hindi took a progressive and modernist turn in the 1930s, led by leading poets of the Chhayavadi era—Nirala and Sumitranandan Pant. Literary criticism in Hindi has also evolved from the early days. However, many of these debates have yet to reach schoolteachers so that they may take alternative stances towards poetry. These live debates have the potential to bring reflexivity in Hindi intelligentsia and make the teaching of Hindi literature in schools more lively.

◆

NOTES

1. http://timesofindia.indiatimes.com/home/education/news/Most-Std-X-students-below-par-in-English-maths-NCERT/articleshow/50475790.cms. Accessed on 24 February 2016.
2. The World Bank data 93% enrollment till 2012. http://data.worldbank.org/indicator/SE.PRM.NENR?order=wbapi_data_value_2012+wbapi_data_value&sort=asc
3. The study was conducted under the supervision of Jane Sahi, Sita School, Bengaluru, and Professor Apoorvanand of Delhi University. It was subsequently presented before the faculty members and students of the postgraduate programme in Education (Elementary) at TISS, Mumbai. The author is grateful for their supervision, feedback and comments.
4. Interview with a member of the textbook committee for primary grades.
5. In an extended introduction written by poet Sumitranandan Pant of his anthology *Pallav*, the resentment of modern educated youths towards medieval value systems took on a linguistic tone. Pant emphasised that Brajbhasha had

a historical role to play, although now the language was not appropriate for expressing modern sensibilities.

REFERENCES

Anderson, Benedict. 1983. *Imagined Communities: Reflection on Origin and Spread of Nationalism*. First Indian Reprint, 2015. Jaipur: Rawat Publications.

Bhabha, Homi K.(Ed.). 1990. *Nation and Narration*. London & NY: Routledge.

Chaudhury, Pravas Jivan. 1965. *Indian Poetics. The Journal of Aesthetics and Art Criticism*, Vol. 24, no. 1, pp. 197–204.

Giroux, Henry A. 1997. *Pedagogy and the Politics of Hope: Theory, Culture, and Schooling*. Boulder, CO: Westview Press.

Kumar, Krishna. 1990. 'Quest for Self-Identity: Cultural Consciousness and Education in Hindi Region, 1880–1950', *Economic and Political Weekly*, Vol. 25, no. 23, 9 June.

NCERT (National Council for Education Research and Training). 2006. 'Position Paper: National Focus Group on Teaching of Indian Languages.' National Curriculum Framework, 2005 (curricular document).

Orsini, Francesca. 1999. 'What did they Mean by "Public"? Language, Literature and the Politics of Nationalism', *Economic and Political Weekly*, Vol. 34, no. 7, 13–19 February.

TEXTBOOKS

Rimjhim. Hindi Textbook for Class V. Delhi: NCERT.

Vasant. Hindi Textbooks for Class VI and VII. Delhi: NCERT.

◆◆

THE MANY AVATARS OF 'EDUCATION'

SATYA SIVARAMAN

My elder brother was just 13 years old when he decided he did not want to live anymore.

He had failed the Class 9 chemistry exam, which meant repeating the year with classmates junior to him. Humiliated by the idea, and petrified by our father's wrath, he broke open a thermometer from the medicine box at home, and swallowed the mercury.

He survived, because his knowledge of chemistry was truly poor. He did not know that in such small quantities elemental mercury would not harm, let alone kill him—most of it sublimating at room temperature anyhow.

Today, three-and-a-half decades later, my brother is a successful entrepreneur, providing jobs to over 20 people. He produces electronic equipment, some of which has been personally designed from scratch.

My brother is one of the lucky ones who, despite such traumatic childhood experiences, somehow survived and mustered enough self-confidence to eventually thrive in a world of ruthless competition. There are thousands of children in our formal educational systems who spend a lifetime plagued by low self-esteem, convinced they are stupid—or what Indian school teachers love to call 'duffers'.

I recount this very personal episode because, when it happened, it led me to think intensely about its implications for my own education, its purpose, and indeed the very idea of life. To draw an analogy: Which other animal species on the planet is likely to share my brother's early experience? Has anyone heard of a young lion jumping off a cliff because it failed to catch a deer in its first chase? Or a bird drowning itself with shame for being unable to fly on its first attempt?

If learning is meant to help the young survive in the world, how does it help to put them through a process that involves building organised hierarchies of the 'clever' and the 'stupid' that leaves many children mentally crippled, disillusioned or dead? Is it, then, all about skilling, or killing, them?

Almost four decades later, there are many more questions I would add, some of them very fundamental. Could it be that the idea of the educational institution being a place where teaching is by teachers, and learning by students, is intrinsically flawed? Why is it assumed that children know nothing at all and need to be 'taught' by adults within the four walls of a school or a college?

John Holt, well-known American educator and critic of schooling, observes in his classic, *How Children Fail*:

> You have only to watch babies and infants, and think seriously about what all of them learn and do, to see that, except for the most grossly retarded, they show a style of life, and a desire and ability to learn, that in an older person we might well call genius. Hardly an adult in a thousand, or ten thousand, could in any three years of his life learn as much, grow as much in his understanding of the world around him, as every infant learns and grows in his first three years. But what happens, as we get older, to this extraordinary capacity for learning and intellectual growth?

A BRIEF HISTORY OF LEARNING

Learning is intrinsic to all living organisms, from the largest mammal to single-cell bacteria. This is simply because learning, even if it is just about the basics of finding food, defending oneself and mating, is critical to the survival of every species. Every little kitten playing with a ball of wool is doing exactly that—learning survival skills; and the newborn baby manipulating the sentiments of powerful adults with its smile is using some newly learnt ones.

In the case of the human species, the quest for knowledge, going beyond the primal instinct of survival, is also fuelled by the phenomenon of 'curiosity' and the excitement of 'solving puzzles' of various kinds. Gazing at the stars in ancient times (or even today) started out perhaps as a form of entertainment, but has contributed to human knowledge and skills as much as farming or fishing, which are clearly linked to survival.

It is the combination of these motivations for learning that has led to an understanding of the laws of nature, the development of sophisticated languages, and writing that has, in turn, contributed to further technological and social development over the millennia. These, together with the collective recording, the processing of information and its transmission to the next generation—an activity broadly called education—has, historically, made humans into the creatures they are today.

> Surviving in the immense diversity of habitats (for humans) depended not on specific genetic adaptations, but on large bodies of culturally transmitted know-how, abilities, and skills that no single individual could figure out in his or her lifetime (Henrich, 2011).

Unlike other species, humans do not have to 'reinvent the wheel', but can draw upon the wealth of knowledge from the past. They are also capable of planning for the future. In a sense, there are no real 'humans' anymore and, instead, what we have are 'super humans', with a tremendous extension of the otherwise limited biological abilities of vision, information processing, physical speed and stamina.

Of course, all this has made *Homo sapiens sapiens,* or the modern human being, the dominant creature on Earth. However, in the times in which we live, it is important to add a caveat: human beings may be 'dominant, as of now', but there is no guarantee that the species itself will necessarily survive forever, let alone dominate anything.

John Leslie, a Canadian philosopher, assesses the probability of humanity failing to survive the next five centuries at 30 per cent in his book, *The End of the World: The Science and Ethics of Human Extinction*'. Sir Martin Rees, Britain's Astronomer Royal, is even more pessimistic, placing the odds that humanity will survive the 21st century at no better than 50 per cent in *Our Final Hour.*

The very fact that the possibility of total planetary annihilation has become technologically feasible calls upon us to take a closer look at the assumptions on which the concepts and processes of learning and education rest.

ENGINEERING A CATASTROPHE

Technological development has played a significant role in shaping major trends in the size of the world population, life expectancy, educational levels, material standards of living, and the nature of work, communication, health care, war, and the impact of human activities on the natural environment. Technology also influences, both directly and indirectly, governance, entertainment, human relationships, and our views on the nature of life and human existence.

> Most differences between our lives and the lives of our hunter-gatherer forebears are ultimately tied to technology, especially if we understand 'technology' in its broadest sense, to include not only gadgets and machines but also techniques, processes, and institutions. In this wide sense we could say that technology is the sum total of instrumentally useful culturally-transmissible information. Language is a technology in this sense, along with tractors, machine guns, sorting algorithms….(Bostrom, 2009: 186–216).

It is hardly surprising that in the last few hundred years since the industrial revolution in Europe, the prestige of technology has risen spectacularly, and it is—in its various forms—the focus of educational policy and priorities the world over. Engineering, which in Victorian England[1] was not considered fit for 'gentlemen', is by far the most prestigious profession across the globe today.

In the United States, those in engineering roles can expect an average salary more than 71 per cent higher than the national average.[2] This figure is perhaps comparable in other parts of the world. The spectacular success of engineering—civil, mechanical, electrical and other branches—has been such that its principles have made inroads into both the social sciences and medicine. For example, there are no real doctors left anymore, with most of them becoming 'medical engineers'; our societies are run, not by politicians, but different kinds of 'political engineers', while religion is managed by 'spiritual engineers'!

In itself, all of this would have been no problem, except that the engineers themselves have little say, and also interest, in deciding how the products they make or help build are going to be used. Popularly portrayed as someone who brings the benefits of science and technology to the world, the engineer is in practice a mere cog in the larger wheel of industry, politics and commerce that far too often operates with ambitions that have little to do with public welfare.

For example, the petroleum or automobile engineer—in the course of doing a job he/she is paid for—does not really care whether the indiscriminate promotion and use of fossil fuels could lead to climate change, with devastating consequences for the entire globe. The professional engineer's blinkered approach is even more apparent in the case of the armaments industry—one deeply dependent on technical expertise, but explicitly used for destructive purposes.

The problem with engineering goes deeper, and is not just about the way it is used by politics or business. Essentially, engineering is the knowledge of manipulating dead, inanimate objects and materials with little understanding of, or respect for, ecological systems. Its objective is to not just mould nature, but also subordinate it permanently, banishing every hint of 'uncertainty' and the non-quantifiable, qualitative processes that are the characteristics of all living organisms. The fewer the variables to deal with the better, is the motto at the heart of engineering that may make for 'stable' structures, but also ones that do tremendous violence to all forms of life that are inherently 'unstable' and dynamic.

The tremendous ecological destruction wrought by the forces of the industrial revolution result from this arrogant attitude towards nature over all other ways of dealing with it. Contrast this approach with that of many indigenous cultures around the world—often described as 'primitive' and backward—which see humans as an integral part of nature and not 'superior' to it in any way.

THE KNOWLEDGE OF THE VICTORIOUS

Precisely, what does 'education' mean? Who specifically decides what is the purpose or the priorities of education? How does one measure the 'benefits' that education is supposed to bestow on human societies?

Of course, there is no single notion of education through human history, or even in the contemporary world, nor is there always a reductionist one-to-one relation between knowledge and those in power. Nevertheless, it is possible to speak in terms of systems/philosophies of education that are more influential, more materially successful, and more ideologically powerful than others—a result of choices made by or imposed on our societies at some point of time in history.

Given the critical role of 'learning' and 'knowledge' in the long, historical process of human survival, conquest and subjugation of the planet, it is not surprising that the idea of what constitutes education has always been very contentious. If the observation and analysis of phenomena in nature gave humans the ability to domesticate other animal species or grow food by farming, it was only a matter of time before these processes were used to 'domesticate' other human beings. Historically, there has always been a struggle for domination between different systems of 'knowledge'. Prioritising one set of information and techniques over another has often been part of a larger struggle for power between different social, economic and political groups.

It is understood that those already in power will try to manipulate the 'software' of the human species to perpetuate their rule while their rivals will create or emphasise their own versions of 'knowledge' in their bid for power. The winners of these struggles have gone on to assert their way of perceiving and explaining the world as being 'obviously' and 'inherently' superior to that of their rivals.

An example of this phenomenon in the current Indian context is the way in which history has become a subject of dispute and controversy, with multiple interpretations jostling for acceptance or domination over others. The use of violence by some players to silence those with different opinions has led to a stormy debate over tolerance and intolerance in Indian society today. The explicit denial of the knowledge of the Vedic scriptures to Sudras in ancient India by Hindu upper castes is an older example of this phenomenon. In our own times, while such crude methods may not always be in vogue, millions are nevertheless denied access to basic sustenance on the basis of gender, caste and, particularly, class.

The prioritisation of some aspects of human knowledge over others for inclusion in the curriculum of educational institutions is also an assertion of power by groups that are already dominant, socially or economically. The trend in recent decades of training for, or promoting, professions that are in 'demand' by private industry is an example of how the very idea of education can be hijacked by specific interest groups.

Another example, at the global level, is the manner in which indigenous societies and cultures everywhere—mostly practising hunting and gathering for survival, and also as a way of life over the millennia—have been displaced and indeed decimated by populations with longer experience of settled agriculture, urbanisation and technological development.

As Jared Diamond argues in his well-known book, *Guns, Germs and Steel*, the deadly combination of these three elements helped modern Europeans conquer the world. This was particularly true in the Americas and Australia, which had populations that were completely helpless, with neither the weapons nor the organisation to match those of the invading Europeans, nor the immunity to survive the diseases they brought with them. Knowledge of a particular kind, in this context, was decisive in determining the outcome of the encounter between Europe and the rest of the globe in favour of the former. Though this was not the first time in history that knowledge played a role in conquest, the significance of European domination is simply that we still live in a world shaped by this phenomenon from around 500 years ago.

Today, if the world learns techniques, skills and knowledge developed foremost in the European context, and uses European pedagogical methods, this is understandably related to their spectacular success in conquering the world and accumulating wealth. As with beauty, power, too, has a way of defining intelligence according to its own image and needs. The powerful are always cleverer and more beautiful than those they vanquish.

In that sense, the identification of what is to be taught as part of the educational process is, very clearly, a political choice and not merely about the dispassionate 'love of learning' or any other such lofty goal. Often, the insistence on sending children to educational institutions is to help them develop the skills to 'fit into the world of work and employment' as part of 'national development'—a euphemism for catching up with the wealthier and technologically advanced West.

It is hardly surprising, then, that many children, not inclined towards the value systems represented by the knowledge imposed on them, simply refuse to show any interest in what is being taught and obediently 'get through' their exams.

CONFORM OR DIE

The debate between different systems of knowledge is clearly not something that is of 'academic interest' alone. The outcome has important implications for the allocation of resources in our societies.

The domination of intellectual labour over manual labour, reflected through vast differentials in wages in favour of the former, is just one example. After all, why should the earnings of a software engineer, or even an artist, be thousands of times more than a farmer's—given the latter's critical role in the biological survival of the human species? Who decides how to prioritise the allocation of resources to different professions? If this is supposed to be done by the 'hidden hand' of the market, then what about the many 'hidden hands' that manipulate the market?

Those willing to accept the idea of knowledge promoted by modern educational institutions, and play by its rules, are rewarded disproportionately in terms of income, status and, as some studies show, even life expectancy. This helps perpetuate the system by sending out the message that education (or what is imposed in its name) is the road to financial and social security and, even, 'self-fulfilment' in life.

A study of the difference in the wages of a family of two college graduates and one of high school graduates in the United States showed that between 1979 and 2012, the gap grew by some USD 30,000, after inflation.[3] Little wonder that in the current global economic scenario, everyone wants to be 'educated' and is willing to beg, borrow or steal to get there.

The distortion of concepts and priorities of education by those in power is further compounded by the fact that, in our times, education has become a vast industry on its own, representing huge earnings and income. If once upon a time learning had an intrinsic value of its own besides ensuring the survival and well-being of the student, today it is a mere commodity to be marketed and sold by the entrepreneurs of education.

The education sector, including expenditure on national education systems, is currently the second-largest global market after healthcare,[4] with an overall global expenditure estimated at USD 4.5 trillion in 2012. This sector is estimated to grow by a compound annual growth rate of 7 per cent over 2012–17, resulting in a global market size of USD 6.3 trillion in 2017. The Indian education sector's market size is expected to reach 6,02,410 crore (USD 109.84 billion) by 2015, almost doubling in size from 2012.[5]

To understand the reasons for the development of education into such an enormous industry, and the appropriation of the world's wealth by the 'educated', it is necessary to take a closer look at the growth of the 'service' sector in the global economy. The service sector produces 'intangible' goods, some well established—government, health, education—and some quite new—modern communications, information, and business services.

Ever since the 1990s, the service sector has been the largest sector in the world, accounting for 63.5 per cent of total global wealth, manufacturing for 30.5 per cent, and agriculture a mere 6.1 per cent.[6] The United States has the largest service sector globally, worth about USD 13.5 trillion.

The service sector is also the largest sector in 194 countries, and in over 30 countries it accounts for more than 80 per cent of their GDP. In the Indian context, in 2014, the service sector accounted for 57.9 per cent of the national economy, manufacturing for 24.2 per cent, and agriculture for merely 17.9 per cent. Over 68 per cent of the Indian population lives in rural areas and it is not surprising that farmers are committing suicide in shocking numbers every year—it is cheaper and quicker to hang oneself than slowly die of hunger.

According to economic theory, as per capita income rises agriculture loses its primacy, giving way first to a rise in the industrial sector, followed by a rise in the service sector. Producing services tends to require more human capital than producing agricultural or industrial goods and, as a result, the demand has grown for more educated workers, prompting countries to invest more in education.

Of course, the theory just discussed hides the fact that the valuation of any human activity is a political act, and those who make the rules of the global economy are bound to assign value to whatever they themselves know best. It is not farmers or workers, but money managers, sitting in their cosy chambers, who decide the price of goods and services, and through that the share of national and global incomes of different professions.

If money managers decide to shift wealth into the hands of 'educated' people like themselves, it would make sense for everyone to try and jump onto the bandwagon of being educated—irrespective of whether or not this concerns any kind of meaningful learning.

Which brings us to the question: Today, if the globe's resources are disproportionately dominated by the 'educated' and 'literate', then is this not the hidden purpose of all education in our times—the justification of already existing unequal power structures, or enabling the theft of common wealth using knowledge as camouflage?

THE UNIVERSITY OF LIFE

One of the more ironical images that emerged from the recent catastrophic floods in Chennai was that of highly-qualified engineers, doctors and managers being rescued from their submerged homes and offices by 'illiterate' fishermen in their boats. Nature—whose wrath was aroused in the form of global warming, at least partly due to the activities of the urban educated—was sending a very clear message. At that moment, amidst the swirling rising waters, there was little debate about who was the more 'learned' of these two different sections of the population. In the middle of the ocean, the man who knows how to swim is worth a dozen rocket scientists.

The other simple lesson that emerges from Chennai is that for all the wealth, power and fame that anyone may acquire, ultimately he/she is always going to be bound by the simple fact of being just a naked, biological animal. At least for now, there are no technologies that promise immunity from the decay that all flesh and blood is subject to, and the anxious search for immortality should stop so that we can live as we really are—mere mortals.

The ideas of endless industrial progress, complete mastery over nature, and conquering the universe through perpetual human innovation for over a century, seem not just unachievable but also quite pointless, if not actually dangerous. Hubris has humbled many a civilisation in human history and in the case of the current one—given its powers of destruction—there may not be even ashes left to rise from.

In 1926, in an essay entitled 'A Poet's School', Rabindranath Tagore points out:

> We have come to this world to accept it, not merely to know it. We may become powerful by knowledge, but we attain fullness by sympathy. The highest education is that which does not merely give us information but makes our life in harmony with all existence.

These are words that ring true even more in our times than in Tagore's own as we stare, as a species, into the abyss of global war, ecological destruction and a deep alienation of the individual from everything around. An education that represents the mere accumulation of information, techniques, and the aggressive pursuit of power and wealth must give way to a different kind of learning that is imbued with a far greater understanding of the place of our species in nature, and the limitations of both human intelligence and actions.

Before we rush to 'educate' more and more people or even talk of 'alternative education', perhaps we should first apologise and return to the so-called 'primitive' and 'illiterate' people of the world what has been stolen from them by the 'educated'—their lands, forests, water, air and way of life. At the same time, we need to have both the courage and humility to start learning from the indigenous people of the world the art and science of treading lightly on Earth—to live like nomads who make no permanent structures and leave no trace of their existence, instead merging into the endless cycles of life and death as do all other living creatures.

If all this sounds too romantic or utopian to pursue, you are welcome to choose your favourite apocalypse on another planet somewhere—please leave mine alone.

◆

NOTES

1. http://www.victorianweb.org/history/gentleman.html
2. http://news.thomasnet.com/IMT/2013/02/19/why-engineers-earn-more
3. http://www.nytimes.com/2014/09/11/business/economy/a-simple-equation-more-education-more-income.html
4. GCC Education Industry Report. 2010. Produced by Alpen Capital.
5. http://www.business-standard.com/article/companies/indian-education-sector-market-size-to-be-110-bn-by-fy15-113012100537_1.html
6. http://statisticstimes.com/economy/countries-by-gdp-sector-composition.php

REFERENCES

Bostrom, Nick. 2009. 'The Future of Humanity', in Jan-Kyrre Berg Olsen, Evan Selinger and Soren Riis (eds.), *New Waves in Philosophy of Technology*. New York: Palgrave McMillan.

Diamond, Jared. 2005. *Guns, Germs and Steel: The Fates of Human Societies*. New York: W.W. Norton & Company.

Henrich, Joseph. 2011. 'A Cultural Species: How Culture Drove Human Evolution', *Psychological Science Agenda,* November. http://www.apa.org/science/about/psa/2011/11/human-evolution.aspx

Holt, John. 1964. *How Children Fail.* New York: Pitman Publishing Corp.

Leslie, John. 1998. *The End of the World: The Science and Ethics of Human Extinction.* US and Canada: Routledge.

Rees, Martin. 2003. *Our Final Hour: A Scientist's Warning: How Terror, Error, and Environmental Disaster Threaten Humankind's Future in this Century—On Earth and Beyond.* New York: Basic Books.

◆◆

A SCHOOL IN A GHETTO
Some Reflections*

FARAH FAROOQI

From 2009 to 2014, I was the Manager of a government-aided, Muslim-majority school, located in the ghetto of Bara Hindu Rao in the walled city of Delhi. About 98 per cent of this school's students and about 80 per cent of its teachers are Muslim. The school's interface with the locality led me to ponder over prejudices towards Muslims, increasing communalisation, and the impact of all this on the life and education of children. I have written about these issues in *Shiksha Vimarsh*, in the form of a diary entitled, 'Ek School Manager Ki Diary Ke Kuchh Panney'. The Diary runs into 19 essays (Farooqi, 2012–16).

If we look at the city of Delhi, relations of class and religious community are woven into its topography. In the last two decades, Muslims have been increasingly confined to urban spaces that can only be called ghettos. These include Idgah, Bara Hindu Rao, Jamia Nagar in south Delhi, and Jaffrabad, Seelampur, etc., in East Delhi. This article describes the Bara Hindu Rao area, captures the life and work of the children of the school, and depicts the problems they face. I comment on the multilayered discourses of discrimination and fear which compel people to live in this 'religiously homogenised' area. Their identity is consolidated and accepted through these discourses, and confers an apparent legitimacy to living in filth and congestion. I also discuss how heterogeneities within Muslims in the ghetto are masked in *burqa* as only an imagined homogenised Muslim identity is thrust upon them. There is a discussion of how the politics of vote is practised around identity and deprivation. Last, but not least, I describe classroom interactions, teacher–pupil relationships, and life at

Winter 2015–Spring 2016, Volume 42, Numbers 3 & 4

school to probe the vexed relationships between the school, the locality and the children.

LIFE AND WORK IN BARA HINDU RAO

There is a dearth of space and public services in this densely packed area, a criss-cross web of narrow lanes. At places, gutters and manholes can be seen overflowing. Some of these lanes are so narrow that you can touch the walls of houses or small (manu)factories called *karkhanas,* if you stand with hands stretched out on both sides. Although these karkhanas churn out business worth crores, the beneficiaries are contractors and employers. Even so, the residents of the locality are mainly workers. Sixty-five per cent of the children of the school toil and live in these karkhanas.

Many karkhanas operate in, and from, one-room houses. In a narrow lane in Ahata Kidara, a single-room, bag-making karkhana doubles up as home. In this 10ft×10ft room, the gas stove and utensils lie scattered on one side. Sewing machines are placed against another wall. Against yet another are stacked both raw material and heaps of cloth bags. In an open alcove are clothes, books and the children's school bags tossed in a disorderly manner, reflecting the chaos and confusion of their lives. It is difficult to imagine seven people sleeping in this cramped space. It is, however, well known that workers in such areas sleep and work in shifts because of the extreme shortage of space. These homes-cum-karkhanas and karkhanas-cum-homes tell their own tale of deprivation, disorder and struggle.

Many children, including a few girls, live with their male relatives, while their mothers and the other women of their families continue to live in their hometown or village. Since there are no adult women present, these young girls have to shoulder domestic responsibilities such as cooking, washing, cleaning, etc. Children like Irshad, a student of Class V, are well aware of their uncertain future with regard to education. Irshad says, 'Didi, I am in Class V and I am already 14. I cannot say for how many years I may be able to continue to study. I do not know for how long my brother can support me as a student.' Irshad and his younger brother Dilshad live in Delhi with their older brother who runs a small belt-making unit. Irshad prepares breakfast and lunch for his two brothers, and two other workers of the karkhana. He attends school from

12:30 p.m. onwards, since our primary school is held in the evening shift. On his return he devotes a few hours to making belts, cooks dinner, and tries to do his homework before going to bed.

The market economy does not allow adults and children to lead a turmoil-free life. Most migrant families are engaged in the informal economy that functions on a piece-rate basis. Entire families work as labourers in the household trade. In conditions of excessive supply of labour, piece-rates carry a low return in the value chain. The children's labour in this work—and many of them put in long hours—remains invisible. In such a situation, unless returns from schooling take place—*and are seen to take place*—the informal sector will continue to grow. Children will remain caught in the web of inter-generational impoverishment comprising low-level education, low wages, and a return to child labour.

The butchers of the Qureshi community live in Qasabpura and Idgah, less than a kilometre from the school. This old habitation was once at the margins of Shahjahanabad. Owing to urban expansion, this population, still marginalised, no longer lives on the physical margins. In 2009, when I took up the position of Manager, hundred-year-old slaughter houses were shifted to Ghazipur *mandi*, 25 to 30 kilometres away from Idgah–Qasabpura. This was the result of Supreme Court orders, the Court ostensibly operating from the 'neo-liberal praxis of aesthetics, safety, health and hygiene' (Ahmad, 2013). The people of the area were passing through a difficult period and thousands lost work as trade suffered. Such income shocks are a hallmark of the area. The sufferers were mostly labourers who had to spend a considerable amount travelling and their net earnings were barely ₹200–300 a day. There is a small percentage of the well-off amongst the Qureshis who saved their people from starvation during this period. The school, too, condoned the fees of a number of Qasabpura children. Despite this, some children left school, taking up petty work to support their families. Since the cattle mandi had been shifted from this 'residential area', marginal meat-traders continued to work stealthily from here, and our little children became part of this trade in turmoil. Buying goats from the mandi, transporting them to the area, slaughtering them, and selling the meat often brought the children and their parents in conflict with the police. The MCD officials, doctors and police went around checking licenses and examining their animals. Community members helped each other during this hard time. To tackle this daily onslaught, they had to bribe the police as well as please the local politician. With the beef controversy in the news at the time of writing, and a government of the religious right at the centre, the area remains under surveillance and in a state of panic because of rumours and false reports.

THE MASKING OF HETEROGENEITIES AND CONFLICTS

At least 65 per cent of the children and parents of our school are those who have migrated to Delhi in the last decade for the sake of work and the former's education. Many of them live and work in the Nabi Karim area. Most are engaged in the manufacture of bags, purses, diaries and belts. Several belong to the Madhubani, Champaran, Sitamarhi and Darbhanga districts of Bihar, but some are also from Uttar Pradesh and Rajasthan. Some have their own manufacturing units, but most sell their labour to karkhanas. A few are financially 'comfortable', while most are on the breadline. They support each other in this far-off land and maintain a distance from those who have been settled here for the past several generations. They say: 'These Dilliwalas sport decent clothes but mouth such abuses, we keep away from them.' The labouring poor, whom I speak of, gain some stability after toiling for a few years. In Nabi Karim, 15 to 20 per cent of the houses are now owned by people from Bihar. Their dwellings may just be a room doubling up as a karkhana, but to have one's own roof is a great blessing. Water is scarce in these areas, the supply of electricity remains erratic, and roads are under perpetual repair. Many people have bought houses in Sarai Khalil, a comparatively cleaner location that boasts DDA flats. At times, the original inhabitants are worried: 'These Biharis are progressing fast, they arrive in a wretched, pitiful condition but slowly they move on.' Recently, a child from Bihar was killed in an accident for which a 'local person' was blamed. When the 'local' people parleyed with a politician for protection, the migrants organised a protest at Jantar Mantar and the culprit was finally arrested. Locals consider themselves the 'original inhabitants'. While they keep reminding the new inhabitants of their 'visitor status', newcomers quietly resist their aggression and try to gain some ground.

The people who have been living in this area for several generations—Muslims—see themselves as divided into three main *biradris* or *zaats* (castes): the Mirdhas, popularly known as tyre-wallahs, who live in *mohullas* adjacent to the school such as Chameleon Road, Mohulla Sheikhiyan, etc.; the Qureshis, who trade in meat; and the Punjabi community, which lives in areas such as Beri-Walah Bagh, Bagheechey Achcheyji and Azad market. Aside from these communities, the Ansari, Saifi, Saqqey and Faqeer live in adjoining mohullas. The Shia community of Shikarpur lives towards Pakki-Gali and most are engaged in the glass trade. Since their total numbers, including those of influential well-off members, are fewer as compared to the earlier mentioned communities, their clout is also less. There has been a gradual migration of affluent Hindus to middle-class localities and an influx of Muslims, especially after the Babri Masjid events of 1992 and the Gujarat genocide of 2002. The Hindus of the area live near Pahari Dheeraj, Filmistan and Chimney Mill. They are quite well-off; most of them are employers and trade in the Sadar Bazar area. Their localities are much cleaner. The mohullas where the Jains live have gates at both exits. Bastis of the Dalit and Khatig peoples are visible near the Nabi Karim area.

The three major Muslim biradris differ from each other in their beliefs related to Islam. The tyre-biradri follows the Barelvi sect. They believe in rituals like *milad*, *vaaz* and *urs*. The Punjabi biradri considers the former's values to be 'incorrect' with respect to their conduct of *bidat,* which means 'un-Islamic innovations' or the pollution of orthodox Islam. The Punjabi biradri interprets Islam in the light of the Quran and Ahadees (narratives about the life of the Prophet). With time, religious beliefs are also undergoing change. Some Barelvis have now adopted the Deobandi point of view under the influence of the Tableeghi-Jamaat. The three biradris differ in rituals and everyday practices as well. Marriages take place within the biradris, but not between communities. Popular impressions, or stereotypes, of the population of Qasabpura are constructed on the basis of their trade: 'they pull out knives at the slightest provocation', 'dangerous people', or 'one should keep away from them'. Every now and then, there are reports of scuffles between residents of Bara Hindu Rao and Qasabpura, and at times between Shia–Sunni children of the school.

For the world beyond this ghetto, these heterogeneities and conflicts are masked under the label of 'Muslim community'. Moreover, the people of this area have consolidated the responses of dominant groups and the media. Hence, they are compelled to take refuge in this ghetto, called *Chhota* Pakistan in some circles.

PERCEPTION OF FEAR AND DISCRIMINATION

At the heart of the ghetto, where the school is located, lies an amalgam of discrimination and fear. The perception that Muslims lack resources and education and that institutions, such as the police and judiciary, are against them is widespread amongst children–adults, rich–poor, *netas*–commoners, and is also reflected in its topography. A multilayered discourse of fear shrouds everyday imagination and conversation. A gentleman has graciously allowed access to a secret passage for escape from his property in the Chimney Mill area, close to the school. I was told: 'God forbid, this will prove to be useful in situations of curfew or riot.' A local politician was invited to unfurl the flag on the occasion of Independence Day. In his speech, he said:

> If someone says to you that this country is not yours, then don't get convinced. Our fathers' and forefathers' remains are buried here. They have sacrificed their lives for the country. This is our nation just as it is theirs...

This sense of fear has been passed down by adults to the children. Once, I was sitting in the Staff Room when a child of Class IV entered with a request to go back home during the break.[1] The vice-principal asked this child, 'Will you be able to go back all the way to your house safely?' The reply was, 'I will go via the Muslim mohullas.' This fear, which results in ghettoisation, is a result of perceived discrimination, and the children are acutely aware of it. I taught a chapter on marginalisation to Class VIII from the textbook, *Social and Political Life, Part III*, published by NCERT. Some of the children's responses, pertaining to the manner in which Muslims are perceived and discriminated against, include:

(i) Villains in films are Muslims.
(ii) If there is a bomb blast somewhere, Muslims are first to be accused.
(iii) Once, my neighbour was looking for a job; members of other communities were unwilling to give her

one. When she got one, she had to undergo a lot of humiliation. Is being Muslim a sin?

(iv) When Muslims were subjected to atrocities and cruelty in Gujarat no one came forward to help them; this happened because no Muslim in Gujarat had a government job.

A number of research studies support the premise that children who perceive discrimination and bias may feel discouraged to strive for academic success as this contradicts the image of education as providing equality of opportunity (Ogbu, 2003). This needs to be examined as one of the factors responsible for glaring dropout rates amongst Muslim children, as observed by the Sachar Committee Report (2006).

An important aspect of this ghetto is that people belonging to a variety of social classes live here, although the percentage of the well-off is tiny. I asked a few relatively affluent people why they chose to live in this congested, unclean area. The reply was, 'Here at least our lives, property and honour are secure. How can we forget Gujarat? Also, when they did not spare the Sikhs in 1984, will they spare us?' Another important reason for this preference is that the culture of Muslims is not respected in the public domain. In fact, it is regarded as lowly and demeaning. The culture evident in public spaces is that of the majority community/communities, which lends them a sense of confidence, whereas the same public culture saps the self-assurance of those from minority communities.

THE SCRAMBLE FOR CRUMBS

A complex web of people lives in the mohullas around the school. This consists of workers, businessmen, service providers, traders, brokers–contractors, the poor and rich, politicians, and social workers. The Residents' Welfare Associations (RWAs) are important actors in any local situation, and the police and the press never far away. Cooperation, clashes, conflicts, selfish interests and politicking—all of these come into play. At times, the school gets caught in this web. Boards bearing the names of RWA members are installed at the entrances and exits of *galis* and lanes. This area came under the sealing drive of the municipal corporation in 2006, resulting in the closure of commercial ventures in residential areas.

This adversely affected the economic condition of the people. Every now and then, one hears that a karkhana has been shut down following allegations of pollution. There are different types of karkhanas manufacturing machine parts, tools, equipment, wires, etc., which consume large amounts of electricity. Locals report that it is almost impossible to make any money at the karkhanas without pilfering electricity. We know the government provides electricity at subsidised rates to big capitalists, such as the Tatas and Ambanis, in special economic zones. In this locality, however, the electricity bill of a karkhana may at times be falsely inflated to lakhs of rupees. In order to rectify this, the police are bribed, and the local politician enticed by feasts. Furthermore, there is a dire lack of civic services in the area and politicians must be pandered to for even basic necessities such as water, electricity and hospitalisation. The obfuscation of the profit–loss mechanism in businesses escalates the need to escape the clutches of the law and the police. Rallying around politicians in order to appease them becomes a necessary evil. Politicians, who act as facilitators, with institutions obeying their directives, are able to establish links with the common man through RWAs and social workers. All, of course, for votes! When a project is completed, the rich of the area organise a small felicitation for *netaji*, who obliges the crowd with speeches and words of wisdom. Being familiar with the locality, I have realised that politicians, even those who appear to be unapproachable, do alight from their pedestals to trap the unwary—the area is bursting at its seams with prospective victims. The graveyard has been encroached upon and tales of litigation, and of people moving in and out of lock-ups, are always in the air.

Given these deprivations and drawbacks, the environment is riddled with conflicts. A flood of 'social workers' in the area—go-betweens—seek to link the 'rulers' and the 'ruled'. Instead of critiquing and pressurising the state and politicians, they are busy concealing the latters' excesses and misdemeanours. Both social workers and politicians gain and grow at the cost of ordinary people as obliging the common man translates into votes in return. It is unfortunate that although 'social workers' are judiciously positioned to stir the consciousness of the people, they stifle it. According to one of our teachers, 'They mentally enslave people. The poor fools' throats become hoarse in shouting slogans in their praise.'

Social workers often visit our school as well and once or twice a year our children, too, come under their obligation when netaji distributes stationery, books and bags, etc., to the children. Once, the principal introduced me to a social worker about whom he said,

> Madam, he is not like the others. He has gently got many things accomplished. We had requested him for computers, which he has arranged through *mantri-sahib*. I received the letter of sanction just today. He has a big list of things he has got arranged through netaji.

It is clear that things get done in the locality through sycophancy and the pull of votes. The computers reached the school just before the enforcement of the code of conduct during the previous general elections. Along with the computers came the legislator—to deliver his speech, to encash the favour, and to preside over thanksgiving and sloganeering. I, too, eulogised and garlanded netaji. Our leaders are charged with the appeasement of Muslims in our country, yet our children are educated not just in politics, but, sadly, petty-politicking as well. The role models for some of our children are people who have 'made it big through short-cuts via netaji'.

DOES THE SCHOOL EMPOWER?

According to McLaren (2007: 187), schools are not just instructional sites, but also cultural arenas where the heterogeneity of ideological and social forms collides in an unremitting struggle for dominance. Thus, it is important to understand the messages of approval and disapproval related to the identities of religion, class and other markers received by the children. A consciousness about these identities and their relationship with larger socio-political structures can give children some insight for transforming their life situation, as well as the structures of oppression and inequality.

There is much concern for discipline in our school, and punctuality is valued. However, many children arrive late, including those who work late hours in factories. Unfortunately, teachers do not seem to grasp their pupils' circumstances; they attribute their lack of control over the children to the latter's upbringing. Either the teachers are unaware of the situation or they just overlook the fact that the children's and parents' routines are linked to the market, which has its own rhythm—it is beyond their control to awaken, eat, sleep and study at fixed hours like members of middle-class families. When I expressed my concern regarding the Board results of our school in the initial days the retort was alarming. I was told that 'Barren land is not farmable; however hard you may try, these people cannot learn.' In this manner, the children's backwardness has been designated as natural, while educators have relieved themselves of all culpability by highlighting their own efforts.

Sometimes, the depiction of the children as the 'Muslim Minority' is not very different from the representation observed in the media or by dominant groups. Teachers, themselves Muslims, say: 'The community is in dire straits. If you go into the localities of the *mian bhais,* you find excessive filth. Look at the areas of Hindus, all spic and span!' Or, 'The community is suffering because nobody is interested in studies. They want to eat chicken everyday; they don't spend money on education. Hindus don't do this; they try to study and advance further, which is why they are progressing.' It is argued that if two groups—one each of Hindus and Muslims, but belonging to a similar class background—are compared, then there would be a difference in cleanliness. The Hindus, it is averred, are more inclined towards hygiene. As described earlier, a single room serves as karkhana in the morning and sleeping space in the evening for 10 to 12 members who use a single toilet. In such a situation, is it not unjust to expect middle-class living standards? Agencies like the Municipal Corporation, active in areas inhabited by the powerful, are unable to perform satisfactorily in congested localities. Hindu neighbourhoods near the school consist of people whose socio-economic status is superior to local Muslims.

Occasionally, teachers also suggest a way out to children battling to improve their life circumstances—an 'easy' way out according to them. This is evident from the reported conversation:

> Teacher Arshi, Class IX, Chapter: 'The Lifeline of the Economic System of the Nation', 27 January 2014
> *Teacher (T): If someone is not able to study or is not able to study further due to some reason, technical education is beneficial for him or her.*
> Child (C I): (Thinking) A person can do a mechanic's job in a garage or work as an electrician as well.
> *T: (Pointing towards the children sitting at the back.) If you get ₹200 daily, will it be advantageous or not?*

C I: No.

T: Why not? (Raising her voice a little.)

C 1: The money will get exhausted daily.

T: Will it benefit you or not?

C 2: If ₹200 is fixed, then obviously it will be advantageous.

C 1: Ma'am, today the rickshaw-wallah charged ₹50.

T: This is too much, you have suffered exploitation.

It is easy to see that this conversation does not in any way help or empower the child or intellectually stimulate him. On the other hand, it is likely to make our working-class children believe that they are condemned to struggle at much the same socio-economic level as their parents, and that they should consider themselves lucky if they are able to eke out a mere existence. When a mockery is made of words like 'exploitation', it seems proper to ask: Are we not partners in the exploitation of our children?

Another conversation on secularism from the same teacher's class demonstrates that the quality of the teaching–learning process does not help children to comprehend the status of their religious group vis-à-vis other groups in society, leave alone think about transforming their life situation.

C: What is meant by secular?

T: Where it has no religion, where the government treats all equally.

C: The Babri Masjid was pulled down in Banaras.

[Although this is factually incorrect, the dialogue is being reported verbatim.]

First the Hindus pulled down the mosque.

T: That is why it was split in three parts. This was a constitutional decision.

C: It was 500 years old.

T: We will talk about this later. The preamble to the Constitution says, 'We the people of India, there should be no religious laws.'

[Quoted verbatim]

C: Should it be Communist?

The teacher ignores the query.

C: There was infighting near Pul Bangash; they put a Maulvi in jail.

T: Leave that aside, have a look at this. This says everybody will be entitled to the right to life.

While the children are struggling to make sense of what secularism means in relation to their real-life situations, this interaction only leads to further confusion. The authority of textbook information is used to assert equality in the eyes of the law. The negation of the children's real-life experiences of discrimination faced by their religious community can further alienate them.

Who will educate children to realise that there is a difference between their own, and their teachers' Muslim identity, both being compounded and intersected by many other identities and social constructs? Moreover, why are they imprisoned in a ghetto? Can there be spaces where these children meet other children from diverse backgrounds and thereby understand themselves, and other groups and contexts as well? The Sachar Committee Report (242) talks of shared spaces, which now seem essential to help people find freedom by relieving themselves and dominant groups from imprisoning 'ghettos' of fear and prejudice. Paying heed to the diversity index of educational institutions will also help in breaking down the walls of alienation. Perhaps, they will help our children in locating better role models.

The controlling regimes of time, discipline, norms and standardised assessments only legitimise the 'social gifts' that few are born into as a 'natural facility'. Instead of enforcing uniform content, could a contextual inquiry related to the socio-cultural and economic structures, which impede the progress of our children, provide an answer? For now, we, as educationalists and teachers, have only dumped our own failure upon them. Some children have internalised these perceptions and say, 'Our teachers work very hard, it's our fault we are not able to deliver.' It is true that many teachers do make an effort, but the system's rigidity and their lack of preparedness hamper processes of change.

In conclusion, I would like to reiterate the community's enormous yearning for education. We need to plan for the children, including girls, who leave the warmth of their native lands to live in Delhi for the sake of 'Education'. Meanwhile, there have been some heart-warming changes in the school. Hope lives on!

◆

* I am grateful to Anil Sethi, Azim Premji University, for editing this article.

NOTE

1. In 2014, because of the dilapidated state of the school buildings, Classes I to X were shifted to a nearby school. A very large number of non-Muslims reside in this area.

REFERENCES

Ahmad, Zarin. 2013. 'Marginal Occupations and Modernising Cities: Muslim Butchers in Urban India', *Economic and Political Weekly*, Vol. xlviii, no. 122, pp. 121–31.

Farooqi, Farah. 2012–16. 'Ek School Manager Ki Diary Ke Kuchh Panney', *Shiksha Vimarsh*. Jaipur: Digantar.

Ogbu, J.U. 2003. *Black American Students in an Affluent Suburb: A Study of Academic Disengagement*. London: Lawrence Erlbaum Associates.

Sachar Committee Report. 2006. 'Social, Economic and Educational Status of the Muslim Community of India: A Report.'

McLaren, P. 2007. *Life in Schools: An Introduction to Critical Pedagogy in the Foundations of Education*. Fifth Edition. US: Pearsons Education.

◆◆

WHAT IS REMEMBERED AND WHAT IS FORGOTTEN

Oral History and Institutional Memory*

INDIRA CHOWDHURY

UNDERSTANDING INSTITUTIONAL MEMORY

Do institutions have memories? Commonly, institutional memories are associated with commemorative events that institutions organise to mark the milestones of their existence. Such events often appear to be internal to the institutions, and trace a trajectory that seems unrelated to the broader socio-economic, political, or cultural, histories of the times. Moreover, institutional commemorative ceremonies and publications are rooted in the present; through such ceremonies institutions sanction, promote and channel institutional memory. Such ceremonies often bear a difficult relationship with the past, as they are often characterised by the unacknowledged forgetting of events and values that had once been a part of institutional life. Speaking of the hold institutional memory exercises over individual memory, anthropologist Mary Douglas says:

> Institutions systematically direct individual memory and channel our perceptions into forms compatible with the relations they authorize. They fix processes that are essentially dynamic, they hide their influence, and they rouse our emotions to a standardized pitch on standardized issues. Add to all this that they endow themselves with rightness and send their mutual corroboration cascading through all the levels of our information system. No wonder they easily recruit us into joining their narcissistic self-contemplation (1986: 92).

If institutional memory exercises such an overpowering hold over individuals, are there ways in which institutional histories might be written that move beyond the 'narcissistic self-contemplation' of institutions? What kind of resources might enable a historian to comprehend the context from which an institution grew and developed? What tools might a contemporary historian use to understand institutional life in the past? In the absence of organised and searchable institutional archives, oral history often serves a compensatory purpose. However, in what ways can memory work with, and against, the flow of institutional memory? This paper draws on the archival oral histories of the Tata Institute of Fundamental Research (TIFR), Mumbai, to explore ways in which oral histories help us understand institutional history.

Oral history, as a methodology, explores individual life stories in order to understand the manner in which meaning is created. As Alessandro Portelli has reminded us:

> But what is really important is that memory is not a passive depository of facts, but an active process of creation of meanings. Thus, the specific utility of oral sources for the historian lies, not so much in their ability to preserve the past, as in the very changes wrought by memory. These changes reveal the narrator's effort to make sense [of] the past and to give a form to their lives, and set the interview and the narrative in the historical context (1990: 52).

The interviews that I conducted for the Archives of the TIFR, between 2003 and 2006, revealed not just the facts related to the creation of the institute but what it meant for the scientists who worked there, what they valued in the institution, and what they learnt from Homi Bhabha—the founder. Looking back, I attempt here to understand: What do people reveal about their experiences when the narratives are institutionally framed? What ideas of self and professional identity come into play when those who work within these institutions record their experiences? And, finally, what kind of interpretative framework would allow us to look at the dissonances within such collections and enable us to move away from the kind of institutional narcissism that Douglas argues institutional frameworks inevitably encapsulate us within? Is it possible to approach the interviews as active instances of memory making, where the interviewees made sense of their experience even as they recounted their experiences of working at the Institute. Without the oral history interviews, I argue, the official institutional history remains static and undisturbed; it is the oral history interviews in the Archives that remind us that dynamic processes underlie institution building. Without the multiple voices of scientists, administrators, and scientific workers and assistants, the 'narcissistic self-contemplation' in which institutions indulge remain an overwhelming declaration that we can only be witnessed and received without generating a complex and critical response.

THE FRAGILITY OF INSTITUTIONAL MEMORY

The TIFR was founded by Homi Bhabha in 1945, with support from the Sir Dorabi Tata Trust, and subsequently became an institution under the Department of Atomic Energy. After Homi Bhabha's tragic death in an air-crash on 24 January 1966, the Institute created a commemorative exhibition, which was first exhibited at the Royal Society in London before being displayed in the auditorium foyer of the Institute from 1967 to 2009. The first photograph that would greet the visitor was a larger-than-life portrait of Homi Bhabha, followed by a photograph of J. R. D. Tata, the longest-serving Chairman of the TIFR Council, with the building of the Institute looming large behind him. In the next photograph, a huge balloon unfolded as it inflated and took off on its journey in the early morning sky as part of a cosmic ray experiment. The exhibition threaded together fragments of the story of the early days of the Institute, documenting the life of the founder and the Institute through pictures and texts. The text and photographs displayed Bhabha's life as an institution builder, presented his vision for science in India (something he shared with Nehru), and confirmed for the viewers the respect and admiration he commanded internationally. The exhibition also included a replica of the largest multiplate cloud chamber in the world built in Ootacamund (Tamil Nadu) in the 1950s by the scientists at TIFR. Simultaneously, the exhibition also channelled institutional memory to summon up the optimistic hopes that were placed in science soon after Indian independence.

This exhibition, as well as the present one that replaced it in 2009 as part of the centenary celebrations of Homi Bhabha, is held together by a larger narrative about the Institution and its founder, and is fuelled by the logic of institutional development. In both, Bhabha is presented as a larger-than-life figure and, indeed, unbeknownst to themselves, most casual visitors end up participating in what Douglas has called 'the narcissistic self-contemplation' of the Institute. But what might be the tools that a historian could use to offer resistance to such a powerful narrative of self-contemplation when writing a critical history of the Institute? In order to frame an answer that would challenge such predetermined narratives, a historian would need to look at alternative historical resources.

In 2002, when I started the work of setting up the TIFR Archives, we were given a very small room inside the foyer of Homi Bhabha Auditorium. In one corner of the foyer, within a glass enclosure, was displayed Bhabha's office, complete with a moulded fibre glass 'tulip chair' designed between 1953 and '56, a black bakelite telephone, his flask, his books, and small wooden and metal sculptures by A. M. Davierwala on the bookshelf. The tulip chair by Eoro Saarinen was designed in the 1950s and it was a curious fact that Bhabha had bought it around the same time that it became a design statement in Europe. Symbolically, this 'tomb' also channelled institutional memory to summon up the optimistic hopes that were placed in science soon after India's independence. But the setting up of this office as a memorial to the founder, I soon discovered, had a complicated story behind it. After Bhabha's tragic death, his office was 'unoccupied' until 2002. That is not to say that the Institute did not have directors after Bhabha—it had four; but none of them occupied the founder's office. In 2002, the furniture of Bhabha's office was moved to the auditorium foyer to be put on display and the fourth-floor office he had occupied became, officially once more, the director's office.

Bhabha's death had cast its long shadow on the Institute, as my oral history interviews with the directors who followed in Bhabha's footsteps revealed. They admitted that they were too shaken by the tragedy to occupy his desk. Over the next 35 years, Bhabha's office remained untenanted until Professor S. S. Jha became Director and decided to preserve the office in the Institute's auditorium. In 2009, when the Institute celebrated the Bhabha centenary, this museum–office was dismantled and replaced by an exhibition on Bhabha's life, his vision, and the visionary quality of his life. The story about Bhabha's office not being occupied from

1966 to 2002 became a lost narrative that could only live on in the archival oral histories that the TIFR Archives has collected and preserved. Ostensibly, it seemed an emotional response to an untimely death—an inability to cope with the loss of a mentor. Even when the impact of the tragedy had dulled, and the Institute grown, the decision to keep the office unoccupied was not revisited, leading to a status quo. Over time, these details dropped out of institutional memory—rather, such memories were relinquished in favour of a grand narrative about science and development, and the visionary quality of Bhabha's institution-building practices. But forgotten narratives actually remind us of the fragility of institutional memory. Oral history can restore part of this forgotten narrative. But do oral histories only serve a compensatory function? Or, do they also offer us other aspects of institutional life to reflect on? In what ways do oral histories challenge institutional memory? And, what do institutional commemoration and individual recollection signify?

COMMEMORATIVE ACTS AND INDIVIDUAL MISREMEMBERING

While conducting oral history interviews with TIFR scientists who had worked closely with Bhabha, I had wondered how the Institute marked the moment of his sudden passing. Almost all the scientists I had spoken to recounted the condolence meeting held at the Institute. Professor Rustom Choksi, Bhabha's close friend and a member of the Council, had addressed the scientists after which they had returned to work, as they believed that the founder would have liked them to carry on working. But the photographs we collected for the Archives hinted at a different story—one that most scientists had temporarily 'forgotten' to mention. The Archives had a set of black and white photographs showing a Parsi Uthamna ceremony being performed in the foyer of the Institute. What did these priests, clad in white, performing rituals for the deceased scientists, signify? Why was this ceremony performed inside the Institute? Was this forgetting an expression of discomfort with religion? Is that why most scientists recalled only the secular ceremony—the Condolence meeting held at the Institute on 25 January 1966, where a resolution was passed placing on record the community's 'sense of abiding sorrow at his death'. The resolution had gone on to confirm the community's appreciation of Bhabha's 'inspired leadership' and expressed its inability to find an appropriate form in which to appreciate 'this most gifted son of India' who, in his lifetime, had 'spurred men on to give of their best'. Not surprisingly, the nationalist dimensions of Bhabha's life had become most significant at this moment, as the resolution went on to state:

> His exemplary patriotism rarely found expression in words; it was in deeds that he strove, together with all his colleagues, young and old, to build with unremitting toil and exalted vision that nobler India in which skilled technology in the service of man would give to the lowliest among us the beginnings of a decent life.[1]

The focus on Bhabha's 'exemplary patriotism' has interesting implications for our understanding of institutional history. Institutional memory had, not surprisingly, deployed the strategy of directing 'individual memory', channelling, as Douglas puts it, 'perceptions into forms compatible with the relations they authorize' (1986: 92). Perhaps, we could comprehend this emphasis on nationalism in the context of the Indo–Pak war, which had ended just a few months before. Or, we could grasp it in the context of the economic and political crisis that was looming over the Indian state at that point. In such circumstances, the nationalist purpose of science had a positive ring to it. Indeed, the rhetoric suited the 'narcissistic self-contemplation' of the institution and endowed it with a legitimacy of purpose.

The condolence meeting that everyone remembered was followed by the other—forgotten—ritual. Writing a personal tribute to Bhabha, Professor Choksi spoke of the reasons for the Uthamna ceremony that was to be held at the Institute two days after the Condolence meeting:

> What was more fitting than that on 26 January, the ceremonial service for him should be held in his own Institute, in that temple that he had built for other worship. There amid the utter serenity and dignity of the long colonnade and the vista of sea and landscape of green lawns and trees, men and women of all faiths could do him their last homage.[2]

Subtly recalling Nehru's oft-quoted lines—'I too have worshipped at the temples of science'—Choksi transformed the secular institutional space into a sacred one within which such a ceremony could be rightfully held. Choksi, Professor of English at Wilson College, Mumbai, had been a member of the board of the Tata Trust when Bhabha had applied for funds to start TIFR in 1944. It was Choksi who had proposed that the Tata Trust support the young scientist 'to the hilt'. Later, in a spirit of affectionate support, Choksi had taken on many tasks at the Institute, sometimes looking into administrative details beyond the call of duty. While Choksi's tribute contextualises the reasons for holding the ceremony at the Institute, it hardly explains why the Parsi ceremony was 'forgotten' by many who had been present.

Armed with archival photographs of the Parsi Uthamna ceremony, I asked scientists and administrators why these death rituals were performed within the Institute premises, at the foot of the library stairs, with the whole Institute gathered outside in the colonnade watching in deep reverence through the glass doors? To my question, some of the senior scientists had but one answer: they wanted to respect the wishes of his mother, Meherbai, who had made this request. In some ways, their answer evaded the deep discomfort that they might have had about a religious ceremony performed within a scientific institution. But their answer pointed to another source of unease—an awkwardness that came from trying to acknowledge the blurred boundaries between the personal and the official that existed in the early history of the Institute.

It struck me that Meherbai had been a presence in the Institute from its beginnings. Even later, she had remained a presence. Scientists as well as the technical and workshop staff often spoke of her gentle interventions.[3] After Bhabha's death, several members of the technical staff had in fact gone to meet her and offer their condolences. Their recollections implied a long-cherished relationship.[4] It was not surprising therefore to see Meherbai's request being honoured by the Institute. But the erasure of this ceremony from institutional memory as well as from individual memory suggests a rupture between the official and the personal, and perhaps at a subterranean level, a split between the scientific and the religious (where the condolence ceremony is remembered and the Uthamna forgotten).

Nevertheless, the misremembering of the condolence ceremony as the only ceremony that took place cannot be attributed to the failure of individual memory: rather, it indicates the ways in which collective memory is shaped within institutions. Maurice Halbwachs had drawn our attention to the social matrix of memory, but had cautioned against the conflation of collective memory and history (1950: 78–86). But memory has also been seen as a significant and interesting resource for history, and Phillippe Ariès has traced the beginnings of historiography to human memory (Hutton, 1988: 311–22). Memory also offers alternative approaches to the past—remembering, forgetting and misremembering offer us ways in which we can understand the significance of past events.[5] In the year that followed Bhabha's death, official commemorative events crowded the horizon for a while: M. G. K. Menon spoke at the Sheriff's meeting in Bombay; the Atomic Energy Establishment was renamed the Bhabha Atomic Research Centre on 14 August 1966; a commemorative stamp was released to honour Bhabha; the approach road to TIFR was renamed Homi Bhabha Road; and, on the first anniversary of his death, J. R. D. Tata gifted the sculptor B. Vithal's Head of Bhabha to the Institute. Two years later, the Institute's auditorium was renamed the Homi Bhabha Auditorium.

With so many tangible commemorative acts, institutional control over memory held sway and the image of the founder as the propagator of scientific temper triumphed. Institutions, after all, as Douglas reminds us, cause its members to 'forget experiences incompatible with righteous image' (1986: 112). It is hardly surprising that intimate relationships, which were enmeshed within the flow of institutional life, were now concealed from view and in its place was installed an official image of the founder whose vision founded and guided the Institute.

UNDERSTANDING INSTITUTIONAL CULTURE THROUGH ORAL HISTORY

Even when official discourse excludes the textures of personal experiences, individual recollections do survive within oral histories collected for the Archives of the Institute. In long oral history interviews, scientists who worked at TIFR recalled and engaged with personal experiences in ways that evaluated, appraised and reflected on the nature of institutional culture, both past and present. It is to these types of resources that we will now turn to understand the relationship between oral history and institutional memory.

M. G. K. Menon joined TIFR in 1955, after he had spent a considerable amount of time at Cecil Powell's laboratory in Bristol. In fact, Menon's experience and his publications would have naturally been accompanied by expectations of a senior position within the Institute. Menon was, however, offered a Readership. Recalling his appointment nearly 50 years later, Menon, who had headed many of India's major scientific institutions, spoke with deep understanding of Bhabha's institution-building practice. The subject of the interviewee's attention in an oral history interview draws often from the interviewee's later experience, and not from the experience she or he had at the time that she or he is speaking about. Therefore, Menon's oral history interview reveals not only the facts of his appointment, but also his appreciation of Bhabha's thinking on institution building—something he experienced later.

> I think he made one quite telling remark. He said that he would have no difficulty in appointing me on the basis of my background as a professor. He said, 'Look! That would not be in the interest of the institution. Not my interest and certainly not in the interest of the others who were already there.'... He said that as it stands at the moment, if you look at the age structure at the institute, they were all older people. Therefore, if somebody new and brash came in with a higher standing in terms of the position or salary, they wouldn't look on it very kindly. They were all doing independent areas of work, and they had accomplished much and were doing it under difficult conditions. Therefore, he said, the best thing would be not to start there. His idea was to appoint me at the bottom of the scale as a Reader. Then he said that 'Once you are here and once they recognize your merit and class and you know what you can deliver, there will be no objection to your going up.'[6]

Contextualising his reasons for not feeling disappointed by Bhabha's offer, Menon recounted that he understood this policy of according credit to those who had worked under difficult conditions within the Institute. Moreover, Menon recounted what characterised the prerequisites of the practice of science at the Institute in the 1950s:

> I didn't feel disappointed at all. There was one good thing in the institution in a certain sense, in those days—it's quite different

> today, let me point out. In those days, very few people in the institute really bothered about what they were titled and called and paid. They wanted to have a position which enabled them to do some thing[s]. And they were interested in a salary, which enabled them to live. I mean, everyone was quite simple and in fact they had all come from an India which was Gandhian in a certain sense.[7]

Menon's elaboration of what characterised the culture at TIFR in the 1950s was gathered not from an initial impression but from his very long association with the Institute, where he would, in course of time, become Director. Interesting in these two excerpts are not the facts of the matter—that he joined because he had made up his mind to return to India; what stands out is what practising science meant to him and the scientists at the Institute. The excerpt also points out the ways in which interviewees often evaluate the present recounting the past ('it's quite different today'). Menon's recollection that status or money were not the primary concerns of scientists, if they were able to do their work, points us towards the larger picture about doing science in India in the 1960s. There were very few institutions that allowed scientists to do their work unfettered by constraints of budgets—universities at that point were no match for an institution like TIFR that had assured funding. So the implications of what scientists desired ('they were interested in a salary which enabled them to live') included the freedom to be able to work on their projects undisturbed. Menon felt that Bhabha's decision to start him at the lower end of the scale held out a lesson in institution building, where it was crucial to hold the balance of the institutional environment nurtured by those who worked at the Institute without a foreign degree. The system of rewards within this setting had to take into account the achievements of locally trained scientists and the accomplishments of those trained abroad. To see the former as being less capable and with fewer achievements would create an imbalance with which it would be difficult to cope. It was also a lesson in fostering collegiality and not violating the atmosphere of trust that the groups had built up.

Lessons in building teams and understanding group dynamics were enduring lessons and recalled by scientists during the oral history interviews. Bhabha played a critical role in shaping institutional norms. He also took care to mentor young scientists in ways of running laboratories. Devendra Lal, the geophysicist who had done his PhD at TIFR and started the C14 lab recounted an incident that taught him not just the necessity of exercising tolerance, but also the need for diversity in the laboratory.

> In my group, I had sometimes been very harsh on people who were not very good and I let them go. So this message somehow or other went to Homi Bhabha. So one day he called me… So he asked me 'Lal, how are you? How is science going?' And he asked me questions. Then he said, 'I want to tell you something—in a group you need people of all kinds.' And he didn't say anything more. He did [not] say, 'I heard that you're firing people'—no such thing. Then he just changed the subject. So he was always very subtle with me. And that one single statement he made, I would never forget.[8]

That the ecosystem of a laboratory needed all kinds of people was the message that remained with Devendra Lal. His recollection of that private moment of mentoring speaks to the history of institution building and the role played by individuals. Oral history, then, is a process that creates meaning for the interviewee in the process of retelling their lives within a historical context. The oral history interview is really a mode of interaction that is actually not about the special knowledge held by an individual scientist. On the contrary, it is an engagement where dialogue engages with memory and history. In each conversation, interviewees recall what a particular event meant for them—for Devendra Lal the conversation with Bhabha is about the diversity of the laboratory and also held lessons about the tone in which a leader could speak to a younger scientist without giving offence.

The distrust of oral history as a source of historical research is conventionally articulated in terms of its lack of 'objectivity'. Oral history, after all, is a subjective process. But oral history is also contextual, and meaning is created through the process by which the interviewer frames the questions. My question about Lal's interaction with Bhabha when he was just a young scientist allowed him to reflect on an incident that shaped him as a scientific leader. This was a moment he remembered because the lessons of the past actually shaped his way of working and enhanced his understanding of human interaction within the laboratory. The recollection of the past, therefore, offers us a glimpse into institutional life that was (the past) and, at the same time, offered an insight into the institutional life Lal himself sought to build when he later headed the Physical Research Laboratory in Ahmedabad and became Visiting Professor at the (future) Scripps Institute of Oceanography at La Jolla. Memories of institutional culture through oral history enable us to understand how institutional memory does not reside only in commemorative acts and official institutional records. Indeed, institutional culture cannot be completely understood from an institution's official records or its commemorative ceremonies, but has to be gathered through individual recollections and reflections, because institutional culture shapes, and is shaped by, individuals who have been a part of institutional life.

CONCLUSION

In what ways can we understand, assess and evaluate institutional memory? What role can oral history play in institutional remembering? Oral history interviews enable interviewees to reflect on the connections between the past and the present. Implicit in the interviews is the acknowledgment that the present has emerged out of the past. In the case of institutional oral histories the values adopted by an institution in the past provide the context for present values. But the reflective nature of oral history also enables the interviewees to meaningfully construct the connection between past and present.

It is oral history that enables private reflections and persuades history to speak to memory.

We, therefore, need to pay attention to these often-lost and frequently ignored narratives for which official institutional documents and institutional modes of commemoration create no space. Yet, when talking to people in the course of conducting oral history interviews, time and again, people recollect their experiences within the workspace, recounting what mattered to them and what they valued within the institution. Only when individual memories are given a space within institutional narratives can we truly understand institutions. It is only then can we critically resist the onslaught of narcissistic accounts that exist in official discourses of institutions.

◆

*I am grateful to the TIFR Archives and all the scientists, administrators and staff with whom I have engaged over the last decade. I have presented parts of this paper at the Centre for the Advanced Study of India, Philadelphia (2011), the Nehru Memorial Museum and Library, New Delhi (2011), and the Godrej Archives Annual Lecture, Mumbai (2013). I am grateful to audiences at these talks for their intervention, and to Vivek Dhareshwar, Ram Guha, Devesh Kapur, Jahnavi Phalkey, and Amrita Shah, for fruitful discussions.

NOTES

1. Resolution passed by TIFR on Homi Bhabha's death, 25 January 1966.
2. See Choksi in 'A World Without Homi Bhabha: A Personal Tribute', dated 31 January 1966. For a longer excerpt see Chowdhury and Dasgupta (2010).
3. G. V. Vasudevachar, Bhabha's first laboratory assistant at Bangalore, who later moved to TIFR, recollected that Meherbai would always ask after the technical staff. 'Once it so happened—we were in Bangalore at the Central Observatory—and all the hotels were closed. Bhabha's mother also was there. Bhabha's mother asked me, "Vasu, have you taken breakfast?" We used to go early morning for launching balloons. So I told her, "No, Madam, today all the hotels are closed." She called Bhabha, "Homi, come here. See people here have not had food." I get tears in my eyes [when I think of it].' Interview with G. V. Vasudevachar by Indira Chowdhury, 24 September 2009.
4. Suresh Sawant recalled that the workers went to see his mother some days later—'I just didn't like to see her cry.' See Chowdhury and Dasgupta (2010: 248).
5. See Portelli (2003) for a deep analysis of 'false memories' and their relationship to history.
6. Interview with M. G. K. Menon, 15 April 2005. TIFR Archives.
7. Ibid.
8. Oral history interview with Devendra Lal, 9 January 2007.

REFERENCES

Choksi, Rustom. 2010. 'A World without Homi Bhabha: A Personal Tribute', 31 January 1966, in Indira Chowdhury and Ananya Dasgupta, *A Masterful Spirit: Homi J. Bhabha 1909–1966*. New Delhi: Penguin, p. 244.

Chowdhury, Indira and Ananya Dasgupta. 2010. *A Masterful Spirit: Homi J. Bhabha 1909–1966*. New Delhi: Penguin, p. 248.

Douglas, Mary. 1986. *How Institutions Think*. Syracuse: Syracuse University Press.

Halbwachs, Maurice. 1980. *Collective Memory*. M. Douglas (ed.). Originally published in 1950. New York: Harper & Row.

Hutton, Patrick. 1988. 'Collective Memory and Collective Mentalities: The Halbwach–Ariès Connection', in *Historical Reflections/Reflexions Historiques*, 15, 2.

Portelli, Alessandro. 1990. 'What Makes Oral History Different?'. *Death of Luigi Trastulli and other Stories*. New York: State University of New York.

———. 2003. *The Order has been Carried Out: History, Memory and Meaning of a Nazi Massacre in Rome*. New York: Palgrave Macmillan.

◆◆

EDUCATION WITHOUT BORDERS

The Asian Imperative

KAVITA A. SHARMA

The international activities of universities have expanded manifold in volume, scope and complexity since the 1990s. International initiatives include study-abroad programmes, franchised foreign degrees, independent institutions based on foreign models, foreign language programmes, and the internationalisation of curricula and programmes to provide cross-cultural understanding. Moreover, cross-border education earns considerable sums for universities and other providers in a world where higher education is becoming increasingly more expensive.

Globalisation and internationalisation have often been used interchangeably, but a distinction can be made between them. Globalisation in the context of education denotes economic, political, societal and other forces that are sweeping 21st-century education inexorably towards greater international involvement. One reason for this is the rise of democracy, as the two are interlinked.

THE IMPACT OF GLOBALISATION AND DEMOCRACY

The demand for higher education is being driven by at least two factors: globalisation and democracy. Globalisation can be seen as the 'widening, deepening, and speeding up of worldwide "interconnectedness"'. It is the

> overarching international system shaping the domestic politics and foreign relations of virtually every country. It involves the inexorable integration of markets, nation-states, and technologies to a degree never witnessed before—in a way that is enabling individuals, corporations, and nation-states to reach around the world farther,

Winter 2015–Spring 2016, Volume 42, Numbers 3 & 4

> faster, deeper, and cheaper than ever before, and in a way that is also producing a powerful backlash from those brutalized or left behind. We have gone from how big is your missile to how fast is your modem? We have gone from a variety of economic ideologies to a choice between, free market vanilla and North Korea (Friedman, 1999).

While the polarities may not be as extreme in today's context as Harvey Feigenbaum observes, it is acknowledged as axiomatic that education and the spread of knowledge are essential to increase international competitiveness because national and global economies are interconnected, and based on information and its exchange.[1]

Globalisation is intimately connected to democracy and the empowerment of individuals who seek opportunities in an increasingly shrinking world. As Friedman points out, two major events have been responsible for this. One is the end of the Cold War that has also been a struggle between two economic systems—capitalism and communism. The other event is the fall of the Berlin Wall on 9 November 1989. Currently, there is primarily one system globally prevalent and while there may be many variations of it, keeping in view the local milieu, everyone has had to orient and adapt to it in one way or another. With the spread of democracy, regulated or centrally planned economies have been giving way to economies governed in consonance with the interests, demands and aspirations of the people, i.e., from ground up, rather than by planning top down.

Individuals push for higher education as they see in it an attractive personal investment, which can bring them rich rewards in terms of long-term income and employability in comparison to individuals with lower formal qualifications. Both these have contributed to the promotion of market elements in higher education, particularly through increased privatisation, which has helped meet the demand for massification, diversification, and the increased access it requires. It has created heterogeneous and complex systems that are required to meet the new and diverse demand that has made it nearly impossible to maintain a pattern of detailed uniform regulation of higher education. Hence, new forms of governance, financing, curricula, and flexible delivery and evaluation systems are needed.

In addition to an increasingly integrated world economy, new information and communications technology, and the emergence of an international knowledge network, the English language has gained in prominence as an international language of communication and work. Without English it is not possible to prepare students for the globalised world, the by-product of which is the internationalisation of higher education. It includes enabling students to study abroad, setting up branch campuses overseas, and internationalising the curriculum or engaging in international partnerships.

The use of English as the lingua franca of university education, and especially for scientific communication, has led to the growing integration of research, and an increase in international labour markets for scholars and scientists. It is aided by Information Technology that facilitates communication, permits efficient storage of information, and the selection and dissemination of knowledge, making it possible to offer academic programmes of all kinds through e-learning. Multinational publishing, technology and communication firms have all grown. Global capital has become interested in higher education and knowledge industries, and is investing heavily not only in research but also in training programmes. The emergence of the 'knowledge society', the rise of the service sector, and the dependence of many societies on knowledge products and highly educated personnel for economic growth are a new phenomenon.

INTERNATIONAL DEBATE

Internationally, there has been much debate and discussion on higher education. October 1998, for instance, was a very significant year for the world of higher education as representatives of 128 nations who were responsible for education, including higher education, in their respective countries met for the first time in Paris under the auspices of UNESCO to discuss issues of common concern and to agree on the general direction that higher education must take in the 21st century. The Conference was unanimously of the view that a renewal of higher education was essential for society as a whole to face emerging challenges. These included the intellectual independence of an individual in creation and appropriate advancement of knowledge, and education and training to shape responsible, enlightened citizens and qualified specialists, without whom no nation could progress economically, socially, culturally or politically. The Declaration of the World Conference emphasised that since society was increasingly knowledge-based, higher education and research had become essential components of the cultural, socio-economic and environmentally sustainable development of individuals, communities and nations. The development of higher education therefore ranked as amongst the highest national priorities of nations throughout the world. Without it, the required human resource could not be created.

The Conference was preceded by widespread mobilisation of partners, national policy makers, institutional leaders, professors, researchers, students, professional sectors, and others. Regional Conferences were held in Havana in November 1996, Dakar in April 1997, Tokyo in July 1997, Palermo in September 1997, and Beirut in March 1998. These were complemented by studies and analyses undertaken by some 50 governmental and non-governmental organisations charged with preparing a series of thematic debates on important issues of higher education. Twelve debates were structured around three main domains:

(i) Higher education and development as requirements for the world of work. Under this were to be considered higher education and sustainable human development contributing to national and regional development; this was to be a continuous process.

(ii) New trends and innovations in higher education that encompass students' vision of higher education for a new society. These would include the use of new information technologies, challenges and opportunities in research, and the contribution of higher education to the educational system as a whole.

(iii) Higher education and its relationship with culture and society. It would have under its umbrella women and higher education; promoting a culture of peace, mobilising the power of culture; and, autonomy and social responsibility.

At the Conference, the delegates dealt with issues pertaining to the changing missions of higher education in the 21st century.

The Conference resolved that, 'Beyond its traditional functions of teaching, training, research and study, all of which remain fundamental', higher education must 'promote development of the whole person and train responsible, informed citizens, committed to working for a better society in the future.' It has led to intense activity around the world as country after country has tried to assess the role of higher education in development and what needs to be further done.[2]

In the year 2000, the Task Force on Higher Education and Society was convened by the World Bank and UNESCO to bring together some of the world's foremost experts on education and development. Based on research, intensive discussion and hearings conducted over a two-year period, it concluded that without more and better education, developing countries would find it increasingly difficult to benefit from a global knowledge-based economy.[3]

THE RISE OF ASIAN COUNTRIES

Just as globalisation has tended to concentrate wealth, knowledge and power in the hands of those already in possession of these, international academic mobility favours well-developed systems of education and institutions. Significant elements of inequality exist in the expanding world of international higher education. Initiatives come from the North and are focused on the South. Ownership of knowledge and knowledge products, and the information technology infrastructure are emphatically in the hands of Northern institutions, corporations and interests. While student-flows tend to move from South to North, other initiatives and programmes flow from North to South. But the good news is that, increasingly, South–South activity is taking place. However, as of now, internationalisation is mainly controlled by the North.

Discussions on cross-border education centre on both the growing numbers of mobile students and branch campuses emerging worldwide, leading to the question whether, in the extreme case, education all over the world eventually becomes mostly foreign.

Asia figures prominently in these discussions because this region supplies the largest number of mobile students. China and India send the maximum number of students to study abroad. The figures of 2015 show that 100,000 students left India to study in the US alone. They now also go to Australia, the UK, Singapore,

Malaysia, Germany and France. The outflow of foreign exchange is estimated at USD 20 billion annually, i.e., India imports education worth USD 20 billion annually. Nevertheless, Asia, too, seems to be gradually adapting to, and innovating in, cross-border higher education to fit both local and regional needs. Rather than merely supplying students to the West, they are beginning to recruit students amongst themselves, and to integrate cross-border provisions in their systems of higher education. Twinning programmes, joint-doctoral programmes, branch campuses, and satellite research centres are now found in countries as varied as Singapore, Vietnam and China (Lee, 2015). In India, they are largely outlawed.

In this process of internationalisation, education hubs are being created that stand out as large-scale initiatives to transform a country, city or zone into an eminent destination for higher education. Several hubs have emerged in Asia in the last two decades. An educational hub treats trans-border education as an instrument of its growth rather than as a supplementary activity. These educational hubs encourage multiple forms of mobility of students, faculty, researchers, programmes and providers. They actively recruit foreign students, researchers, training providers and even multinational companies. The most common discourse is globalisation and internationalisation, but the underlying rationales are many and varied. Many observers assume that student fee and the earnings they bring are the main motif—and this is mainly correct—but other rationales well beyond economic interests also cannot be denied. These are talent development, educational capacity and soft power. Further, the rationales are not stagnant. Policy rationales fluctuate according to the on-going developments in local, regional and global political economy. Educational hubs see cross-border education as a critical plank of development that involves substantial participation from multiple individuals and institutions, both local and foreign. In Asia, Singapore, Malaysia and Hong Kong have emerged as important educational hubs.

The idea of an educational hub emerged in the late 1990s in Qatar, Singapore and Malaysia (ibid.). These countries were also early pioneers in cross-border education in terms of twinning and franchised programmes, and branch campuses. Nevertheless, it took about 10 years before the hubs appeared in the first decade of the 21st century.

RATIONALES

The main rationales for developing educational hubs are economic benefits, talent development, educational capacity and soft power. The development of higher education and research hubs benefits economies by upgrading technology and providing better research facilities. Industry grows, and more patents are filed. The educational capacity of the country improves; the standards of existing universities rise as well. Local students are exposed to a global environment, which makes them capable of job mobility throughout the world. Gradually, the universities can be more selective about the students they enrol and set their own standards. Often, universities augment their revenue by charging a differential fee from foreign students. Alternatively, they may, as in Singapore, provide a fee waiver if, after graduation, a student is prepared to work for a specified number of years. Finally, the city where the university is located benefits as large numbers of foreign students live there, and are visited by friends and family. Not only does its economy improve, but it becomes more cosmopolitan. Of course, what goes without saying are the soft-power benefits that internationalisation brings. When students from different parts of the world live and study together they develop bonds that last a lifetime. They have a special place in their hearts for the country where they have spent perhaps the best years of their youth, making it a lifelong point of reference.

REGIONAL GROUPS

Not only individual countries, but also groups of states are creating educational hubs. For example, when organisations such as the Association of Southeast Asian Nations (ASEAN) and the Southeast Asian Ministers of Education Organization (SEAMEO) were established in the 1960s, their prime objectives were to achieve political confidence and facilitate collaboration amongst themselves. The rapid expansion of trade and economic activities in the region, and increasing globalisation, accompanied by the influence of the Bologna process, allowed nation states in these organisations to collaborate in a wide range of activities, including education. Collaboration in education has also grown between Southeast Asian countries and East Asian countries (ibid.). In 1989, the Asia Pacific

Economic Cooperation (APEC) was created with 12 Asia–Pacific economies. Three more—China, Hong Kong and Chinese Taipei—joined APEC in 1991. Since 1997, ASEAN has undertaken various collaborative activities with three East Asian countries—China, Japan and South Korea—to foster educational collaboration. This has led to the emergence of a new regional organisation, ASEAN Plus Three (APT or ASEAN+3).

It is significant that since the early 1990s, East Asian countries too have placed great emphasis on developing close linkages and collaborations with their partners in the region. This is especially true of China, Japan and South Korea. In 2010, the three countries jointly launched the Campus Asia Project, a regional response to globalisation and worldwide competition in higher education. The aim was to make universities in Japan, China and South Korea places where students and professors from diverse cultural and regional backgrounds could come together and realise the merits of each other's universities. In particular, the Campus Asia Project also aims to stimulate the regional mobility of students, faculty and researchers to enable further collaboration in higher education. Within the framework of this programme, the three countries have formulated national policies and strategies to further integrate their educational systems. These initiatives include the provision of financial support to build intra-regional university networks, design joint curricula and joint-degree programmes that combine the cultural and academic strengths of the three countries, and provide more English-taught degree programmes. Currently, major universities in China, Japan and South Korea are expanding their English language lectures and degree programmes for undergraduate and graduate studies in order to attract more students from other northeast Asian countries, i.e., not only from China, Japan and South Korea, but also from North Korea, Mongolia and the eastern regions of Russia.

As a consequence, the region has seen a growth in personal movement. With respect to student mobility, according to UNESCO statistics for 2013, about half the students from Asia and the Pacific studying abroad actually do so within the region, compared to 36 per cent in 1999. In some countries and territories, such as Indonesia, Japan, South Korea, Vietnam, Hong Kong and Macao, students from Asia and the Pacific accounted for more than 90 per cent of foreign students. In China, Japan and South Korea, the lists of the top five countries of origin of foreign students comprise, in addition to the United States, countries of the region—Vietnam, Thailand, Malaysia, Mongolia, and Taipei, China. The rapid increase in student mobility has paralleled corresponding growth in the regional mobility of academics. A gradual increase in the number of full-time foreign faculty members from neighbouring countries are employed in higher educational institutions in China, Japan and South Korea. For example, the number of full-time faculty members from Asia, especially from China and South Korea, at Japanese universities had grown considerably by 2013. Also, by 2009, of the 345 full-time foreign faculty members at the University of Tokyo, 212 were from Asia. This means that the largest percentage of full-time foreign faculty members are from Asia. Similarly, the number of full-time faculty members from China and Japan at Korean higher educational institutions has tripled between 2003 and 2012.

SINGAPORE

As Jack T. Lee has pointed out, Singapore realised in the 1980s that its manufacturing sector was severely limited by its small size and cheaper production emerging elsewhere in Asia (ibid.). At that time economic growth depended on manufacturing and services, and Singapore continued as a manufacturing country until the recession of 1985–86. This forced it to identify 11 promising service industries through which it could diversify its portfolio, education being one of them. But the government could not commercialise it because of socio-political sensitivities, until the Asian financial crisis in 1997. The aim was to make Singapore the 'Boston of the East'. Considering the state of education in Singapore at that time, the idea was met with great scepticism, both at home and abroad. Undeterred, Singapore launched its World Class University programme in 1998 to attract at least 10 internationally reputed universities to set up campuses. It also divided its education sector into six segments: (i) elite world-class universities, (ii) local universities, (iii) applied research, (iv) corporate training, (v) primary education, and (vi) testing services. While capability development and talent attraction were presented as rationales, the chief motive was revenue generation. Over the next 10 years, Singapore consolidated the initiatives taken and added some more. The key actors in developing Singapore as an educational hub were its Economic Development Board, followed by the agency for Science, Technology and Research. The Ministry of Education was only peripherally involved.

MALAYSIA

Malaysia too used the idea of the educational hub to solve its chronic problem of trade deficit in the service sector. Malaysia has aspired to be a high-income country since the 1990s when Prime Minister Mahathir launched his seminal blueprint—Vision 2020. It was realised that one important factor contributing to its service deficit was the large number of students studying overseas. The country's Malay majority was economically disadvantaged as compared with Chinese and Indians. Affirmative actions in terms of ethnic quotas were put in place, leading to an exodus of students who now could not find places at the local universities. Although quotas were abolished in 2002, enrolment data continued to be skewed.

Private universities emerged rapidly in the 1980s and 1990s to absorb the unmet demand from public universities. These began to partner with foreign universities to deliver twinning and franchise programmes. The 1997 Asian crisis hit this sector badly and, as a result, few Malaysian students could go abroad to study as part of their training programme requirements. Hence, the private universities entered into agreements with their foreign partners to allow them to deliver the entire programme in Malaysia, converting the twinning into a franchise programme. This fuelled the idea that Malaysia could become an educational hub—by opening its private education sector to international students and marketing the country's low cost of living. The plans for the educational hub concept can be prominently seen in the New Economic Model, 2010; the Economic Transformation Plan, 2010; and, the National Higher Education Strategic Plan, 2020. Unlike Singapore, the main driving force in Malaysia is the Ministry of Higher Education.

HONG KONG

Hong Kong began implementing the idea of emerging as an educational hub later than Singapore and Malaysia. In the late 1990s, some references are found in policy documents that show a desire to enrol students from Mainland China. In 2004, the Chief Executive of Hong Kong named Education as one of the potential industries that could contribute to the city's economic growth to make it 'Asia's World City'. However, visible strategies to attract more non-local students appeared only in 2007. The worldwide recession in 2008 motivated the government to undertake an economic review and it was proposed that Hong Kong expand its expertise beyond financial services. Six industries were recommended for this: medical services, education services, environmental industries, innovation and technology, testing and certification, and cultural and creative industries. A large number of Mainland Chinese students began to enrol, motivated by the city's high-quality universities, as well as civic freedoms that Hong Kong gave them.

NATIONAL INITIATIVES

In parallel with the regionalisation of higher education in Asia, many countries have developed strategies of internationalisation in higher education to respond to the challenges of globalisation. While there are individual differences, the main objectives of these policies and strategies are generally concerned with a further expansion of personal mobility across borders, and the incorporation of international perspectives and content into teaching and research (Huang, 2015). They also include the provision of joint- or double-degree programmes, the establishment of branch campuses in partnership with foreign institutions, the delivery of English-taught programmes, the building of a regional hub, and supporting several selected universities or disciplines with enlarged budgets to become world-renowned institutions or departments. In East Asia, before the mid-1990s, the internationalisation of Chinese higher education mainly meant sending students abroad and attracting international students to Chinese campuses, as well as the implementation of English-taught degree programmes. Since the mid-1990s, however, the Chinese government has implemented new national policies. In 1995, the first document—'Contemporary Regulation on Operation of Higher Education Institutions in Cooperation with Foreign Partners'—was released. Project 211 and Project 985 were launched, which have been carried out to build several world-class universities in China in the near future.

The Japanese government made conscious efforts from the 1980s to the 1990s to enable the acceptance of international students. It developed national policy, which was implemented in 1983, to host 100,000 overseas students by the year 2000. More recently, internationalisation in higher education in Japan has entered a new phase, with new characteristics. First, the Japanese government has begun to revise legislation concerning the approval of foreign institutions in Japan, and to adopt new strategies for recognising cross-border or transnational branches and programmes. This approval makes it possible for foreign educational activities or services to be recognised by Japanese universities, and allows Japanese students to apply to foreign educational programmes or institutions in Japan. Meanwhile, more and more Japanese institutions have attempted to export their educational activities by providing transnational programmes in other countries. Second, in June 2001, the Japanese government set the goal of fostering its 'Top 30' universities toward the attainment of top global standards. Later, the programme was converted into a scheme of cultivating Centers of Excellence in the 21st Century (COE21). It focused on nine key disciplines for which the central government expanded the budget: life sciences, medical sciences, chemistry, material sciences, mathematics, physics, earth sciences, information technology, and electrical and electronic engineering. The government hopes that the quality of research activity in Japanese higher education can be enhanced, and an increased international dimension can be integrated into campus research activities.

In 2009, the Japanese government launched a new Global 30 Programme. Its primary aim is to attract 300,000 foreign students by 2020, tripling the current number. In order to achieve that goal, 13 universities, including seven national and six private universities, were selected to play a central role in its implementation. They were required to accept many more international students and to provide at least two English-taught degree programmes. In 2012, the Japanese government employed another strategy to develop global human resources in Japan, in response to the demand of big enterprises in the context of increased global economic competition. Although there is still some debate about the interpretation of the phrase 'global human resources' by individual universities, industry and stakeholders in Japan, according to the government report, the aim is to develop the soft skills of their people. They are to acquire the ability to think independently, be more easily understood by their colleagues, customers and acquaintances, make their minds more supple so that they are able to understand multiple points of view, and use that to build synergies. The effort is to understand different perspectives from different cultures, and to create new values.

The Korean government announced its first national plan on the internationalisation of higher education in 1996. This was the Initial Plan for Opening the Higher Education Market to Foreign Countries, and was a response to the upcoming WTO negotiations. This plan was based on the idea that importing higher education services in close collaboration with overseas partners would be an efficient and practical way to meet the challenges of internationalisation. In 1999, the Korean government started the Brain Korea 21 project for the purpose of building world-class graduate schools and nurturing the development of research personnel. The second stage began in 2006. Although Korean higher education has already moved to a stage of near universal access, it has very few research-intensive universities. Many Korean academics believe that only two or three universities are really research intensive, and the huge majority of their universities are oriented towards teaching. Therefore, the objective of Brain Korea 21 is to establish the research-focused university system and attract expert personnel, including academics who are internationally recognised in their disciplines, and researchers with an international reputation. In 2008, another national strategy called the World Class University Project was implemented. It is expected that these inbound top scholars will be able to undertake joint research and co-author with local professors and researchers, and therefore raise the ranking of Korean universities in major global university ranking systems. Similar policies can also be found in other Southeast Asian countries.

In South Asia, perhaps the South Asian University (SAU) comes nearest to bringing students of all the SAARC countries together in one University. Established by all the SAARC countries in 2010, it stands out as an effort of regional cooperation. Tertiary education—vocational, professional and academic—is key in building the economies of developing nations such as ours. Priority has to be given to the reduction of poverty through sustainable economic growth, for which higher education is critical. In most of our countries, however, higher education is far from what it should be. The challenge is to make the system more inclusive for the disadvantaged and improve the quality. This requires large financial outlays.

In most of South Asia, the GER is very low, ranging from 5–6 per cent to about 17–20 per cent. That higher education holds the key to prosperity, both of the individual and society, has also been emphasised by all UN bodies since 2000. Developing countries such as ours are, however, caught in the dilemma of competing globally, while simultaneously addressing local concerns with inadequate resources; typically have huge populations, poor school infrastructure and an inequitable distribution of opportunities and resources; and suffer from social stratification and stultifying cultural norms. These are interrelated issues.

Today, South Asia is embroiled in all kinds of conflicts and hostilities. Clearly, we can prosper only through cooperation. We need to remember our shared geography and rich cultural heritage, our philosophy, the synergies in arts and crafts, music, poetry and theatre, mythology and folklore, the living knowledge systems coming to us from the past, and ways of life. It is essential that we take a long view stretching back to the centuries gone before us, rather than see the short and the immediate in which are present conflicts of our own making and those caused by a divisive colonial heritage, not including Nepal and Bhutan. For this, while we need academic excellence, we also need to inculcate in our students democratic ideals, tolerant world views, multi-cultural perspectives and critical, thoughtful and compassionate minds and hearts. In a globalised world, which is unable to break away from the shackles of the nation state, SAU strives to dissolve borders in a region that has a shared common history, and create leaders of tomorrow who will strive to work to fulfil the aspirations and needs of the region.

We live in a globalised world in which survival and progress depend on creating a knowledge in which universities have to play a vital role. We have an abundance of talent in South Asia, but a paucity of resources and opportunities. We lose a lot of our talent and skilled human resource to the more developed economies of the West. We need to create opportunities at home so that people return, or stay to make a more equitable society in which there is economic growth and progress for all. Together with opportunities at home, a passion for nation building has to fire the imagination of our young people as only then will there be a determined resolve to make the country, and thereby the region, progress. Men and women have to be educated in a way that they acquire human values, a commitment to social justice, and are imbued with a critical and scientific outlook.

The responses playing out in the world to meet the twin challenges of globalisation and democracy are also being reflected in India. Obviously, the public higher education system will have to cope with it but it is not likely to be able to meet the huge demand for higher education. Also, education and employment, having got firmly linked to higher education, questions are becoming insistent about its relevance and quality. The need to simultaneously expand to increase access, create equity and tackle the issues of relevance and quality by upgrading existing institutions and establishing new ones, has put a strain on the resources available for the public funding of higher education and given rise to private education. Even the government has allowed elements of private education to enter the public sector universities and colleges through mechanisms like 'self-financing courses' that run concurrently with public funded programmes. Self-financing institutions have also been affiliated to public universities and they now far outnumber public-funded colleges. Most of them are in the southern states of India. Many private deemed universities have emerged which indicates that the government seeks private help and, lacking a transparent policy or legislation, has taken this route to enable private institutions to flourish. There is another group of private institutions in the non-university sector that are run by private and corporate initiatives such as NIIT and APTEC. By law they cannot award degrees, but they attract students because of the quality and relevance of their programmes and training they offer.

However, the acceptance of private higher education will essentially depend on the role of the government. The government has to be clear, and build a national consensus on the issue. At the moment there is divergence and the public perception is negative with a fair justification. At the same time, paradoxically, the private sector continues to grow while policy lags behind. Therefore, either the benign negligence of the private sector or allowing its covert entry will not do. The government must decide whether it needs the private sector for resource mobilisation and its other strengths. If indeed it does, then it must facilitate the private sector and see it as complementary to its task of discharging its responsibility of expanding the base of higher education. The first and most important step is appropriate legislation because it will embody the will of the state and bring about clarity on the rules of the game. It will prevent perpetual litigation and help emphasise quality private participation. Regulation implemented with integrity can lead to open and transparent policies that can attract big corporations with enough funds to establish quality institutions and the staying power to not expect immediate returns. Lacking a national legislation, many states have already enacted for the establishment of private universities, sometimes with disastrous consequences as in Chhattisgarh. Hence state legislation is not enough, and the national policy must be spelt out clearly with its three basic components: promotion, facilitation and regulatory control.

Right now Indian higher education appears to be stuck in a quagmire. It is clear that India is affected by global trends but is unable to deal with them. If it has to meet these challenges, it has to systematically create an internationally competitive academic system. For this it will have to rise above ideological biases and politics to reform its outmoded structures of academic governance and delivery systems, and build a national consensus by a continuous centre-state dialogue on higher education, both in the public and private sectors. A tall order perhaps but without it the Indian higher education system can neither deliver nationally nor can it compete globally. It is imperative for India and other Asian countries, competing with the best, to think and act both locally and globally. They must create an eco-system of education which is inclusive, diverse, flexible and strives for excellence; for all Asian countries this is the Asian imperative.

◆

NOTES

1. Harvey B. Feigenbaum. 'Globalization and Cultural Diplomacy.' Centre for Arts and Culture, www.gsfc.nasa.gov
2. World Conference on Higher Education. 'Higher Education in the Twenty-First Century: Vision and Action', UNESCO, Paris, 5–9 October, 1998, unesdoc.unesco.org/images/0011/00163/116345e.pdf

3. 'Higher Education in Developing Countries: Perils and Promise', February 2000, siteresources.worldbank.org/INTAFRREGTOTEJA/Resources/Peril_of Globalization," Asia: The Next Higher Education Superpower?

REFERENCES

Friedman, Thomas L. 1999. *The Lexus and the Olive Tree*. New York: Farrar, Strauss and Giroux.

Futao, Huang. 2015. 'Internationalization in Higher Education in the Era of Globalization', in Rajika Bhandari and Alessia Lefébure (eds.), *Asia: The Next Higher Education Superpower?* New York: IIE and the AIFS Foundation.

Lee, Jack T. 2015. 'Education Hubs in Asia: A Common Façade for Uncommon Visions', in Rajika Bhandari and Alessia Lefébure (eds.), *Asia: The Next Higher Education Superpower?* New York: IIE.

◆◆

CONTRIBUTORS

APOORVANAND is Professor of Hindi, University of Delhi. He was part of the core group that designed the National Curriculum Framework for School Education in 2005; member of the national Focus Group on Teaching of Indian Languages (NCERT); and on the Committee to advise on Renovation and Rejuvenation of Higher Education in India, 2008. He currently edits *Alochana*, a quarterly journal of criticism.

DIPTA BHOG is co-founder of Nirantar, a centre for gender and education in Delhi. She has worked as a journalist; women's rights activist; and Women's Literacy, Adult and Girls Education at the level of programme design, implementation, policy and impact. Bhog initiated a newspaper, *Khabar Lahariya,* in 2002, and has been involved in training the team of rural women journalists.

DISHA MULLICK works with a collective of rural women to produce, and distribute, print and digital news in north India. Prior to this, she worked with Nirantar on various field and research projects on women and education, and in publishing.

FARAH FAROOQI is Professor of Education, Jamia Millia Islamia, Delhi. She has contributed to textbooks on Environmental Studies for Classes III to V, and to books for teachers and teacher-trainees (both NCERT). She has recently published her experiences as Manager of a school in Old Delhi in the form of a diary, *Shiksha Vimarsha*. Farooqi has contributed to *Economic and Political Weekly*, *Learning Curve*, and *The Friday Times* (Lahore).

INDIRA CHOWDHURY heads Centre for Public History, Srishti Institute of Art, Design and Technology, Bengaluru. She holds a PhD in

History from School of Oriental and African Studies, London. Her book, *The Frail Hero and Virile History*, was awarded the Tagore Prize in 2001. She is President of both Oral History Association of India and International Oral History Association.

JYOTSNA JHA presently heads Centre for Budget and Policy Studies, Bengaluru. Trained as an economist, Jha has led many research initiatives, and has several books and publications to her credit. She has written primarily on education, gender and other development-related issues. Previously, she worked as an adviser to Social Transformation Programmes Division at the Commonwealth Secretariat, London.

KAVITA A. SHARMA is presently President, South Asian University, New Delhi. She taught at Hindu College for 37 years, before serving as its Principal for the next ten. She was then Director, India International Centre, New Delhi. Her books include *Hindu College, Delhi—A People's Movement* and *National University of Educational Planning and Administration: A Transformational Journey*, among others. She contributes to research journals, and participates in seminars and conferences on higher education, gender issues, diaspora and the Mahabharata.

KISHORE SINGH served with UNESCO for several years, and has long-standing professional experience in the field of the right to education. As UN Special Rapporteur on the Right to Education since August 2010, he presents Annual Reports on areas of priority concern to both Human Rights Council and United Nations General Assembly. Singh remains engaged in informal consultations with state representatives, international organisations and civil society.

MANABI MAJUMDAR is Professor of Political Science, Centre for Studies in Social Sciences, and is also affiliated with Pratichi Institute, both in Kolkata. Her research interests include areas of politics of education, social exclusion and democratic politics.

MANOJ KUMAR currently works with School of Education, Azim Premji University, Bengaluru. Kumar's interests lie in the teaching of language and literature in school, children's literature, in-service teacher education, and in broader sociological reflections on education. Besides teaching, he enjoys writing for children. Room to Read, India, has recently published his book, *Sabse Bada Chhata* (The Biggest Ever Umbrella).

MARY E. JOHN is currently Senior Fellow, Centre for Women's Development Studies, New Delhi, and was Director of the Centre from 2006 to 2012. She has written widely on subjects related to feminism and women's studies. Recent publications include *Planning Families Planning Gender* (co-authored), *Women's Studies in India: A Reader* (edited) and the issue of *Seminar* on 'Democratising Knowledge' (guest editor).

PRADEEP CHAKRAVARTHY is an HR consultant with more than 20 years of experience with Cognizant, Infosys and McKinsey. He is also an historian and has been writing on Tamil Nadu's history and art for more than a decade, with five published books in this field. Based in Chennai, he has recently begun to curate heritage tours in Tamil Nadu.

PUSHPA SUNDAR has over 30 years of experience in the field of development and civil society and has since worked with, and consulted for, Ford Foundation, FICCI and World Bank, among others. Sundar's published works include *Beyond Business: From Merchant Charity to Corporate Citizenship*; *For God's Sake: Religious Charity and Social Development in India*; *Giving with a Thousand Hands: The Changing Face of Indian Philanthropy* (forthcoming).

ROMILA THAPAR is Professor Emerita of History, Jawaharlal Nehru University, New Delhi. She has researched and written on early Indian history, and on historiography.

SALAI SELVAM works at the Azim Premji Foundation. She has been long active in the women's movement and in alternative education contexts.

SANGRAM MUKHERJEE is Research Associate, Pratichi Institute, Kolkata, focusing on both quantitative and qualitative methods of social science research.

SATISH DESHPANDE teaches Sociology at Delhi University. His areas of interest include caste and class inequalities, the theory and practice of social justice, higher education, and social science teaching, including in Indian languages. Deshpande's most recent books are *Beyond Inclusion: The Practice of Equal Access in Indian Higher Education* and *The Problem of Caste*, both edited volumes.

SATYA SIVARAMAN is a print and broadcast journalist, and health communicator with over 30 years of experience in different parts of the world, mainly South and Southeast Asia. Currently, he works as the Communications Advisor on a project for Uppsala University, Sweden, that seeks to raise global awareness and initiate action against the abuse of antibiotics.

SATYAJIT DHANANJAYAN is a professional photographer based in Chennai. He has been freelancing since 1999.

SUDHANSHU BHUSHAN is Head, Department of Higher and Professional Education, NUEPA. Bhushan conducts and guides research, and provides policy support to the government, UGC and the Planning Commission of India. Recent publications include *Quality Assurance of Transnational Higher Education: Australia and India Experiences*; *Public Financing and Deregulated Fees in Indian Higher Education*; and *Restructuring Higher Education in India.*

TEJASWINI NIRANJANA heads Centre for Indian Languages in Higher Education, Tata Institute of Social Sciences, Mumbai, and is Distinguished Adjunct Professor of Humanities at Lingnan University, Hong Kong.

UDAYA KUMAR teaches English at Jawaharlal Nehru University, New Delhi.

V. GEETHA is a feminist historian who writes in Tamil and English on anti-caste movements, gender, caste and education. She is currently Editorial Director, Tara Books.

◆